Evolving Finance, Trade and Investment in Asia

The year 2015 witnessed significant events in the area of finance, trade and investment, which brought Asia to the centre of the world stage. The Trans-Pacific Partnership reached its basic agreement among the 12 member countries in October; the Chinese Yuan was included into the Special Drawing Rights basket of currencies at the International Monetary Fund in November; the ASEAN Economic Community came into force; and the Asian Infrastructure Investment Bank was established with the 57 founding members in December.

Within and outside the region, there is an urgent need to understand the underlying economic structures that brought about these events, which have global implications. The Centre on Asia and Globalisation at the National University of Singapore launched a series of conferences on 'Evolving Finance, Trade and Investment in Asia' with the aim of strengthening research capacity in Asia to influence regional policymaking. Looking forward, the conference will provide an annual platform for scholars to discuss the latest findings and to disseminate them to business leaders and policymakers.

This book contains scholarship presented at the inaugural international conference in September 2015, and was originally published as a special issue of the *International Economic Journal*.

Tomoo Kikuchi is a Senior Research Fellow at Centre on Asia and Globalisation, Lee Kuan Yew School of Public Policy, National University of Singapore, and a Guest Research Fellow at the Keio Global Research Institute at Keio University, Tokyo, Japan.

T0346598

Evolving Finance, Trade and Investment in Asia

Edited by
Tomoo Kikuchi

LONDON AND NEW YORK

First published 2018 by Routledge

2 Park Square, Milton Park, Abingdon, Oxfordshire OX14 4RN
52 Vanderbilt Avenue, New York, NY 10017

Routledge is an imprint of the Taylor & Francis Group, an informa business

First issued in paperback 2019

Copyright © 2018 Korea International Economic Association

British Library Cataloguing in Publication Data
A catalogue record for this book is available from the British Library

ISBN 13: 978-1-138-72139-5 (hbk)
ISBN 13: 978-0-367-22953-5 (pbk)

Typeset in Minion Pro
by RefineCatch Limited, Bungay, Suffolk

Publisher's Note
The publisher accepts responsibility for any inconsistencies that may have arisen during the conversion of this book from journal articles to book chapters, namely the possible inclusion of journal terminology.

Disclaimer
Every effort has been made to contact copyright holders for their permission to reprint material in this book. The publishers would be grateful to hear from any copyright holder who is not here acknowledged and will undertake to rectify any errors or omissions in future editions of this book.

Contents

Citation Information   vii
Notes on Contributors   ix

Introduction: Evolving Finance, Trade and Investment in Asia   1
Tomoo Kikuchi

1. The Role of China, Japan, and Korea in Machinery Production Networks   5
Ayako Obashi & Fukunari Kimura

2. Global Value Chains and China's Exports to High-income Countries   27
Yuqing Xing

3. Rethinking the Exchange Rate Impact on Trade in a World with Global
Value Chains   40
Kevin C. Cheng, Gee Hee Hong, Dulani Seneviratne & Rachel van Elkan

4. Exchange Rates and Production Networks in Asia: A Twenty-first Century
Perspective   53
Willem Thorbecke

5. Mega-FTAs and the WTO: Competing or Complementary?   67
Shujiro Urata

6. Heterogeneous Patterns of Financial Development: Implications for
Asian Financial Integration   79
Linh Bun & Nirvikar Singh

7. Regional Financial Integration in East Asia against the Backdrop of
Recent European Experiences   108
Ulrich Volz

8. Does Inflation Targeting in Asia Reduce Exchange Rate Volatility?   130
Alice Y. Ouyang & Ramkishen S. Rajan

Index   149

Citation Information

The chapters in this book were originally published in the *International Economic Journal*, volume 30, issue 2 (2016). When citing this material, please use the original page numbering for each article, as follows:

Introduction
Evolving Finance, Trade and Investment in Asia
Tomoo Kikuchi
International Economic Journal, volume 30, issue 2 (2016), pp. 165–168

Chapter 1
The Role of China, Japan, and Korea in Machinery Production Networks
Ayako Obashi & Fukunari Kimura
International Economic Journal, volume 30, issue 2 (2016), pp. 169–190

Chapter 2
Global Value Chains and China's Exports to High-income Countries
Yuqing Xing
International Economic Journal, volume 30, issue 2 (2016), pp. 191–203

Chapter 3
Rethinking the Exchange Rate Impact on Trade in a World with Global Value Chains
Kevin C. Cheng, Gee Hee Hong, Dulani Seneviratne & Rachel van Elkan
International Economic Journal, volume 30, issue 2 (2016), pp. 204–216

Chapter 4
Exchange Rates and Production Networks in Asia: A Twenty-first Century Perspective
Willem Thorbecke
International Economic Journal, volume 30, issue 2 (2016), pp. 217–230

Chapter 5
Mega-FTAs and the WTO: Competing or Complementary?
Shujiro Urata
International Economic Journal, volume 30, issue 2 (2016), pp. 231–242

Chapter 6

Heterogeneous Patterns of Financial Development: Implications for Asian Financial Integration
Linh Bun & Nirvikar Singh
International Economic Journal, volume 30, issue 2 (2016), pp. 243–271

Chapter 7

Regional Financial Integration in East Asia against the Backdrop of Recent European Experiences
Ulrich Volz
International Economic Journal, volume 30, issue 2 (2016), pp. 272–293

Chapter 8

Does Inflation Targeting in Asia Reduce Exchange Rate Volatility?
Alice Y. Ouyang & Ramkishen S. Rajan
International Economic Journal, volume 30, issue 2 (2016), pp. 294–311

For any permission-related enquiries please visit:
http://www.tandfonline.com/page/help/permissions

Notes on Contributors

Linh Bun is a Graduate Student at the Department of Economics, University of California Santa Cruz, CA, USA.

Kevin C. Cheng is a member of the Research Department at the International Monetary Fund, Washington DC, USA.

Gee Hee Hong is a member of the Research Department at the International Monetary Fund, Washington DC, USA.

Tomoo Kikuchi is a Senior Research Fellow at the Centre on Asia and Globalisation, Lee Kuan Yew School of Public Policy, National University of Singapore, Singapore, and a Guest Research Fellow at the Keio Global Research Institute, Keio University, Tokyo, Japan. His research areas include international economics and economic growth and development.

Fukunari Kimura is Chief Economist at the Economic Research Institute for ASEAN and East Asia (ERIA), Jakarta, Indonesia, and a Professor at the Faculty of Economics, Keio University, Tokyo, Japan. His primary expertise is in international trade and development economics.

Ayako Obashi is an Assistant Professor at the School of International Politics, Economics and Communication, Aoyama Gakuin University, Tokyo, Japan. Her fields of interest are international economics and trade policy.

Alice Y. Ouyang is Professor at the China Academy of Public Finance and Public Policy, Central University of Finance and Economics, Beijing, China.

Ramkishen S. Rajan is a Professor of International Economic Policy at the School of Policy, Government and International Affairs (SPGIA), George Mason University, Fairfax, VA, USA, as well as a Visiting Professor at the Lee Kuan Yew School of Public Policy, National University of Singapore, Singapore. His research areas include macroeconomic management and Asian economic regionalism.

Dulani Seneviratne is a member of the Research Department at the International Monetary Fund, Washington DC, USA.

Nirvikar Singh is a Distinguished Professor at the Department of Economics, University of California Santa Cruz, CA, USA. His research interests include political economy and economic development.

Willem Thorbecke is a Senior Fellow at the Research Institute of Economy, Trade and Industry, Tokyo, Japan. His expertise is in monetary economics, financial economics, and international economics.

Shujiro Urata is a Professor at the Graduate School of Asia-Pacific Studies, Waseda University, Tokyo, Japan and a Senior Research Advisor at the Economic Research Institute for ASEAN and East Asia (ERIA), Jakarta, Indonesia. His expertise is in international economics and development economics.

Rachel van Elkan is Chief of the Regional Studies division in the Asian and Pacific Department, International Monetary Fund, Washington DC, USA.

Ulrich Volz is Head of the Department of Economics at SOAS University of London, UK; Senior Research Fellow at the German Development Institute, Bonn, Germany; Chaire de recherche Banque de France at EHESS, Paris, France; and Honorary Professor of Economics at the University of Leipzig, Germany. His areas of expertise include money, finance, international economic interdependencies, and global economic governance.

Yuqing Xing is a Professor of Economics and the Director of Asian Economic Policy at the National Graduate Institute for Policy Studies, Tokyo, Japan. His research focuses on trade, exchange rates, FDI, and regional economic integration.

Introduction: Evolving Finance, Trade and Investment in Asia

Tomoo Kikuchi

Centre on Asia and Globalisation, Lee Kuan Yew School of Public Policy, National University of Singapore, Singapore

The year 2015 witnessed significant events in the area of finance, trade and investment, which brought Asia to the centre of the world stage. The Trans-Pacific Partnership (TPP) reached its basic agreement among the 12 member countries in October; China's Yuan was included into the Special Drawing Rights basket of currencies at the International Monetary Fund (IMF) in November; the ASEAN Economic Community (AEC) came into force on 31 December; and the Asian Infrastructure Investment Bank (AIIB) was established with the Article of Agreement signed by the 57 founding members in December. There is an urgent need within and outside the region to understand the underlying economic structures that brought about these events, which have global implications. The Centre on Asia and Globalisation has launched a series of conferences on 'Evolving Finance, Trade and Investment in Asia' with the aim of strengthening research capacity in Asia to influence regional policymaking. Looking forward, the conference will provide an annual platform for scholars to discuss the latest findings and to disseminate them to business leaders and policymakers. This special issue of the *International Economic Journal* includes a selection of papers that were presented at the inaugural international conference, which took place at Lee Kuan Yew School of Public Policy, National University of Singapore on 16–17 September 2015. The conference brought together prominent economists who are experts in the fields of finance, trade and investment in Asia.

Fukunari Kimura (Keio University and Economic Research Institute for ASEAN and East Asia) and Ayako Obashi (University of Wisconsin and Keio University) confirm that China had become increasingly influential on the international stage through establishing a dominant position in production networks. By employing a new method of analysing finely disaggregated international trade data between 2007 and 2013, Kimura and Obashi find that China became the number one player in machinery production networks not only in trade values but also in the diversity and density of the export production pairs. While China's machinery export growth was mostly attributed to the intensive margin, China also built more trade relationships of existing products with new destination countries. Meanwhile, South Korea extended its production networks by transforming the product and destination composition in the exports of machinery final production, in line with China's expansion. Japan lost its relative importance in the regional as well as global context. Kimura and Obashi warn that the recent slowdown of the Chinese economy may affect other countries much more than before, and they recommend that China should further reduce its tariff barriers in the Regional Comprehensive Economic Partnership (RCEP) negotiations.

Yuqing Xing (National Graduate Institute for Policy Studies) argues that China's processing exports benefit substantially from the spillover effects of Global Value Chains (GVCs) in brands, global distribution networks, and technological innovations of leading multinational firms. With more than 50% of Foreign Value Added (FVA) embedded in processing exports, China's competitiveness in processing exports is determined by foreign contents rather than China's comparative advantage and indigenous technological innovation. By taking part in GVCs, Chinese firms bundle low-skilled labour services with globally recognised brands and advanced technology, and then sell them to global consumers. Xing's regression analysis shows a significant positive correlation between the share of processing exports and the income of importing countries, providing empirical evidence on the facilitating role of GVCs for 'Made in China' products to penetrate high-income markets such as the United States and Japan. Moreover, the cross-country heterogeneity of processing exports suggests that China actually captures relatively more value added from its exports to low-income countries than to high-income ones.

With a GVC, imports, which represent FVA, are used as inputs into the production of exports, making them complements in production with Domestic Value Added (DVA). Therefore, a country's exports contain both DVA and FVA. As a result, it is reasonable to expect that GVC-related trade responds differently than traditional trade in 'single-country' goods to changes in the exchange rate. Keving C. Cheng, Gee Hee Hong, Dulani Seneviratne, and Rachel van Elkan (IMF) use a recently-released Organisation for Economic Co-operation and Development (OECD) – World Trade Organization (WTO) database on trade in value added and found out that the strength of the exchange rate elasticity depends on the foreign content in a country's GVC exports, with a larger foreign share working to dampen the response. Many countries have foreign input shares that cause GVC-related exports (and import) elasticities with respect to their own exchange rate to be less than – but close to – zero. These findings imply that for products manufactured within a GVC, competitiveness is defined at the level of the entire supply chain. This reflects that the price of the final product depends on the exchange-rate-adjusted prices of all the individual countries' inputs, weighted by their respective value-added contributions. In particular, exchange rate changes by small DVA contributors have little effect on their own value added or the value added of others in the same supply chain. On the other hand, exchange rate changes in countries that are large contributors to the final product generate spillovers to their smaller GVC partners, tending to obviate traditional 'beggar-thy-neighbour' concerns among countries within the same GVC. Thus, somewhat paradoxically, a high degree of trade interconnectedness through GVCs may dampen the sensitivity of trade and trade balances to the real exchange rate. Therefore, larger exchange rate movements are needed to achieve a given change in the trade balance in a country whose exports are produced mainly in a GVC, especially if the country is a relatively small contributor to the total value added of the supply chain.

Willem Thorbecke (Research Institute of Economy, Trade and Industry) studies how exchange rates in supply chain countries remain important for explaining China's processing exports, which are the final goods produced using parts and components imported from East Asia. Thorbecke concludes that when upstream countries do not let their currencies appreciate in the face of enormous current account surpluses, no amount of Yuan appreciation will rebalance China's half a trillion dollar surplus in processing trade. However, not only do firms from different countries cooperate extensively through production fragmentation, they also compete in selling goods to third markets. For this reason, a country such as South Korea in 2015 resisted currency appreciation even when its current account surplus was approaching 9% of GDP because it didn't want to lose price competitiveness relative to Japan. One way out of this impasse is for East Asian countries to allow their currencies to appreciate together in response to market forces. If they appreciated in concert, then any loss of competitiveness relative to other East Asian countries would be small. The effect on real effective exchange rates in East Asian countries would also be attenuated because the currencies of neighbouring countries with whom they trade intensively would also be appreciating.

2015 marks the twentieth anniversary of the establishment of the WTO. The Doha Development Agenda (Doha Round), the first multilateral trade negotiation under the auspices of the WTO, began in 2001, but the negotiations haven't made much progress because of the differences toward trade liberalisation among the WTO members. Meanwhile, recent years have witnessed the emergence of mega-Free Trade Agreements (FTAs), which involve many countries and encompass bilateral and multilateral FTAs, including the TPP and RCEP, and the Transatlantic Trade and Investment Partnership (TTIP) involving the US and the European Union. Shujiro Urata (Waseda University) examines the relationship between these mega-FTAs and the WTO. Urata argues that it is possible to consider mega-FTAs and plurilateral agreements as the means to achieve a free and open world trade environment under the WTO by taking alternative approaches, which can limit the number of countries and the number of issues and areas, respectively. To achieve these objectives, it is important for the mega-FTAs to accept new members, and for the plurilateral agreements to share the benefits with the non-negotiating members on the Most Favoured Nation (MFN) basis.

Even after the global financial crisis, which included financial contagion across national boundaries, there is a continued interest in financial integration, especially in East Asia and the Asia Pacific. Recent empirical works suggest that financial integration within the region has been increasing, but it still remains below what might be most beneficial. Linh Bun and Nirvikar Singh (University of California, Santa Cruz) propose and construct a measure of differences in the patterns of financial development, and compared differences in the patterns with differences in the levels of financial development. For 14 economies of the Asia Pacific region, Bun and Singh calculate differences in levels and patterns of financial development for different years and vectors of components for overall financial development. They also illustrate how groupings of countries can be constructed through cluster analysis, and how the clustering differed when based on patterns versus levels of financial development. These kinds of calculations can be a useful preliminary tool for assessing the prospects for beneficial financial integration among a given set of economies.

Ulrich Volz (University of London and German Development Institute) discusses recent trends in regional financial integration in East Asia and ASEAN's current regional integration efforts against the backdrop of three decades of European financial integration experience. In reviewing Europe's two recent major financial crises, Volz illustrates the risks associated with comprehensive capital account liberalisation. The European experiences suggest that ASEAN members need to be very cautious in implementing their ambitious financial integration agenda formulated in the AEC Blueprint 2025 published in November 2015. The lesser-developed ASEAN countries need to be cautious with gradual capital account liberalisation and work towards strengthening domestic financial systems and financial governance capacities. The European experiences clearly show the importance of targeted macro-prudential policies in the absence of capital controls. They also underpin the importance of developing an adequate region-wide regulatory and supervisory framework to minimise the risks associated with regional financial integration.

Inflation targeting has become a popular option among many developing economies including those in Asia. Despite a gradual move towards inflation targeting, many Asian economies remain concerned about exchange rate variability. Motivated by this, Alice Ouyang (Central University of Finance and Economics) and Ramkishen S. Rajan (National University of Singapore and George Mason University) study the impact of inflation targeting on real exchange rate volatility in Asian economies. In particular, using a panel of 37 developing economies for the period 2007–2012, the paper explores the impact of inflation targeting on real exchange rate volatility as well as in terms of its two component parts, i.e. relative tradable prices across countries (external prices) and the sectorial prices of tradable and non-tradables within countries (internal prices). They find that while there is no evidence that inflation targeting regimes have faced greater real effective exchange rate volatility than other regimes, both Asian and non-Asian inflation targeting regimes do seem to experience lower variability in internal prices than other countries. Even though inflation targeters in developing countries tend to have lower inflation compared with other regimes, this is not the case for Asia. However, Asian inflation targeters do experience lower inflation rates in comparison with other Asian economies.

Overall, Kimura and Obashi, and Xing show how China has become the dominant player in GVCs. Thorbecke and Cheng et al. show how GVCs have changed the impact of exchanges rates on trade balances. Urata provides a perspective on how the TPP, RCEP and other mega-FTAs can be complementary to the WTO. Bun and Singh measure and compare differences in patterns of financial development with differences in levels of financial development. Volz illustrates three decades of European experience with financial integration and draws lessons for financial integration in ASEAN. Ouyang and Rajan analyse the effects of inflation targeting on exchange rate volatility. I am convinced that readers will benefit from examining these papers, which have the most up-to-date data sets and policy-relevant implications facing Asia in the realm of finance, trade and investment.

Acknowledgments

I would like to thank the Centre on Asia and Globalisation at the Lee Kuan Yew School of Public Policy, National University of Singapore for funding the conference 'Evolving Finance, Trade and Investment in Asia'.

The Role of China, Japan, and Korea in Machinery Production Networks

Ayako Obashi[a,b] & Fukunari Kimura[b,c]

[a]Department of Economics, University of Wisconsin-Madison, USA; [b]Faculty of Economics, Keio University, Tokyo, Japan; [c]Economic Research Institute for ASEAN and East Asia (ERIA), Jakarta, Indonesia

ABSTRACT
China, Japan, and Korea have been the three largest players in East Asian machinery production networks. This paper employs a new method of analyzing finely disaggregated international trade data that applies the concept of zero trade flows, least-traded goods, and intensive/extensive margins of trade growth and scrutinizes changes in the role of China, Japan, and Korea in machinery production networks between 2007 and 2013. We find, first, that China became a dominant player in the global machinery production networks in terms of both export values and the diversity and density of product-destination pairs. Second, the growth of Korea as machinery parts and components suppliers was also salient while Korea's dependency on China was sharply enhanced. Third, Japan kept being stagnated, and the machinery production links between Korea and Japan were substantially weakened.

1. Introduction

Since the 1990 s, East Asia has led the world in the formation of production networks in machinery industries.[1] In particular, the People Republic of China (hereafter China), Japan, and the Republic of Korea (hereafter Korea) have continuously been important players in East Asia. We, however, have recently observed drastic changes in the balance among these three countries. In the Global Financial Crisis, the performance of these countries widely differed. China conducted an unprecedented macro stimulus to keep rapid economic growth. Korea took advantage of the Chinese boom and extended production networks. Japan was kept stagnant and confronted various difficulties including natural and man-made disasters. It is thus worth reviewing the recent development of East Asian production networks, focusing on China, Japan, and Korea.

This paper sticks to international trade data and explores the analytical possibilities of a recently developed empirical method. We first separate machinery parts and components

---

[1] East Asia here is defined as so-called ASEAN+6, namely, the Association of Southeast Asian Nations (ASEAN) member countries, China, Japan, Korea, Australia, New Zealand, and India.

from machinery final products so that peculiar characteristics of intermediate goods transactions can be highlighted. And then, in addition to the traditional trade value approach, we apply concepts of zero trade flows, least-traded goods, and intensive and extensive margins of trade growth (Besedeš & Prusa, 2011; Debaere & Mostashari, 2010; Kehoe & Ruhl, 2013). This empirical approach is very effective and articulate in quantifying the development of production networks, or how and to what degree countries participate into production networks.

In our companion paper on ASEAN (Obashi & Kimura, 2015), we traced out the catching-up process of latecomers by measuring the degree of participation in production networks from the perspective of export product and destination diversification. In cases of China, Japan, and Korea, we would like to overview competition and collaboration among these leading countries in the world in the formation of production networks. As will be shown below, for China, Japan, Korea and other big players in production networks, the export product mix was already fully diverse and saturated in the base year of our analysis. Thus, the concept of 'the proportion of non-zero to potential product-destination pairs' proposed by Baldwin and Harrigan (2011) is particularly useful in analyzing big players in production networks. That is, the current paper puts relatively more emphasis on counting the number of actually-occurred, non-zero product-destination pairs relative to the number of potential pairs, the latter of which also differs across exporter countries. In addition, we employ the concept of 'least-traded goods' proposed by Kehoe and Ruhl (2013), which is useful to explore the importance of the ins and outs of product-destination pairs, i.e., the extensive margin, for big players in production networks by decomposing the growth in exports into intensive and extensive margins. We find contrasting performance in operating production networks in the three countries of our interest.

This paper is structured as follows: the next section explains the laborious data construction to make the dataset clean. The third section develops empirical analysis on the three country's machinery export data. Starting with checking export/import shares of machinery parts and components and final products, we check the positioning of the three countries, the ins and outs of export product-destination pairs, and the extensive and intensive margins of export growth. The fourth section focuses on machinery trade among three countries. The final section concludes the paper.

2. Data Description

International trade data used throughout the paper are obtained from the UN Comtrade Database. We use import statistics, whenever they are available, from the standpoint of reliability. Most countries report country of origin as a partner in import statistics and last known destination as a partner in export statistics. Import statistics appear to be more reliable because the country of origin is more closely verified due to tariff regulations although the final destination may not be known at the time of export.

We use import statistics for the years 2007 and 2013, based on the 1996 version of the Harmonized System (HS) product classification.[2] To count the number of products traded

---

[2] The import statistics that we use are originally reported based on the HS 1996 classification or are converted to the HS 1996 classification if a country originally reported based on the other version of classification. We employ the HS 1996 classification although a substantial number of countries reported based on a newer version of classification, even for 2007, because Indonesia, which is one of East Asian countries of particular interest to the authors, reported based on

and trading partner countries in a consistent manner, we restrict our attention to a group of 136 countries that are the UN member states and are reporters of import statistics both for 2007 and 2013. In addition, we include a few East Asian countries including Brunei Darussalam (hereafter Brunei), Lao People's Democratic Republic (hereafter Laos), and Myanmar, with some modifications: first, because Brunei did not report import statistics for 2007, we instead use those for 2006. Second, Myanmar has reported trade statistics based on the HS classification, but only for 2001 and 2010, since 2000. We use Myanmar's import statistics for 2001 and 2010 instead of those for 2007 and 2013, respectively. Third, Laos has reported trade statistics only for limited years, 1962–1974, based not on the HS classification but on the Standard International Trade Classification (SITC; rev. 1). We instead use export statistics reported by Laos' trading partners, i.e., mirror data, for both 2007 and 2013.[3]

By so doing, we are able to analyze all potential bilateral trade flows between $136 + 3 = 139$ countries, including all East Asian countries of interest, in two points of time, basically 2007 and 2013. In other words, we deal with $139 \times 138 (= 139 - 1$ (the reporter country itself)) $= 19,182$ potential exporter-importer pairs.[4] By excluding the reporter country itself from a set of the partner countries, we remove obvious re-imports from our data set.

Based on the HS classification, manufactured goods range from HS 28 to HS 92. Among them, machinery includes all goods classified as part of general machinery (HS 84), electric machinery (HS 85), transport equipment (HS 86–89), and precision machinery (HS 90–92) industries. We group respective HS product codes, at the most disaggregated level, into machinery parts and components and final products.[5]

3. China, Japan, and Korea and World Trade in Machinery

Using highly disaggregated international trade data at the HS six-digit product level, we explore how and to what degree China, Japan, Korea, and other countries participate in international production networks in the machinery industry. In Subsection 3.1, we begin with an analysis of the proportion of machinery parts and components in the total exports and imports based on the traditional value data. The following four subsections then examine the degree of participation into the production networks based on a novel approach on the diversification of products exported and export destination market countries, through sorting out features of world exports of machinery from ten leading countries. After an initial overview using the value data in Subsection 3.2, we count the number of exported products and destination markets in an informative way in Subsections 3.3 and 3.4. The

---

the HS 1996 classification for 2007. The available annual data for 2014 already account for more than 90% of the world trade value, according to the UN Comtrade (accessed on 16 October 2015), and consist of a number of reporter countries; however, we use 2013 as the latest year of our analysis because Vietnam, one of the East Asian countries of interest, has yet to be included as a reporter in the data for 2014.

[3] See the Appendix for a list of countries included in the dataset.

[4] The aggregated total values of imports to the selected 136 reporter countries from 138 partner countries (= 136 + 3–1) account for more than 90% of annual total imports to all reporter countries available in the UN Comtrade Database from all partner countries with which ISO 3166-1 alpha-3 country codes are assigned, both for 2007 and 2013.

[5] See Kimura and Obashi (2010) for the list of machinery parts and components at the HS (four- and) six-digit level for different versions of the HS classification.

importance of ins and outs of products and destinations in a country's exports is further explored by decomposing the export growth into intensive and extensive margins in Subsection 3.5.

3.1. Machinery Shares in Manufactures Exports and Imports

To explore how and to what degree China, Japan, Korea, and other countries participate into international production networks, let us begin by comparing countries using the proportion of machinery parts and components in the total exports and imports of manufactured goods. In Figure 1, a pair of stacked bars shows the percentages of machinery in country's manufactures exports to (the left bar) and imports from the world (the right bar). For each stacked bar, the dark colored portion represents the percentage accounted for by parts and components (labelled as 'P&C') while the light color portion for final products ('FP'). We focus on the 20 leading countries in world exports of machinery parts and components, including China, Japan, and Korea, that are selected based on the average value of exports in 2007 and 2013. The bars for the top 20 exporters are in descending order, from left to right, in terms of the machinery parts and component shares in exports.

Figure 1 gives an overall picture of how the degree of integration into, and the way of participating in international production networks, differs across the top 20 exporters. For China, for example, the percentage of machinery parts and components is about 20% in the total manufactures exports while the corresponding percentage stands at around 40% in the imports. At the same time, the percentage of machinery final products is relatively high, compared with parts and components, ranging from 35 to 45%, for the export side. Similar patterns are observed for Mexico and Thailand. Such patterns can be considered as indicating these countries' role as the world's factory in the sense that they import a large amount of intermediate goods for the final assembly of products to be sold domestically or to be exported.

Korea, together with the Philippines and Malaysia, is one of the countries that have strikingly high percentages of machinery parts and components, exceeding 40% for the export side and 30% for the import side. The percentages accounted for by machinery final products, on the other hand, are relatively limited. Such high percentages of machinery parts and components both for the export and import sides would reflect these countries' active participation in back-and-forth transactions of intermediate goods across borders.

In addition to the Philippines, Malaysia, Korea, and Mexico, Japan is another country that is highly dependent on machinery exports. In contrast to Korea, the percentages of machinery final products in Japan's total manufactures exports and imports are almost comparable in magnitude to the corresponding figures for parts and components. Austria and France show the similarity in the proportion of machinery final products to parts and components; however, it is striking that the relative importance of machinery in the total exports from Japan is much higher than those countries' levels, accompanied by a high percentage of machinery parts and components, exceeding 35%, for the export side.

3.2. Ten Leading Countries in World Exports of Machinery

In this and the following few subsections, we aim to elicit features of world trade in machinery, with special interest to China, Japan, and Korea, by focusing on the leading countries

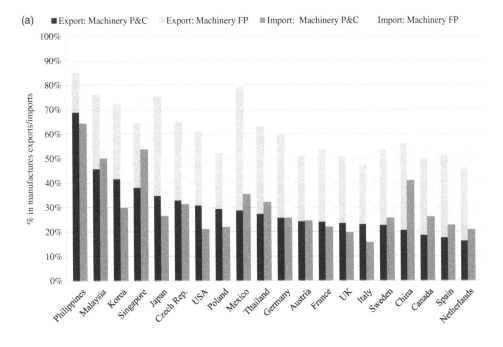

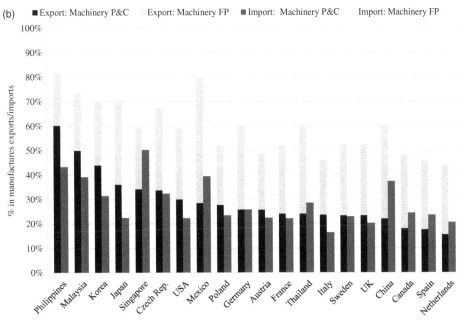

Figure 1. Machinery shares in total manufactures exports to and imports from the world.
Source: UN Comtrade Database (mainly, import statistics reported by selected countries, based on the HS 1996 classification, at the six-digit level).
Notes: Machinery industries are defined as HS 84-92. Product groupings, i.e., parts and components (P&C) and final products (FP), follow Kimura and Obashi (2010). Top 20 exporter countries of machinery parts and components (selected based on the average export value in 2007 and 2013) are listed on the horizontal axis, in descending order, from left to right, in terms of the machinery parts and components shares in exports.

Table 1. Overview of world exports of machinery.

Top 10 exporters of machinery parts and components		Export value (millions, constant US $)		Growth rate, 2007–13	Cumulative share in the total world trade, in 2013
		2007	2013		
1	China	228,266	344,601	51%	14%
2	USA	292,682	301,182	3%	26%
3	Germany	287,146	281,220	−2%	38%
4	Japan	241,098	229,652	−5%	47%
5	Korea	140,333	193,299	38%	55%
6	France	106,967	97,254	−9%	59%
7	Malaysia	72,585	86,462	19%	63%
8	Italy	90,389	85,036	−6%	66%
9	Mexico	60,545	78,100	29%	69%
10	UK	78,497	67,465	−14%	72%
Top 10 exporters of machinery parts and components		Export value (millions, constant US $)		Growth rate, 2007–13	Cumulative share in the total world trade, in 2013
		2007	2013		
1	China	387,393	590,311	52%	21%
2	Germany	380,732	367,774	−3%	33%
3	USA	285,599	288,809	1%	43%
4	Japan	277,627	217,163	−22%	51%
5	Mexico	105,444	139,241	32%	56%
6	Korea	102,550	112,558	10%	60%
7	France	129,345	111,898	−13%	64%
8	UK	89,422	83,353	−7%	66%
9	Italy	92,849	79,345	−15%	69%
10	Netherlands	78,031	72,013	−8%	72%

Source: UN Comtrade Database (mainly, import statistics reported by selected countries, based on the HS 1996 classification, at the six-digit level), IMF IFS Database (US CPI).

Notes: See notes of Figure 1. By product grouping, top 10 exporter countries are listed in descending order, in terms of the export value in 2013. China, Japan, and Korea are countries of interest in the paper and are therefore highlighted. Export values are deflated by the consumer price index (CPI) in the US to obtain a constant dollar series, and are rounded off to the million. All figures expressed in percentage terms are rounded off to the whole number.

in world exports of machinery parts and components and of machinery final products. For each of the product groupings, we select ten leading exporter countries in terms of the total value of exports to the world in 2013. Table 1 provides an initial overview of world exports of machinery. By product grouping, the values of exports in 2007 and 2013 and growth rates of export values between the two years are reported in the left part of the table. The cumulative shares in the total world trade of the product grouping concerned are in the rightmost column.

First and foremost, China achieves outstanding performance in exports of both machinery parts and components and final products. For machinery parts and components, China was ranked fourth, following the United States of America (USA, hereafter the US), Germany, and Japan, in 2007, but expanded exports by 51%, which is the highest rate of growth among the ten leading exporters, and has come out on top as of 2013. For machinery final products, China was already in the top spot in 2007, and further increased exports by 52% in the period from 2007 to 2013. As of 2013, China leads the value of exports of machinery final products by a large margin, achieving the export value 1.6 times larger than that of the second-ranked Germany.

In contrast to China, Japan has decreased the value of exports of machinery, especially for final products, by −22%, which is the lowest rate of (negative) growth among the ten leading exporters. For machinery parts and components, while Japan slightly decreased exports in the period 2007–1013, Korea increased exports by 38% and, as a result, Korea has got close to the export value of Japan.

In 2013, both for machinery parts and components and for final products, the four largest exporter countries in the world are China, the US, Germany and Japan. About a half of the total world trade in machinery parts and components (47%) and in final products (51%) is accounted for by the four leading exporters. In addition, the ten leading exporters as a whole engage in more than 70% of the world trade in machinery parts and components and in final products.

3.3. Number of Export Products and Destinations

Departing from simply looking at the value of trade, we turn our interest to counting the number of products traded and the number of trading partner countries and sorting out the pattern of export product and destination diversification.[6] In addition to merely counting the numbers of exported products and destination market countries, we examine how many potential export flows, i.e., product-destination pairs, a country is actually involved in. To do so, we follow Baldwin and Harrigan (2011) to define a zero at the most disaggregated level, as a country's export flow, which could have occurred but did not. That is, a zero occurs when a country exports a certain product at the HS six-digit level to at least one country but not to all countries in the sample. By so doing, zero export flows consist only of goods actually produced in the exporting country. Furthermore, in identifying a zero export flow, we restrict attention to destination countries to which the exporter country sells at least one product classified under the product grouping concerned. In other words, we exclude exporter-importer country pairs with no trade in the product grouping at all from our analysis. Naturally, on the other hand, actually-occurred export flows are referred to as non-zeros.

In Figure 2, the light colored bars represent the numbers of non-zero product-destination pairs in country's exports of machinery parts and components and of machinery final products to the world for 2007, and the dark color bars for 2013. The proportions of non-zero to potential product-destination pairs are reported on top of the corresponding bars. The numbers of products exported to at least one country and the numbers of destination market countries with non-zero trade of the product grouping concerned in 2007 and 2013 are shown in the lower part of the figure. The number of products classified under machinery parts and components and final products at the six-digit level of the HS 1996 classification is 445 and 729, respectively. And the maximum possible number of destination countries is 138. As in Table 1, we focus on the ten leading exporter countries for each product grouping, in terms of the total value of exports in 2013, and the top ten exporters are listed in descending order, from left to right.

For all the ten leading exporter countries, the number of machinery parts and components exported shows a slight decrease from 2007 to 2013. The decrease in the number of machinery final products exported is much larger in magnitude. For machinery parts and components as well as final products, every country's export product mix appears

---

[6] We here simply employ a cut-off of $0 to determine whether a good is traded or not in a particular period, although employing an alternative cut-off when analyzing the importance of the extensive (relative to intensive) margin of trade growth in Sections 3.5 and 4.3.

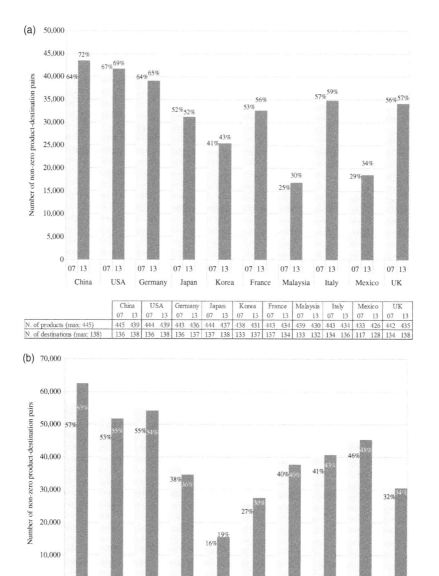

Figure 2. Number of products and destinations in machinery exports.
Source: UN Comtrade Database (mainly, import statistics reported by selected countries, based on the HS 1996 classification, at the six-digit level).
Notes: See notes of Figure 1. By product grouping, top 10 exporter countries are listed in descending order, from left to right, in terms of the export value in 2013. In order to count the number of products traded and trading partner countries, we employ a cut-off value of $0 to determine whether or not a product is traded between a particular exporter-importer country pair.

to already hit the ceiling. Meanwhile, the number of destination countries in a country's exports of machinery parts and components trends upward for most of the ten countries except France and Malaysia. The similar upward trends in the diversification of destination countries are observed for exports of machinery final products from all the ten countries.

Despite the slight decrease in the number of products exported, the number of non-zero product-destination pairs in country's exports of machinery parts and components has increased, driven by the diversification of destination countries, in the period 2007–2013 for all the countries except Japan. Reflecting the increase in the number of non-zero product-destination pairs, these countries, in contrast to Japan, experienced a rise in the percentage of non-zero product-destination pairs, which indicates that their export product-destination mix has become not only more geographically diverse but also denser. Similarly, the increase in the number of non-zero product-destination pairs and the simultaneous increase in the percentage of non-zero product-destination pairs are observed for exports of machinery final products from most countries, but the exceptions include not only Japan but also Germany and the US. Nevertheless, the most notable is Japan, whose export product-destination mix has become less diverse in the product space and less dense to the greatest extent, both for machinery parts and components and for final products.

China had a predominantly high number of non-zero product-destination pairs, both in exports of machinery parts and components and of final products, as of 2007, and has further increased the number of pairs sharply. In 2013, not only does China lead the value of exports of machinery, but it also leads the number and the percentage of non-zero product-destination pairs. China has developed trade relationships of 43,410 and 62,443 product-destination pairs and is actually involved in 72% and 63% of the potential product-destination pairs for machinery parts and components and for final products, respectively. The numbers of non-zero product-destination pairs in exports of machinery parts and components and of final products from China are 1.4 to 2.3 times higher than the levels of Japan and Korea.

3.4. Ins and Outs of Export Product-destination Pairs

Looking into changes in the number of (non-zero) product-destination pairs in country's exports, Figure 3 reveals the ins and outs of product-destination pairs that are going on underneath the surface. A country experiences a change in the number of product-destination pairs, i.e., at an extensive margin, by exporting a new product that has never been exported or by exporting an already exported product to a new destination country which had not previously had the product.[7] The 'ins' of product-destination pairs occur through entries of products to a country's export product mix or through entries of destinations to a country's product-specific destination mix. Similarly, the 'outs' of product-destination pairs occur through exits of products from a country's export product mix or through exits of destinations from a country's product-specific destination mix.

To be more precise, for exporter country m, we define the set of non-zero product-destination pairs in period $t = \{t_0, t_1\}$ as I_t^m. We define the set of product-destination pairs

---

[7] To the authors' knowledge, Besedeš and Prusa (2011) is one of few previous studies that examine changes in a country's exports to the world by decomposing the extensive margin into the new product margin and the new destination margin. We follow Besedeš and Prusa's way of thinking of the extensive margin. Other studies such as Kehoe and Ruhl (2013) focus only on the new product margin because they examine changes in trade patterns for a selected country pair.

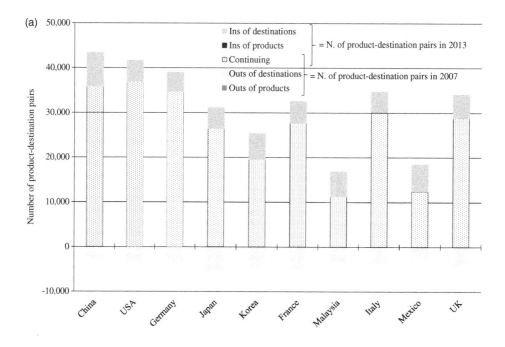

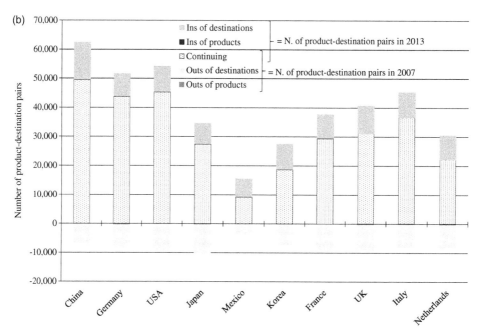

Figure 3. Number of product-destination pairs in machinery exports: ins and outs.
Source: UN Comtrade Database (mainly, import statistics reported by selected countries, based on the HS 1996 classification, at the six-digit level).
Note: See notes of Figure 2.

with non-zero trade, i.e., being active, in both periods as $I^m = I^m_{t0} \cap I^m_{t1}$. We define the set of product-destination pairs that are active not in t_0 but in t_1 as $EN^m = I^m_{t1} \setminus I^m$, which corresponds to either (i) entries of products to country m's export product mix, ENP^m, or (ii) entries of destinations to country m's product-specific destination mix, END^m. Similarly, we define the set of product-destination pairs that are active in t_0 but not in t_1 as $EX^m = I^m_{t0} \setminus I^m$, which corresponds to either (i) the exits of products from country m's export product mix, EXP^m, or (ii) the exits of destinations from country m's product-specific destination mix, EXD^m. Note that the number of non-zero product destination pairs in the base year equals the sum of continuing pairs and outs, $I^m_{t0} = I^m + EXP^m + EXD^m$, while the number for the ending year is the sum of continuing pairs and ins, $I^m_{t1} = I^m + ENP^m + END^m$.

The stacked bars in Figure 3 show the composition of changes in the number of product-destination pairs in a country's exports of machinery parts and components and of machinery final products to the world between 2007 and 2013, by counting the number of pairs classified under the five different types: continuing, I^m; ins of products, ENP^m; ins of destinations, END^m; outs of products, EXP^m; and outs of destinations, EXD^m. As in Figure 2, the ten leading exporter countries are listed in descending order, from left to right.

For all the ten leading exporter countries, a substantial amount of entries and exits of destinations to and from a country's product-specific destination mix of machinery parts and components and of final products is going on beneath the surface. Meanwhile, no substantial amount of ins and outs of products is observed, reflecting the fact that every country's product mix was already fully diverse in the base year of 2007. For machinery parts and components, the ins and outs of destinations reached the level ranging from 12% (Germany) to 49% (Malaysia) and from 8% (China) to 31% (Malaysia) of the number of continuing pairs, respectively. The corresponding figures for machinery final products are much larger: ins range from 18% (Germany) to 68% (Mexico) and outs are from 13% (China) to 37% (Japan and Korea). These observations suggest that countries have undergone a non-negligible downsizing of the product-specific destination mix for some products while diversifying the destination mix for the other products, during the period of only six years.

In particular, the sharp increase in the number of product-destination pairs in China's exports of machinery parts and components and of final products is driven by a large amount of ins of destinations, accompanied with a relatively small amount of outs of destinations compared to other countries. The noticeable decrease in the number of product-destination pairs in Japan's exports of machinery, on the other hand, is driven by a large amount of outs and a limited amount of ins of destinations.

3.5. Intensive and Extensive Margins of Export Growth

To further explore the relative importance of ins and outs of product-destination pairs in country's exports, we decompose the growth in country's total exports into intensive and extensive margins. In line with the methodology proposed by Kehoe and Ruhl (2013), we classify a good as not traded if its annual value of trade is zero or very little, instead of employing $0 (as we did in Sections 3.3. and 3.4) or other fixed cut-offs. For each exporter-importer country pair, we order goods from the smallest to the largest annual value of trade recorded for the base year, and create the set of least-traded goods (including goods that are not actually traded) so that the set accounts for cumulatively 10% of the total merchandise trade. We define the cut-off value of tradedness to be the annual value of trade of the first good that would not be included in the set of least-traded goods for the base year. The set of least-traded goods in the ending year is made up of all the goods whose annual value of trade is less than the cut-off value defined above. In what follows, least-traded goods are regarded as 'non-traded' and the set of traded goods is simply the complement of the set of least-traded goods.

We then decompose the growth in country m's exports into contributions of the five different types of product-destination pairs discussed in Section 3.4: I^m, ENP^m, END^m, EXP^m, and EXD^m. Once again, note that we here distinguish between traded and non-traded product-destination pairs, employing the cut-off à la Kehoe and Ruhl (2013) that varies across exporter-importer country pairs, unlike the preceding subsections that deal with non-zero product-destination pairs and zeros by employing a cut-off of $0. The country m's trade growth is decomposed as follows:

$$\frac{\sum_{i \in I_{t_1}^m} x_{i,t_1}^m - \sum_{i \in I_{t_0}^m} x_{i,t_0}^m}{\sum_{i \in I_{t_0}^m} x_{i,t_0}^m} = \underbrace{\frac{\sum_{i \in I^m} -(x_{i,t_1}^m - x_{i,t_0}^m)}{\sum_{i \in I_{t_0}^m} x_{i,t_0}^m}}_{\substack{\text{Continnuing} \\ \text{product—destination} \\ \text{pairs} \\ \| \\ \textbf{Intensive margin}}}$$

$$+ \underbrace{\underbrace{\frac{\sum_{i \in ENP^m} x_{i,t_1}^m}{\sum_{i \in I_{t_0}^m} x_{i,t_0}^m}}_{\text{New products}} + \underbrace{\frac{\sum_{i \in END^m} x_{i,t_1}^m}{\sum_{i \in I_{t_0}^m} x_{i,t_0}^m}}_{\text{New destinations}} - \underbrace{\frac{\sum_{i \in EXP^m} x_{i,t_1}^m}{\sum_{i \in I_{t_0}^m} x_{i,t_0}^m}}_{\text{Old products}} - \underbrace{\frac{\sum_{i \in EXD^m} x_{i,t_1}^m}{\sum_{i \in I_{t_0}^m} x_{i,t_0}^m}}_{\text{Old destinations}}}_{\substack{\| \\ \textbf{Extensive margin}}},$$

where the value of country m's exports for product-destination pair i in period t is denoted by $x_{i,t}^m$.

The stacked bars in Figure 4 show the contributions of the five different types of product-destination pairs to the growth in a country's exports of machinery parts and components and of machinery final products to the world between 2007 and 2013. The diamond-shaped dot indicates the growth rate of the country's total export values of the product grouping concerned in the period 2007–2013. As in Figures 2 and 3, the top ten exporter countries are listed in descending order, from left to right.

Overall, the growth in country's exports of machinery parts and components and of final products is mostly attributed to the intensive margin. Although the growth contribution of the net extensive margin is limited relative to the intensive margin, looking into the contents of the extensive margin reveals non-negligible contributions of ins of new destinations and outs of old destinations to the total growth rate of exports of machinery beneath the surface, although the contributions offset each other. In particular, although the total growth rates are limited or even negative in some cases, the US, Germany, Japan, and Italy experienced a substantial change in the composition of export values of machinery parts

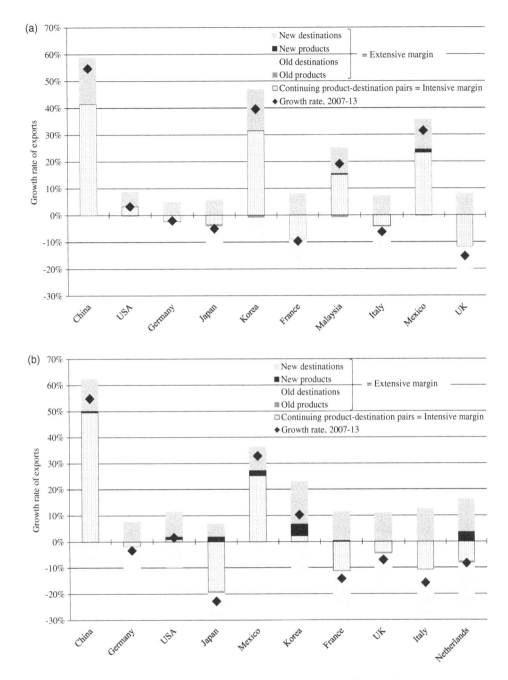

Figure 4. Decomposition of growth in machinery exports: Intensive and extensive margins.
Source: UN Comtrade Database (mainly, import statistics reported by selected countries, based on the HS 1996 classification, at the six-digit level).
Notes: See notes of Figure 1. By product grouping, top 10 exporter countries are listed in descending order, from left to right, in terms of the export value in 2013. To determine whether or not a product is traded between a particular country pair in the base year of 2007, we employ Kehoe and Ruhl (2013)'s method of calculating cut-off values varying across exporter-importer country pairs. For each country pair, the same cut-off value is used to determine the tradedness in the ending year of 2013.

and components through the growth contribution of the turnover of destinations. Similarly, for Germany, the US, and the United Kingdom (UK), the turnover of destinations substantially affects the composition of export values of machinery final products. Notice that the (gross) growth contributions of new and old destinations are not necessarily consistent with the simple counting of ins and outs of destinations relative to the number of continuing product-destination pairs (explored in Section 3.4 and Figure 3).

A remarkable exception is Korea, for which the (net) extensive margin makes up more than three-quarters of the total export growth rate (10%) in exports of machinery final products. More than half of the (net) extensive margin is accounted for by the product margin rather than by the destination margin. Nevertheless, the (gross) growth contributions of ins and outs of destinations are even more strikingly large, although they offset each other. These observations suggest that Korea has undergone a drastic transformation of the composition of export values of machinery final products through the ins and outs of economically important destinations with which Korea has a non-negligible amount of trade and by starting to export a non-negligible amount of new products.

4. Trade in Machinery among China, Japan and Korea

Given the data examinations on world trade in machinery, with special interest to China, Japan and Korea, we next explore how trade relationships between these big three exporter countries in the East Asian region have been changing. In Section 4.1, we begin with an overview of intra-East Asian exports of machinery from the big three, showing the importance of intra-East Asian destination markets for the machinery exports from the big three as well as confirming the dominance of the big three over the trade in machinery inside the East Asian region. The following two subsections look into changes in the structure and margins of the growth of bilateral trade within the big three by machinery subsector.

4.1. China, Japan, and Korea's Intra-East Asian Exports of Machinery

Table 2 provides an overview of intra-East Asian exports of machinery from each country of the big three. By product grouping, the values of intra-East Asian exports in 2007 and 2013 and growth rates of export values between the two years are reported in the left part of the table. The proportions of intra-East Asian exports in the country's total exports of the product grouping concerned to the world are reported in the middle part of the table, followed by the cumulative shares in the total intra-East Asian trade of the product grouping concerned. For reference, figures for bilateral trade within the big three are also reported to be compared with the aggregated regional figures. For each product grouping, the big three countries are listed in descending order, in terms of the total value of intra-East Asian exports in 2013.

First of all, Table 2 confirms the dominance of the big three exporter countries over the trade in machinery inside the East Asian region. The big three exporters as a whole make up more than 71% and 73% of the total intra-East Asian trade in machinery parts and components and in machinery final products in 2013, respectively.

The most notable change in intra-East Asian exports of machinery from the big three is that China and Korea greatly expanded their exports by more than 50% while Japan's exports have remained stagnant in the period from 2007 to 2013. Such contrasting growth

Table 2. China, Japan, and Korea's intra-East Asian machinery exports: Overview.

Machinery parts and components

	Export value (millions, constant US $)		Growth rate, 2007-13	Share in country's total exports to the world		Cumulative share in the total intra-EA trade, in 2013
	2007	2013		2007	2013	
Korea's intra-EA exports	89,996	137,877	53%	64%	71%	25%
to China	59,877	98,478	64%	43%	51%	
to Japan	11,678	7,043	−40%	8%	4%	
China's intra-EA exports	83,966	131,302	56%	37%	38%	48%
to Japan	27,370	32,807	20%	12%	10%	
to Korea	17,890	25,703	44%	8%	7%	
Japan's intra-EA exports	123,884	125,849	2%	51%	55%	71%
to China	62,980	63,692	1%	26%	28%	
to Korea	16,534	15,755	−5%	7%	7%	

Machinery final products

	Export value (millions, constant US $)		Growth rate, 2007-13	Share in country's total exports to the world		Cumulative share in the total intra-EA trade, in 2013
	2007	2013		2007	2013	
China's intra-EA exports	81,690	144,695	77%	21%	25%	42%
to Japan	28,766	51,472	79%	7%	9%	
to Korea	9,895	13,331	35%	3%	2%	
Japan's intra-EA exports	73,556	74,061	1%	26%	34%	64%
to China	27,807	31,899	15%	10%	15%	
to Korea	12,475	8,755	−30%	4%	4%	
Korea's intra-EA exports	21,263	32,326	52%	21%	29%	73%
to China	8,117	15,677	93%	8%	14%	
to Japan	2,682	3,947	47%	3%	4%	

Source: UN Comtrade Database (mainly, import statistics reported by selected countries, based on the HS 1996 classification, at the six-digit level), IMF IFS Database (US CPI).
Notes: See notes of Figure 1 and Table 1. East Asia here consists of ASEAN+6. By product grouping, exporter countries are listed in descending order, in terms of the intra-East Asian export value in 2013.

rates between rapidly-growing China and Korea and a stagnant Japan are similar to what we observed for their total exports to the world in Section 3.2 (and Table 1). For intra-East Asian trade in machinery parts and components, Japan has been displaced by the rapidly-growing Korea and China at the top of the exporters. As of 2013, the intra-East Asian exports of machinery parts and components from the big three countries are comparable in value to each other. For machinery final products, on the other hand, China has remained in the first place, leaving the other two far behind. In 2013, intra-East Asian exports of machinery final products from China are twice as large as Japan's exports in value terms. The value of intra-East Asian exports of machinery final products from Korea is still less than a half of Japan's exports, although Korea shows strong growth in the period 2007–2013.

Meanwhile, all the big three countries tend to increase the intra-East Asian exports at a more rapid rate than the overall exports to the world, resulting in the growing importance of intra-East Asian destination markets. In particular, the percentage of intra-East Asian trade in the overall exports of machinery parts and components from Korea to the world was 64% in 2007 and further increased to a strikingly high level of 71% in 2013. For machinery final products, Japan is the most highly dependent on intra-East Asian destination markets, and the percentage of intra-East Asian trade was increased from 26% in 2007 to 34% in 2013.

Comparing figures for bilateral trade within the big three to the aggregated regional figures reveals that Korea has expanded exports of machinery parts and components, becoming more and more dependent on China rather than intra-East Asian destination markets in general. The percentage of exports to China in the overall exports of machinery parts and components from Korea to the world was 43% in 2007 and 51% in 2013. That is, more than 70% of Korea's intra-East Asian exports of machinery parts and components are shipped to China in 2013. In contrast, despite the high growth in the intra-East Asian exports as well as in the overall exports to the world, Korea's exports of machinery parts and components to Japan decreased by 40%. As a result, the percentage of exports to Japan in the overall exports of machinery parts and components from Korea to the world was only 4% in 2013. Similarly, the increasingly high dependence on China as a destination, accompanied by the weakened trade relationship with Korea, is observed for Japan's exports of machinery parts and components and of final products.

4.2. Overview by Machinery Subsector

Looking into bilateral trade in machinery subsectors among China, Japan, and Korea, we examine how these big three countries have constructed trade relationships with each other and how the trade patterns among the big three have changed in the period from 2007 to 2013. In the left part of Table 3, the values of trade in 2007 and 2013 and growth rates of trade values between the two years are reported for respective exporter-importer country pairs within the big three, by machinery subsector and by product grouping. The proportions of the trade between the exporter-importer country pair in the exporter country's total exports of the sector-product grouping concerned to the world are reported in the middle part of the table. The numbers of products traded in 2007 and 2013, the numbers of those traded in both years, i.e., continuing products, the numbers of those traded not in 2007 but in 2013, i.e., ins of products, and the numbers of those traded in 2007 but not in 2013, i.e., outs of products, are in the right part of the table. The number of products classified under each sector-product grouping, i.e., the maximal possible number of products traded, is noted on the top row of the corresponding section of the table. By sector-product grouping, exporter-importer country pairs are listed in descending order, in terms of the value of trade in 2013.

First, electric machinery parts and components make up 40% of the total bilateral trade in machinery within the big three in 2013. The most notable feature of trade in electric machinery parts and components within the big three is an increase of transactions between China and Korea. On the one hand, Korea's exports to China have expanded by 94% while its exports to Japan have decreased by almost half (–46%) in the period 2007–2013. Korea's exports to China have become more than twice as large as Japan's exports to China, which have ceded the top spot to Korea's exports to China as of 2013. On the other hand, China's exports to Korea have increased at a rate (47%) greater than its exports to Japan (22%). As a result, China's exports to Korea outweigh its exports to Japan in 2013.

Similar trends are observed for trade in transport equipment and in precision machinery, both for parts and components and for final products. For those other than trade in

Table 3. Machinery trade among China, Japan, and Korea: Overview.

	Trade value (millions, constant US $)		Growth rate,	Share in country's total exports to the world		N. of products				
	2007	2013	2007–13	2007	2013	2007	2013	Continuing	Ins	Outs
General machinery parts and components								(max: 186)		
Japan to China	12,091	14,381	19%	15%	18%	176	173	170	3	6
China to Japan	9,539	10,358	9%	10%	9%	165	164	159	5	6
Korea to China	7,587	6,689	−12%	29%	24%	164	165	159	6	5
Japan to Korea	4,264	4,924	15%	5%	6%	179	176	175	1	4
China to Korea	3,834	3,902	2%	4%	3%	172	175	169	6	3
Korea to Japan	2,395	2,222	−7%	9%	8%	161	157	151	6	10
General machinery final products								(max: 325)		
China to Japan	13,574	19,513	44%	8%	8%	267	270	252	18	15
Japan to China	15,196	12,181	−20%	21%	23%	293	288	280	8	13
Korea to China	4,325	7,458	72%	18%	27%	272	266	254	12	18
China to Korea	4,051	5,645	39%	2%	2%	270	292	264	28	6
Japan to Korea	6,659	3,455	−48%	9%	7%	278	276	260	16	18
Korea to Japan	946	719	−24%	4%	3%	228	226	201	25	27
Electric machinery parts and components								(max: 144)		
Korea to China	35,255	68,412	94%	43%	55%	131	125	124	1	7
Japan to China	37,990	32,473	−15%	36%	38%	134	131	131	0	3
China to Korea	12,159	17,880	47%	11%	10%	133	130	130	0	3
China to Japan	14,172	17,307	22%	13%	10%	131	129	128	1	3
Japan to Korea	9,222	7,740	−16%	9%	9%	130	130	127	3	3
Korea to Japan	7,145	3,876	−46%	9%	3%	127	124	120	4	7
Electric machinery final products								(max: 149)		
China to Japan	11,974	27,691	131%	6%	10%	107	108	106	2	1
China to Korea	4,981	6,002	20%	3%	2%	110	113	110	3	0
Japan to China	5,501	5,533	1%	14%	19%	111	107	106	1	5
Korea to China	2,306	3,623	57%	7%	12%	102	95	91	4	11
Korea to Japan	1,516	2,905	92%	4%	9%	98	100	94	6	4
Japan to Korea	1,999	1,424	−29%	5%	5%	108	110	107	3	1
Transport equipment parts and components								(max: 44)		
Japan to China	4,727	7,023	49%	14%	16%	39	38	37	1	2
Korea to China	1,373	3,173	131%	14%	18%	31	35	30	5	1
China to Japan	1,428	2,691	89%	10%	10%	37	37	34	3	3
China to Korea	619	1,257	103%	4%	4%	37	40	36	4	1
Korea to Japan	432	749	73%	4%	4%	31	29	28	1	3
Japan to Korea	1,111	624	−44%	3%	1%	41	38	37	1	4
Transport equipment final products								(max: 88)		
Japan to China	3,794	7,281	92%	3%	7%	55	47	42	5	13
Korea to China	848	2,208	160%	2%	5%	36	34	25	9	11
China to Japan	1,042	1,225	18%	6%	4%	45	52	37	15	8
Japan to Korea	1,890	1,166	−38%	1%	1%	58	58	52	6	6
China to Korea	425	774	82%	2%	3%	50	53	43	10	7
Korea to Japan	45	45	0%	0%	0%	40	40	30	10	10
Precision machinery parts and components								(max: 71)		
Korea to China	15,663	20,204	29%	68%	85%	56	56	54	2	2
Japan to China	8,172	9,815	20%	44%	50%	63	62	61	1	2
China to Korea	1,278	2,664	108%	11%	16%	63	63	62	1	1
Japan to Korea	1,937	2,468	27%	10%	12%	59	58	57	1	2
China to Japan	2,232	2,451	10%	19%	14%	66	63	63	0	3
Korea to Japan	1,706	196	−89%	7%	1%	56	47	47	0	9

(*continued*).

Table 3. Continued.

	Trade value (millions, constant US $)		Growth rate,	Share in country's total exports to the world		N. of products				
	2007	2013	2007-13	2007	2013	2007	2013	Continuing	Ins	Outs
Precision machinery final products								(max: 167)		
Japan to China	3,316	6,905	108%	15%	23%	142	135	132	3	10
China to Japan	2,175	3,043	40%	11%	10%	138	134	127	7	11
Japan to Korea	1,927	2,710	41%	9%	9%	141	138	135	3	6
Korea to China	637	2,389	275%	22%	36%	124	118	111	7	13
China to Korea	437	910	108%	2%	3%	139	143	136	7	3
Korea to Japan	175	278	59%	6%	4%	114	99	90	9	24

Source: UN Comtrade Database (mainly, import statistics reported by selected countries, based on the HS 1996 classification, at the six-digit level).

Notes: See notes of Figure 1 and Table 1. Machinery includes general machinery (HS 84), electric machinery (HS 85), transport equipment (HS 86-89), and precision machinery (HS 90-92). By machinery subsector and by product grouping, exporter-importer country pairs are listed in descending order, in terms of the trade value in 2013.

precision machinery parts and components, however, Japan's exports to China have also increased steadily and are still more than twice as large as Korea's exports to China in 2013.

Second, China's exports to Japan have remained a lead in bilateral trade in electric machinery final products within the big three and further increased by 131% in the period 2007–2013. As of 2013, China's exports of electric machinery final products to Japan are more than quadruple the second-ranked China's exports to Korea in value terms. Korea's exports of electric machinery final products to Japan also showed a strong growth (92%), although the value is still relatively limited in 2013. In addition, China's exports of general machinery final products to Japan have increased steadily in the period 2007–2013 and have come out on top of the bilateral trade within the big three as of 2013.

Third, bilateral trade in general machinery parts and components within the big three show a different picture of Japan's presence as an exporter. In addition to the fact that Japan's exports to China have continued to lead by a substantial margin, Japan's exports of general machinery parts and components to China and to Korea achieved a higher growth than other exporter-importer country pairs in the period 2007–2013.

Lastly, the number of products actually traded between the big three countries tends to be saturated relative to the maximal possible number for machinery parts and compo-nents than for final products. In particular, the numbers of electric machinery parts and components and of precision machinery parts and components bilaterally traded within the big three appear to already hit the ceiling, showing a slight downward trend in the period 2007–2013. Additionally, an increasing number of products traded is noticeable for exporter-importer country pairs including China in the sample period. Bilateral exports of machinery parts and components to China have a tendency to be diversified in the prod-uct space while exports of final products from China tend to experience the export product diversification.

4.3. *Intensive and Extensive Margins of Trade Growth*

We further explore the relative importance of ins and outs of products in bilateral trade among China, Japan, and Korea. In an analogous way to what we did in Section 3.5 (and Figure 4), we decompose the growth of bilateral trade in machinery, by subsector and by

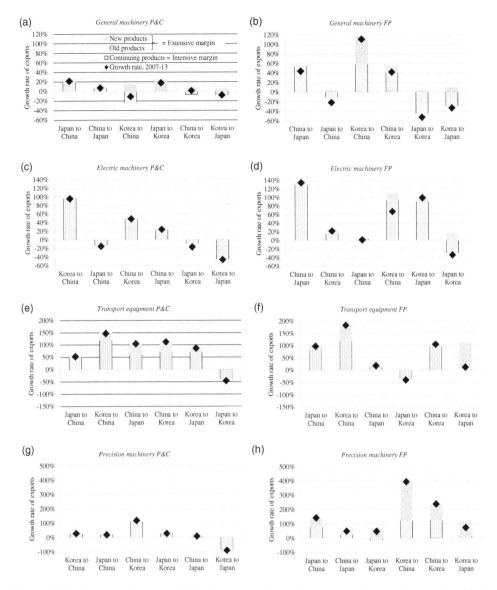

Figure 5. Machinery trade among China, Japan, and Korea: Intensive and extensive margins of trade growth.
Source: UN Comtrade Database (mainly, import statistics reported by selected countries, based on the HS 1996 classification, at the six-digit level).
Notes: See notes of Figure 4. Machinery includes general machinery (HS 84), electric machinery (HS 85), transport equipment (HS 86-89), and precision machinery (HS 90-92). By machinery subsector and by product grouping, exporter-importer country pairs are listed in descending order, from left to right, in terms of the trade value in 2013.

product grouping, into intensive and extensive margins. The stacked bars in Figure 5 show the contributions of continuing products, new products, and old products to the growth in bilateral trade of the sector-product grouping concerned between 2007 and 2013. The diamond indicates the growth rate of the exporter-importer country pair's total trade value of the product grouping concerned in the period 2007–2013. As in Table 3, for each sector-product grouping, exporter-importer country pairs are listed in descending order, from left to right, in terms of the value of trade in 2013.

The growth of bilateral trade in machinery parts and components within the big three is mostly attributed to the intensive margin in the period 2007–2013, with an exception of Japan's exports of general machinery parts and components to Korea. The (net) extensive margin accounts for about 90% of the total growth in Japan's exports of general machinery parts and components to Korea, which suggests that Japan steadily increased exports to Korea through the export product diversification, or by starting to export a non-negligible amount of new products. The relative importance of the extensive margin, particularly of the growth contribution of ins of new products, is also observed for China's exports of transport equipment parts and components to Japan and to Korea to some, although relatively limited, extent.

Compared with the trade growth in machinery parts and components, the growth of bilateral trade in final products within the big three shows a tendency to be accounted for by the intensive margin to a lesser extent. In particular, about a half or more of the total trade growth in precision machinery final products is attributed to the (net) extensive margin rather than the intensive margin. The most prominent example is the strikingly high growth (393%) in Korea's exports of precision machinery final products to China, which is attributed largely to ins of new products (287 out of 393 percentage points, or more than 70% of the total growth). The growth in Korea's exports of general machinery final products to China is also driven by the export product diversification to a considerable extent. Another interesting thing to note is that the (gross) growth contributions of ins and outs of products are strikingly large, although they almost totally offset each other, in Korea's exports of transport equipment final products to Japan. Behind the resulting low growth rate of the trade value, Korea appears to have undergone a drastic transformation of the composition of its exports of transport equipment final products to Japan through the ins and outs of economically important products.

5. Conclusion

This paper employs newly developed analytical method of zero trade flows, least-traded goods, and intensive and extensive margins of trade growth and analyzes the recent changes in machinery production networks extended by China, Japan, and Korea between 2007 and 2013. Our empirical approach is proved to be very effective and articulate in shedding light on the structure and the evolution of production networks. We found drastic changes in East Asian production networks within such a short period. China became a number. 1 player in machinery production networks not only in trade values but also in the diversity and density of export product-destination pairs. Although the outstanding growth of China's machinery exports was mostly attributed to the intensive margin, China actively built more trade relationships of existing products with new destination countries. Korea took advantage of China's dynamism and extended its production networks. Meanwhile, Korea underwent a drastic transformation of the product and destination composition in the exports of machinery final products. Japan remained stagnated and lost its relative importance in the regional as well as global context.

This result has profound policy implication. First, the dominant position of China in production networks means that China became increasingly influential to the whole world. Of course, exports and imports by China are not wholly attributed to Chinese firms; the role of multinational enterprises including Japanese and Korean firms is still substantial in China's international trade. But still, the importance of China as a center of production networks is obvious. This implies, for example, that the recent slowdown of the Chinese economy may potentially cause much larger impacts than before on countries that are connected with China by production networks. Another concern is China's passive attitude toward mega-FTAs. Mega-FTAs are now regarded as important policy channels to improve international business environment for production networks through setting up a high standard of trade/investment liberalization and a prototype of new international rules. However, in the negotiation over Regional Comprehensive Economic Partnership (RCEP) or ASEAN + 6 FTA, China, together with India, continuously tries to keep the liberalization level as low as possible. As a result, the modality of negotiation was set in the Economic Ministers Meeting held in August 2015 with the tariff removal ratio of only 80%. It was a bad timing because, just after this, in October 2015, the Trans-Pacific Economic Partnership (TPP) negotiation reached a rough agreement. China is now a responsible player in production networks and thus should engage itself in getting proactively involved with the establishment of a novel international economic order for production networks.

Second, Korea has achieved a lot of progress in the degree of participating in production networks, although it has strengthened the dependency on China in an extreme manner. Korean chaebols extend their production networks in China and other parts of East Asia, while keeping largely closed to Korean connections. This means that Korean firms might be less prone to being influenced by the performance of Chinese firms than Japanese firms. However, in the past few years, the Korean economy decelerated its growth seemingly due to the slowdown of China. Production links between Korea and China should be investigated further at the micro level.

Third, the poor performance of Japan in 2007–2013 was due to various negative shocks: the Global Financial Crisis, the East Japan Earthquake, extraordinary yen appreciation, confusing economic policies, and others. Since the end of 2012, 'Abenomics' has been effective for returning to the '2007 normal' but does not seem to push up the potential growth rate of the Japanese economy. Although manufacturing employment is still sustained at least in medium and large-scale firms, the nature of activities left over in Japan must be scrutinized.

Acknowledgements

The authors would like to thank the organizers, particularly Professor Tomoo Kikuchi, and the participants of the Inaugural International Conference, Centre on Asia and Globalization, Lee Kuan Yew School of Public Policy, National University of Singapore held in Singapore on 16–17 September 2015.

References

Baldwin, R., & Harrigan, J. (2011). Zeros, quality, and space: Trade theory and trade evidence. *American Economic Journal: Microeconomics, 3*(2), 60–88. doi:10.1257/mic.3.2.60

Besedeš, T., & Prusa, T. J. (2011). The role of extensive and intensive margins and export growth. *Journal of Development Economics, 96*, 371–379. doi:10.1016/j.jdeveco.2010.08.013

Debaere, P., & Mostashari, S. (2010). Do tariffs matter for the extensive margin of international trade? An empirical analysis. *Journal of International Economics*, *81*, 163–169. doi:10.1016/j.jinteco.2010.03.005

Kehoe, T. J., & Ruhl, K. J. (2013). How important is the new goods margin in international trade? *Journal of Political Economy*, *121*, 358–392. doi:10.1086/670272

Kimura, F. & Obashi, A. (2010). International production networks in machinery industries: Structure and its evolution (ERIA Discussion Paper Series ERIA-DP-2010-09). Retrieved from the Economic Research Institute for ASEAN and East Asia (ERIA) website: http://www.eria.org/ERIA-DP-2010-09.pdf

Obashi, A. & Kimura, F. (2015). Deepening and widening of production networks in ASEAN. Manuscript submitted for publication.

Appendix. Countries included in the dataset

- *Reporters of import statistics based on the HS 1996 classification for 2007 and 2013* (136 countries): Albania, Algeria, Andorra, Antigua and Barbuda*, Argentina, Armenia, Australia, Austria, Azerbaijan, Bahamas, Bahrain, Barbados, Belarus, Belgium, Belize, Benin, Bolivia, Bosnia Herzegovina, Botswana*, Brazil, Bulgaria, Burkina Faso, Burundi, Cabo Verde, Cambodia, Canada, Central African Rep., Chile, China, Colombia, Congo, Costa Rica, Côte d'Ivoire, Croatia, Cyprus, Czech Rep., Denmark, Dominican Rep., Ecuador, El Salvador, Estonia, Ethiopia, Fiji, Finland, France, FS Micronesia, Gambia*, Georgia, Germany, Ghana, Greece, Guatemala, Guyana, Hungary, Iceland, India, Indonesia*, Ireland, Israel, Italy, Jamaica, Japan, Jordan, Kazakhstan, Kenya, Kiribati, Kuwait, Kyrgyzstan, Latvia, Lebanon, Lithuania, Luxembourg, Madagascar, Malawi, Malaysia, Maldives, Malta, Mauritania*, Mauritius, Mexico, Mongolia, Montenegro, Morocco, Mozambique, Namibia, Netherlands, New Zealand, Nicaragua, Niger, Nigeria, Norway, Oman, Pakistan, Palau, Panama, Paraguay, Peru, Philippines, Poland, Portugal, Qatar, Rep. of Korea, Rep. of Moldova, Romania, Russian Federation, Rwanda, Samoa*, Sao Tome and Principe*, Saudi Arabia, Senegal, Serbia, Singapore, Slovakia, Slovenia, Solomon Islands, South Africa, Spain, Sri Lanka, Sweden, Switzerland, TFYR of Macedonia, Thailand, Togo, Tunisia, Turkey, Uganda, Ukraine*, United Kingdom, United Rep. of Tanzania, Uruguay, USA, Venezuela, Viet Nam, Yemen, Zambia, and Zimbabwe.
- *Countries included in our sample with modification* (three countries): Brunei Darussalam (whose import statistics for 2006 are used instead of those for 2007), Lao People's Democratic Republic (for which export statistics reported by trade partners are used), and Myanmar (whose import statistics for 2001 and 2010 are used instead of those for 2007 and 2013, respectively).

Notes
The country names listed above follow abbreviations used in the UN Comtrade Database (our source of data). * indicates that a country originally reported based on the HS 1996 classification for 2007 (this is not applicable to 2013 for all the listed countries). For countries without *, we use converted data. China includes only mainland China. Because the statistical territory of China's external trade statistics coincides with its customs territory which does not cover the separate customs territories of Hong Kong and Macau, the UN Comtrade Database practically treats mainland China and those Special Administrative Regions (SARs) separately. France includes Monaco. Norway includes Svalbard and Jan Mayen. Switzerland includes Liechtenstein. USA includes Puerto Rico and the US Virgin Islands.

Global Value Chains and China's Exports to High-income Countries

Yuqing Xing

National Graduate Institute for Policy Studies, Minato-ku, Tokyo, Japan

ABSTRACT

This paper argues that global value chains (GVCs) have functioned as a vehicle for 'Made in China' products to enter international markets, especially markets of high-income countries. The analysis of the paper focuses on China's processing exports, a subset of GVC activities. It demonstrates that, by participating in GVCs Chinese firms bundle processing exports with advanced technologies and globally recognized brands of lead firms, and then sell them to consumers of international markets through distribution networks of GVCs. Using panel data of bilateral processing exports covering more than 100 of China's trade partners, the paper shows empirically there exists a significantly positive correlation between the share of processing exports and the income of trading partners, implying that processing trade is an effective means for 'Made in China' products to enter high-income countries. The cross-country heterogeneity of processing exports also indicates China captures relatively more value added in its exports to low-income countries than to high-income countries.

1. Introduction

After three and half decades of rapid economic growth, China has surpassed Germany, Japan and the US and emerged as the largest exporting nation. 'Made in China' products are now ubiquitous in markets of both developed and developing countries, ranging from labor-intensive products, such as T-shirts and shoes to high-tech products such as mobile phones and digital cameras. For some consumers outside of China, it seems impossible to live without 'Made in China' products (Bongiomi, 2008).

Why are China's exports so competitive in the global market? What are the major forces driving the worldwide expansion and diversification of its manufacturing exports? Many academic scholars and China observers have tried to answer the questions from various aspects. A plethora of articles analyzing drastic growth of China's exports have been published in academic journals, magazines and newspapers. According to these studies, fundamental factors determining significant growth and worldwide expansion of China's exports include: (1) abundant labor endowment and corresponding comparative advantage in labor-intensive products (Adams, Gangnes, & Shachmurove, 2006; Wang, 2006);

(2) reforms of domestic institutions, such as the transition to a market oriented economy, the adoption of export-led growth strategy and unilateral trade liberalization (Hu & Khan, 1997; Lin, Cai, & Li, 2003); (3) improved market access for China's exports through institutional arrangements, namely the WTO membership, bilateral and multilateral free trade agreements and the abolishment of multi-fiber arrangement (Branstetter & Lardy, 2006; Prasad, 2009); (4) exchange rate regime adopted by the Chinese government and undervalued currency (Marquez & Schindler, 2007; Thorbecke & Smith, 2010); and (5) massive inflows of export oriented foreign direct investment (Whalley & Xin, 2010; Zhang & Song, 2000).

With a population of more than 1.4 billion, China is naturally endowed with comparative advantage in labor-intensive products. Assuming other factors determining global competitiveness are equal across countries, the relatively low labor cost should grant Chinese exports an edge over their competitors. Without any doubts, trade liberalization since 1990s in terms of tariff reductions and trade facilitations has substantially improved the market access of Chinese exports. Comparative advantage and trade liberalization arguments, however, mainly emphasize production costs and barriers to cross-country flows of goods, they fail to take into consideration the critical roles performed by the organization structures of modern trade in promoting China's exports, in particular its successful penetration into high-income countries. Those arguments actually leave many important questions unanswered. Without foreign brands, could 'Made in China' products maintain the same competitiveness? Whenever Apple launches new cutting-edge products, the shipment of Apple products from China to the rest of the world increases and continues to grow along with the rising popularity of Apple products. To whom should be given credits for the increase, innovative American company Apple, or assembler Foxcon, a Taiwanese company located in mainland China, which has been banking on cheap Chinese labor?

In the classic models of Ricardo and Heckscher-Ohlin, comparative advantage represents a sole factor determining competitiveness and trade patterns. Today's trade, nonetheless, is not 'wine for clothes'. The proliferation of global value chains has transformed trade in goods into trade in tasks (Grossman & Rossi-Hansberg, 2008). Many firms located in various geographic locations jointly deliver ready-to-use products to consumers of the global market. The comparative advantage of an individual country cannot decide the competitiveness of products manufactured along GVCs. Brands, global distribution networks and technology innovations perform far more important roles in determining winners and losers. GVCs are particular relevant to China's exports, as about half of its manufacturing exports are assembled with imported parts and components, and most so-called 'Made in China' products either carry brands owned by multinational enterprises (MNE) or are distributed by global retail giants such as Wal-Mart.

In this paper, we attempt to interpret China's export boom in the context of value chains. We argue that GVCs have been functioning as a vehicle for Chinese exports entering international markets, especially markets of high-income countries. By successfully plugging into GVCs, Chinese firms have been able to bundle their low-skilled labor services with globally recognized brands and advanced technologies of MNEs, and then sell them to consumers of international markets. GVCs are actually a catalyst for 'Made in China' products; strictly speaking, they show China's value added embedded in its manufacturing exports, being bought and consumed in various nations. Continuous technology innovations, aggressive promotions on brand and the worldwide development of distribution networks by lead firms of GVCs, constantly expand and create new demand, which in turn raises demand for tasks performed by Chinese firms integrated with supply chains and this eventually enhances China's exports.

To establish this argument, we first examine tasks performed by Chinese firms in GVCs and domestic value added in its exports. The analysis starts with a case of the iPhone, of which has China been the exclusive exporter, then extends the coverage to high-tech products, where China claims to be the No. 1 exporter in the world (Meri, 2009), and further expands the scope to processing exports, which includes both high-tech and ordinary manufacturing goods.

Following the descriptive analysis, we empirically analyze the intensity of processing exports in China's bilateral trade and its correlation with the income of destination markets. Processing exports refers to exports manufactured or assembled with imported parts and components. Assembly and processing are typical segments of value chains and belong to low value added tasks. Processing exports not only reveal tasks the Chinese firms perform, but also provide a direct measure of exports associated with GVC participation. The empirical investigation is based on a unique panel data set, covering China's processing exports to more than 100 economies from 1993–2013. We find China's processing exports mainly end up with high-income countries and the intensity of processing exports, defined as the share of processing exports in bilateral exports has a significantly positive relation with the income of destination markets, implying that processing exports has functioned as an effective means for 'Made in China' products to enter markets of high-income countries. China's exports to high-income countries benefit substantially from GVC's spillover effects associated with brands, distribution networks and technology innovations.

The rest of the paper is organized as follow. In Section 2, we will briefly summarize spillover effects of GVCs to Chinese firms involved in supply chains. The analysis focuses on spillover effects of brands, distribution networks and technology innovations; Section 3 will discuss the roles and tasks performed by Chinese firms in exports manufactured and traded along GVCs. The discussion concentrates on representative products – iPhone, high-tech products and processing exports; in Section 4, we will investigate the relative importance of processing exports in China's bilateral trade, and empirically analyze the correlation between the intensity of processing exports and the income of its trading partners; Section 5 summarizes the main findings of the paper.

2. Spillover Effects of Global Value Chains

A global value chain comprises a series of tasks necessary for delivering a product from its inception to final consumers in international markets, including research and development, product design, manufacturing parts and components, assembly and distribution, which are carried out by firms located in various countries (Gereffi & Karina, 2011). According to governance structures, GVCs can be classified into producer-driven and buyer-driven value chains. Producer-driven chains are generally developed by technology leaders in automobiles, aircrafts, computers, semiconductors and other capital-intensive industries; buyer-driven chains are typically developed by large retailers, branded marketers and branded manufacturers (Gereffi, 1999). In the context of a property-rights model, the characterization of ownership allocation along value chains can also depend on incentives to integrate suppliers and the elasticity of demand faced by final-good producers (Antràs & Chor, 2013).

Technology advancement, unprecedented liberalization in trade and investment and profit seeking behaviors of MNEs have been driving the emergence of GVCs in the last decades (OECD, 2013). Today, most manufacturing commodities are actually produced and traded along value chains. GVCs have also been extended into business process and management, such as software development and maintenance and voice services. Like an invisible hand, GVCs have interconnected national economies. The economic integration through value chains is fundamentally market driven and tends to be more stable and effective than that led by institutional arrangements or defined by conventional arms-length trade. The theory of international trade suggests that specializations according to comparative advantage improve the efficiency of resource allocations and hence the welfare of trading nations. Compared with conventional specializations on industries or products, specializations on tasks defined by value chains further refine specializations among nations and enhance the efficiency of resource allocations, consequently raising the productivity and economy growth of all economies involved.

Here we would like to emphasize spillover effects of GVCs at micro-level and discuss how spillover effects generated by intangible assets of lead firms, such as brands, distribution networks and technology innovations, help Chinese firms overcome entry barriers of international markets and achieve dramatic global expansion. Cheap labor is often addressed as a comparative advantage of Chinese firms. It seems that as long as companies could manufacture products at competitive costs, they would be able to sell their products and compete in the global market. As a matter of fact, the competition in the global market is much more complicated than this kind of simple reasoning. Production costs are just one of many factors deciding the success in international markets. As barriers to entry in manufacturing fall, intangible assets such as brands and global distribution networks have turned into major hurdles to firms of developing countries, which strive to take part in the world market (Kaplinsky, 2000).

Generally, consumers of developed countries tend to be brand oriented and have high willingness to pay for particular brands. Brands are one of the critical factors that determine consumers' choices (Bronnenberg, Dube, & Gentzkow, 2012). Owing to asymmetric information, consumers regard brands as an assurance of product quality. Switching costs may also undermine consumers' willingness to substitute preferred brands with new alternatives. Consumers' biases to particular brands grant advantage to incumbent producers and raise barrier to new entries. For instance, branded clothing constitutes the majority of the European clothing market, with around 80% market share. So only 20% is left to private labels and non-branded clothing (Thelle, Jeppesen, & Hvidt, 2013). Despite more than three decades high growth, Chinese firms have not nurtured a significant number of globally recognized brands. So far, only one Chinese brand, Huawei, is on the list of 2014 global brands. Creating and sustaining global brands requires lavish advertising budgets and global promotion campaigns, which is beyond the capacity of most Chinese firms when they in the early stage of their development. Owners of global brands usually lead buyer-driven value chains (Gereffi, 1999). By plugging into buyer-driven value chains as assemblers, part producers, or original equipment makers, Chinese firms are able to circumvent the disadvantage in brands and take advantage of consumers' preferences towards international brands. Compared with non-branded products with equal or even lower costs, the labels of international brands strengthen the competitiveness of 'Made in China' products and enhance their appeal to consumers. The preferences of brand-oriented consumers are implicitly transformed into the demand for 'Made in China' products. Without any doubts, China's exports would fall substantially if the attached foreign brands were removed.

In addition, to a large extent, new and fast growing markets have been nurtured by technology innovations and product inventions. Revolutionary innovations in information and communication technology (ICT) have given rise to a variety of new products, such as laptop computers, smart phones and tablets, thus dramatically stimulating consumers' demand beyond traditional commodities. In 2012, ICT goods emerged as some of top products traded globally. The world imports of ICT goods rose to US$2 trillion, about 11% of world merchandise trade and exceeded trade in agriculture and motor vehicles (UNCTAD, 2014). If not all, then most intellectual properties of ICT products are owned by the MNEs of developed countries. Compared with established MNEs, Chinese firms do not have comparative advantage in high-tech products. Constrained by limited human resources, insufficient investment in research and development, and relatively short learning-by-doing history, Chinese firms face challenges to market products with their own intellectual properties and compete with incumbent technology leaders. The global expansion of value chains, on the other hand, offers an alternative for Chinese firms to participate in the markets of high-tech products and benefit from the fast growing demand for these products, regardless of their disadvantages. By participating in the value chains of high-tech products and specializing in low value added segments, such as assembly and production of low-tech components, Chinese firms are able to join the value creation processes of high-tech products and grow together with lead firms. The unit value added of the segment may be relatively small, for instance assembly adds only $6.5 per iPhone (Xing & Detert, 2010). The sheer size of the world market implies a huge growth potential and economies of scale. Being a part of value chains, Chinese firms can enjoy the spillover effect of lead firms' technology innovations. It is imperative to clarify that the spillover emphasized here differs from that defined in conventional literature of technology and productivity growth. It refers to an opportunity of joining and benefiting from markets of high-tech products, where Chinese firms have neither the necessary intellectual properties nor comparative advantage. As a matter of fact, China's leading positions in exports of laptop computers, digital cameras, mobiles and other ICT products have been achieved via specializing on low value added task-assembly of those products rather than on indigenous technology innovations.

Finally, selling products in world markets requires global distribution networks. The existence of a basic marketing and distribution infrastructure is a prerequisite for supply and demand to be interconnected with one another. The buyer–seller links between exporters and overseas buyers is an important channel for the diffusion of knowledge and information (Wgan & Mody, 1992). In any value chains, lead firms are buyers and responsible for marketing and distribution. They set up product standards and instruct suppliers upstream of chains about what to be produced. Through such contacts suppliers learn the nature of the potential market, and lead firms exercise direct quality control and often transfer valuable design, packaging and production know-how to suppliers (Gereffi, 1999). Hence, the required buyer–seller relations for exporting commodities to foreign markets are naturally built in GVCs. For firms without their own global distribution networks, joining GVCs can mitigate information deficiency, reduce transaction costs and facilitate market access. Taking advantage of GVC's spillover effects in distribution networks, Chinese firms involved in GVCs have not only entered the world market successfully, but have also been free of concerns about marketing their products to consumers in dispersed geographic locations. For example, Wal-Mart, if counted as a 'nation', is the seventh largest trading partner of China and imports more than $18 billion goods from China annually (Lee, Gereffi, & Barrientos, 2011). The retail networks of Wal-Mart provide an essential marketing and distributions infrastructure for 'Made in China' products. Chinese suppliers use the retail networks as a vehicle to reach consumers in the US and in other foreign markets.

3. GVCs and Global Expansion of China's Exports

In this section, we will take a few representative goods as examples to intuitively illustrate the contribution of GVCs to the global expansion of Chinese exports. Since the launch of the first generation iPhone, China has been the exclusive exporter of iPhones. In 2009, it exported 11.3 million iPhones valued at $2.0 billion to the US. In spite of rising wages and the cumulative appreciation of the Yuan, China's iPhone exports to the US continued to grow and surged to $8.5 billion, more than triple the figure in 2012. During the same period, the Chinese Yuan appreciated 8.2% against the US dollar from $1 equals 6.83 Yuan to 6.31 Yuan. The average annual wage of Chinese workers rose close to 50% from 34,000 Yuan to 50,000 Yuan. In terms of exchange rates and wages, China's comparative advantage in labor costs actually deteriorated, and thus cannot explain the drastic increase in iPhone exports.

Furthermore, that China exports iPhones to the US, where the iPhone was invented, appears inconsistent with classic theory of comparative advantage. The strange trade pattern, however, can easily be explained by GVCs. On the back of each iPhone, there is a statement 'Designed by Apple in California. Assembled in China'. The message unambiguously reveals the actual task performed by China in manufacturing iPhones. Compared with other smart phones, the iPhone is the most expensive, with a more than 60% gross profit margin (Xing & Detert, 2010). The value chain of the iPhone is governed by Apple. Therefore, the competitiveness of the iPhone and its fast global expansion should be attributed to the technology innovations of Apple rather than China's comparative advantage – i.e. low labor cost. It is critical to emphasize that what China exports via the iPhone is the services of low-skilled labor but not advanced technology. It is the iPhone supply chain that provides an opportunity for Chinese firms to sell labor services to all users of iPhones. The international production fragmentation of the iPhone enables Chinese firms to be one of the beneficiaries of Apple's technology innovations.

iPhone trade is not unique. Most of China's exports in high-tech products follow the same fashion. They are manufactured and delivered through various GVCs. In recent years, high-tech products have emerged as a major export item, accounting for about one third of China's total manufacturing exports. In 2012, China exported US$600 billion high-tech goods, more than ten times higher compared with in 2002. The exponential growth of high-tech exports has been driven by the extension of high-tech supply chains into China. To a great extent, it is international fragmentations of high-tech manufacturing processes

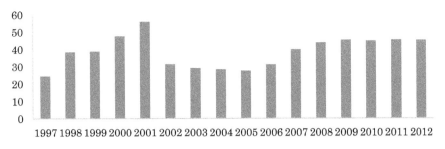

Figure 1. The domestic value added of China's processing high-tech exports.
Source: Xing (2014a).

that bring Chinese firms into the game of exporting high-tech products. In order to utilize China's abundant labor, many high-tech MNEs have relocated manufacturing facilities into China or outsourced low value added tasks to firms there. According to Xing (2014b), foreign invested firms produce more than 80% of China's high-tech exports. More importantly, about 80% of China's high-tech exports falls into the category of processing trade and has relatively low domestic value added. Domestic value added in exports measures the dependence of exports on foreign contents and vertical integration of its industries with international production networks. Figure 1 shows the share of domestic value added of China's processing of high-tech exports from 1997 to 2012. It was as low as 25% in 1997 and gradually increased to 45% by 2012. Despite a substantial increase in domestic contents, foreign value added remains above 50%, suggesting that processing of high-tech exports is a result of GVC operations. Given that most key components used in high-tech exports are imported and Chinese firms perform mainly low skilled tasks, the technology sophistication of China's high-tech exports is primarily determined by the technology innovations of lead firms. In other words, technology spillovers of GVCs raise the sophistication and the competitiveness of China's processing high-tech exports, thus eventually fostering its rapid expansion in the global market. Some researchers (e.g. Branstetter & Lardy, 2006) argue that these products are not high-tech but commodities as they can be manufactured in large volumes. We do not agree with this argument. These products still represent technology frontiers, but tasks performed by Chinese firms, such as assembly and making non-core components, are low skilled.

To investigate the critical role of GVCs beyond high-tech exports, we extend the discussion into processing exports, a subset of GVCs' activities. Since China adopted an export-led growth strategy, processing exports has been promoted as a major trade regime. In 2012, it amounted US$860 billion, about 42% of China's total exports. During the high growth period of 1997–2007, it grew faster than ordinary exports and generally exceeded 50% of China's total exports (Figure 2). Foreign invested firms play a dominant role in processing exports and are responsible for more than 75% (Ma & Assche, 2011) of this work. The analysis on the geographic origins of processing imports, the inputs used for producing exports and the destination markets of processing exports shows that East Asian economies are the major origins while G-7 countries are the main destinations (Xing, 2012). The triangle trade pattern formed by processing trade outlines an aggregated GVC with China in the middle. Similar to processing high-tech exports, foreign value added accounts for a large portion of the value added in processing exports too.

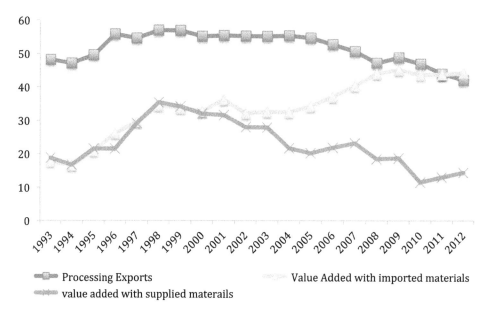

Figure 2. Processing exports and the domestic value added.
Source: Xing (2014a).

Figure 2 shows the estimated domestic value added in two distinct groups of processing exports: one with imported materials and the other with materials supplied by foreign contractors. In the former, the share of domestic content averaged 33%, while in the latter it was 23% during the period of 1993–2012. Significantly, a low share of domestic value added suggests excessive dependence of processing exports on foreign contents and a high degree of vertical integration with foreign firms. In fact, in the case of processing exports with supplied materials, Chinese firms simply assemble supplied parts and components together and then send the assembled products to foreign contractors, who are responsible for product designs, material procurements and marketing. Therefore, through different channels and at different fragments of GVCs, brands, distribution networks and technology innovations of lead firms have all contributed to rapid growth and impressive global expansion of China's processing exports.

4. Processing Exports and China's Exports to High-income Countries

China has turned into the largest import source of the US, Japan and the European Union. Shares of China's exports in these markets are disproportionally high compared with its weight in the world economy. Generally, the markets of high-income countries tend to be more competitive and thus more challenging for firms of developing countries to enter and gain market share. As argued above, firms participating in GVCs are able to benefit from brands, technology innovations and distribution networks, which are indispensable for competing in the global market. A few studies (e.g. Ma & Assche, 2011; Xing, 2012) show that China's processing exports mainly end up in the markets of the US, Japan and the EU. By definition, processing exports are synonymous with GVCs. The significant presence of processing exports actually underline the vehicle role of GVCs in facilitating 'Made in China' products to enter high-income countries.

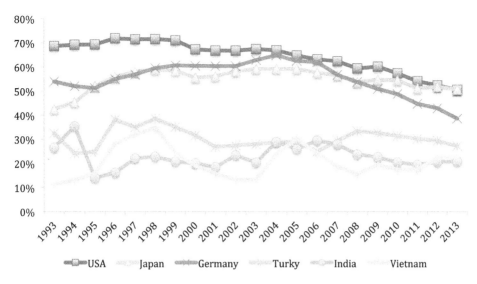

Figure 3. Intensities of processing exports in China's exports to selected countries.
Source: Authors' calculation.

To empirically investigate the vehicle role of processing trade, we first calculate the shares of processing exports in China's exports to six individual countries: the US, Japan, Germany, Turkey, India and Vietnam. All of these countries are important trading partners of China and represent high, middle and low-income countries respectively. Figure 3 summarizes the results from 1993 to 2013. It is straightforward to see a divergence between high-income (the US, Japan and Germany) and low-income (India and Vietnam) countries. In the former, processing exports accounted for more than 55% on average while in the latter about 20%. Specifically, processing exports comprised about 65% of China's exports to the US on average and even exceeded 70% during the period of 1996–1999. Before 2005, processing exports to both Japan and Germany grew rapidly, much faster than ordinary exports. As a result, the share of processing exports to Japan rose to 59% in 2005 from 43% in 1993 while to Germany it increased to 62% from 54%. In recent years, shares of processing exports gradually declined from a peak but remained more than 50% for the US and Japan.

On the contrary, processing exports on average accounted for 30% of China's exports to Turkey, 23% to India and 21% to Vietnam during the period – much lower than to high-income countries. The simple descriptive statistics imply that processing exports mainly target high-income countries. To examine the stability of the correlation, we expand the sample size by including all of China's partners in processing exports in 2012. The sample consists of 115 countries. We use the sample to draw a scatter chart of the share of processing exports versus the income of destination markets. Figure 4 shows the scatter chart, where the vertical axis denotes the share of processing exports and the horizontal axis GDP per capita. The logarithm of both variables is used in the chart. It unambiguously reveals a positive log-linear relation between the share of processing exports and the income, suggesting that the proportion of processing exports is an increasing function of the income of destination markets.

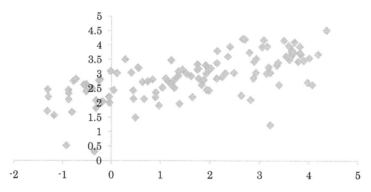

Figure 4. The correlation between the share of processing exports and the income of China's trading partners in 2012.
Source: authors' calculations.

Figures 3 and 4 provide intuitive evidence on the possible correlation between the share of processing exports and the income of China's trading partners. Now we turn to regression analysis of the relationship.

To formally test the correlation, we specify the regression model as

$$\ln(p_{jt}) = \alpha + \beta_1 \ln(y_{jt}) + \beta_2 \ln(ex_{ust}) + \beta_3 EA + \beta_4 WTO + \beta_5 Epot + \beta_6 t + \mu_{jt}$$

where p_{jt} represents the share of processing exports in China's exports to country j, defined as a ratio of processing exports to total exports to country j in year t. The specified model can be considered as a derivative of two gravity equations, one is a gravity equation of processing exports and the other a gravity equation of total exports. Since the GDP of China and its trading partners as well as geographic distance are usually included in gravity equations, these variables are assumed to be cancelled after the first gravity equation is divided by the second one. y_{jt} denotes GDP per capita of country j. It measures the preferences of foreign consumers to processing exports. As argued above, consumers of developed economies tend to have strong preferences toward branded and technology goods. Figure 3 and 4 intuitively suggest a positive correlation between the intensity of processing exports and the income level of China's trading partner. y_{jt} is the focus of the estimation. ex_{ust} represents the nominal exchange rate of The Yuan to the US dollar, calculated as the price of the US dollar in terms of the Chinese Yuan. We use the exchange rate of the Yuan to the US dollar rather than bilateral exchange rates for two reasons. First, more than 80% of China's exports are priced and settled in the US dollar. Second, processing exports is a subset of GVC's activities. In general, only one currency, usually the US dollar, is used to settle transactions between firms involved in the same GVCs.

EA is a dummy variable, proxying the impact of GVCs in East Asia. GVCs show significant regional bias. Chinese companies engaging in processing exports mainly take part in production networks in East Asia. It is necessary to include a dummy variable to capture the regional bias. *EA* takes the value 1 if j belongs to East Asia, zero otherwise. *WTO* is another dummy, testing the impact of China's entry to the World Trade Organization in 2001. It is equal to 1 after 2001, zero otherwise. *Epot* is also a dummy variable and identifies trading partners serving as an entrepôt, where a substantial part of China's exports to these economies is re-exported to third countries. Hong Kong, Macao and Luxembourg

Table 1. Processing exports and income of trading partners.

	(1)	(2)
Variables	OLS estimation	Fixed effect
ln(y)	0.299***	0.705***
	(0.00777)	(0.0984)
ln(ex)	0.372**	0.392***
	(0.153)	(0.121)
EAD	0.539***	
	(0.0275)	
WTO	−0.0381	−0.0391
	(0.0492)	(0.0330)
Eport	0.123**	
	(0.0500)	
t	−0.00655	−0.0157***
	(0.00507)	(0.00435)
Constant	8.276	23.29***
	(10.32)	(8.500)
Observations	2401	2401
R-squared	0.434	0.722

Notes: standard errors are in parentheses, with *** (**,*) denotes statistical
significance at 1% (5%, 10%) level.
Source: authors' calculations.

are defined as entrepôts in the estimation. Independent variable T is employed to capture the trend of processing exports.

Data used for the estimation are drawn from various sources. Statistics on bilateral processing exports and total exports covering 21 years from 1993–2013 are provided by the office of China Customs. GDP per capita and foreign exchange rates are downloaded from the World Development Indicators of the World Bank and the International Financial Statistics of the International Monetary Fund. After preparing variables for estimation, there are 2401 observations. We test the stationarity of dependent variable $\ln(p_{jt})$ and the result shows that it is stationary. Table 1 reports estimation results based on the ordinary least squared (OLS) and the fixed effect models. Estimates of the OLS are listed as a reference. Here we only explain estimates of the fixed effect model.

The R-squared shows that the fixed effect model can explain 72% of the variation of the dependent variable. The coefficient of GDP per capita y is 0.705 and statistically significant at 1%, implying that the share of processing exports to high-income countries is larger than that to low-income countries. It supports our hypothesis that processing exports function as an effective vehicle for Chinese exports to enter markets of developed countries. A 1% increase in GDP per capita will be expected to raise the share of processing exports 2 percentage point. The coefficient of exchange rate ex_{ust} is 0.392 and statistically significant at 1%. ex_{ust} is the price of the dollar in terms of the Chinese Yuan. The positive coefficient implies that the depreciation of the Yuan against the US dollar would increase the share of processing exports and vice versa. According to the estimate, a 1% appreciation of the Yuan would give rise to a 1.48 percentage point decrease in the share of processing exports. The Chinese Yuan has appreciated about 35% cumulatively against the US dollar since 2005. Meanwhile, the share of processing exports in China's total exports fell to 39% in 2013 from its peak of 57%. The empirical result provides evidence that the appreciation of the Yuan undermined China's comparative advantage in the assembly task of GVCs, thus undercutting overall growth of China's exports. The estimated coefficient of dummy variable T is

−0.0157 and is statistically significant at 1%, suggesting that the share of processing exports trended lower. The WTO dummy is positive but insignificant.

Moreover, the empirical result reveals that China's processing exports are not uniformly distributed across trading partners, and there exists significant cross-country heterogeneity. As demonstrated above, processing exports incorporate more than 50% of foreign value added. To a large extent, the share of processing exports determines the proportion of domestic value added embedded in China's bilateral exports. The low intensity of processing exports implies high domestic value added. In other words, China captures relatively more value added in its exports to low-income countries compared with that to high-income ones.

5. Concluding Remarks

As the center of global assembly, Chinese exporting firms have been closely integrated with GVCs. Besides intrinsic comparative advantage, rapid growth and worldwide expansion of China's exports should be examined in the context of GVCs. To investigate the contribution of GVCs to China's exports, in particular exports to high-income countries, we focus on processing exports, a subset of GVC activities. Our analysis shows that China's processing exports benefit substantially from spillover effects of GVCs in brands, global distribution networks and technology innovations of lead firms. By taking part in GVCs, Chinese firms bundle low-skilled labor services with globally recognized brands and advanced technology, then sell these services to global consumers. More than 50% of foreign value added imbedded in processing exports suggests that, to a large extent, the competitiveness of processing exports is determined by foreign contents rather than China's comparative advantage and indigenous technology innovations.

Processing exports actually function as a vehicle for 'Made in China' to enter the markets of high-income countries. While shares of processing exports to high-income countries, such as the US and Japan exceed more than 50%, the share to low-income countries is as low as 20%. The regression analysis shows that there exists a significant positive correlation between the share of processing exports and the income of import countries, providing empirical evidence on the facilitating role of GVCs for 'Made in China' products to penetrate the markets of high-income countries. The cross-country heterogeneity of processing exports suggests that China actually captures relatively more value added from its exports to low-income countries than to high-income ones.

References

Adams, G. F., Ganges, B., & Shachmurove, Y. (2006). Why is China so competitive? Measuring and explaining China's competitiveness. *World Economy*, 29, 95–122.

Antràs, P., & Chor, D. (2013). Organizing the global value chain. *Econometrica*, 81, 2127–2204.

Bongiomi, S. (2008). *A year without 'Made in China': One Family's true life adventure in the global economy*. New Jersey: Wiley.

Branstetter, L., & Lardy, N. (2006). China's embrace of globalization. NBER Working Paper 12373.

Bronnenberg, B. J., Dube, J. H., & Gentzkow, M. (2012). The evolution of brand preference: Evidence from consumer migration. *American Economic Review*, 102, 2472–2508.

Egan, M. L., & Mody, A. (1992). Buyer-seller links in export development. *World Development*, 20, 321–334.

Gereffi, G. (1999). International trade and industrial upgrading in the apparel commodity chain. *Journal of international Economics*, 48, 37–70.

Gereffi, G., & Karina, F. (2011). *Global value chain analysis: A primer*. Durham, NC: Center on Globalization, Governance and Competitiveness, Duke University.

Grossman, G. M., & Rossi-Hansberg, E. (2008). Trading tasks: A simple theory of offshoring. *American Economic Review*, 98, 1978–1997.

Hu, Z. F., & Khan, M. (1997). Why is China growing so fast? *IMF Staff Papers*, 44(1), 103–131.

Kaplinsky, R. (2000). Globalization and unequalization: What can be learned from value chain analysis? *The Journal of Development Studies*, 37, 117–142.

Lee, J., Gereffi, G., & Barrientos, S. (2011, November). Global value chains, upgrading and poverty reduction. *Capturing the Gains, Brief Notes*.

Lin, J. Y., Cai, F., & Li, Z. (2003). *The China miracle*. Hong Kong: The Chinese University Press.

Ma, A. C., & Assche, A. V. (2011). China's role in global production networks. Retrieved from SSRN: http://ssrn.com/abstract = 2179940.

Marquez, J., & Schindler, J. (2007). Exchange rate effects on China's trade. *Review of International Economics*, 15, 837–853.

Meri, T. (2009). China passes the EU in high-tech exports. Science and Technology, Eurostat Statistics in Focus. Retrieved from http://epp.eurostat.ec.europa.eu/cache/ITY_OFFPUB/KS-SF-09-025/EN/KS-SF-09-025-EN.PDF.

OECD (2013). *Interconnected economies: Benefiting from Global Value Chains*. Paris: OECD.

Prasad, E. (2009). Is the Chinese growth miracle built to last? *China Economic Review*, 20(1), 103–123.

Thelle, M. H., Jeppesen, T., & Hvidt, M. (2013). *Unchaining the supply chain: How global branded clothing firms are contributing to the European economy*. Copenhagen: Copenhagen Economics.

Thorbecke, W., & Smith, G. (2010). How would an appreciation of the Renminbi and the East Asian currencies affect China's exports? *Review of International Economics*, 18(1), 95–108.

UNCATD (2014). Global imports of information technology goods approach $2 trillion. Retrieved from www.uncatad.org.

Wang, Y. (2006). Cheap Labor and China's export capacity. In K. H. Zhang (Ed.), *China as the World Factory* (pp. 69–82). London: Routledge.

Whalley, J., & Xin. X. (2010). China's FDI and non-FDI economies and sustainability of high Chinese growth. *China Economic Review*, 21(1), 123–135.

Xing, Y. (2012). Processing trade, exchange rates and China's bilateral trade balances. *Journal of Asian Economics*, 23, 540–547.

Xing, Y. (2014a). Measuring value added in PRC's exports: A direct approach. ADBI Working Paper 493, Asian Development Bank Institute.

Xing, Y. (2014b). China's high-tech exports: myth and reality. *Asian Economic Papers*, 13(1), 109–123.

Xing, Y., & Detert, N. (2010). How the iPhone widens the United States trade deficit with the PRC. ADBI Working Paper 257, Asian Development Bank Institute.

Zhang, K. H., & Song, S. (2000). Promoting exports: the role of inward FDI in China. *China Economic Review*, 11, 285–396.

Rethinking the Exchange Rate Impact on Trade in a World with Global Value Chains

Kevin C. Cheng, Gee Hee Hong, Dulani Seneviratne & Rachel van Elkan

International Monetary Fund, NW, Washington DC, USA

ABSTRACT

Global value chains (GVCs) are a prominent feature of global production and trading systems. Using the OECD-WTO database on trade in value added, this paper examines the exchange rate elasticities of GVC-related exports and imports and compares them with elasticities for trade in traditonal goods. We find that a real depreciation raises both the foreign and domestic value-added content of GVC-related exports. The size of these elasticities is found to be smaller when the import content of GVC exports is larger. Among the key policy implications of these results is that exchange rate changes by small contributors of value added have little effect on their own production or the production of their supply chain partners. On the other hand, large contributors to the value-added of the final product create spillovers to their smaller supply chain partners, obviating traditional beggar-thy-neighbor concerns.

1. Introduction

Greater technological complexity of products, lower transport and communication costs and reduced barriers to foreign trade have enabled the cross-border fragmentation of production into global value chains (GVCs). In a GVC, numerous countries add value at different stages in the overall production process, and imported intermediate products are transformed and then re-exported. Goods generated in GVCs are therefore multi-country products. This contrasts with the traditional view of international trade, in which products are made in their entirety within a single country and shipped as final goods to export markets. About a third of the value of world trade consists of GVC-related intermediate products.[1]

Within a GVC, imports – which represent foreign value added (FVA) – are used as inputs into the production of exports, making them complements in production with domestic value added (DVA). Therefore, a country's exports contain both DVA and FVA. As a result, it is reasonable to expect that GVC-related trade responds differently compared with traditional trade in 'single-country' goods to changes in the exchange rate. Understanding how exchange rate changes affect cross-border trade and trade balances

---

[1] Because intermediate products traverse international borders multiple times, this leads to the well-documented result that GVCs tend to swell the amount of international trade.

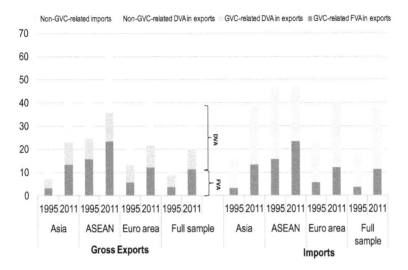

Figure 1. Decomposition of gross exports and imports, 1995 and 2011 (in percent of GDP). *Source*: OECD-WTO TiVA database; and authors' estimates.

has become all the more important in view of the large exchange rate realignments among major reserve currencies in recent years. In particular, policymakers will tend to be more interested in how DVA – which determines competitiveness and ultimately GDP – and the trade balance respond to exchange rate changes, than in what is happening to gross trade flows.

This paper examines the impact of exchange rate changes on GVC-related exports and imports and contrasts the response to that of traditional non-GVC products. It also looks at how exchange rate movements impact the trade balance. In order to address these questions, we rely on a recently-released OECD-WTO database on trade in value added. Due to the relative novelty of this dataset, we discuss upfront the concepts and terminology that are used in this paper.

As illustrated in Figure 1, total gross exports comprise exports produced within a GVC as well as other, non-GVC exports. Gross GVC exports can, in turn, be divided into DVA and FVA components, both of which are subsequently exported as inputs into the next stage of the supply chain. On the other hand, non-GVC exports consist primarily of DVA. Therefore, gross exports constitute both DVA and FVA. Gross imports encompass GVC–related imports – which is the FVA component of GVC-related exports – and non-GVC-related imports. Because FVA in GVC exports appears in both gross imports and gross exports, it does not affect the size of the trade balance. It is apparent from the figure that GVC-related gross exports (sum of DVA and FVA in GVCs) have grown considerably as a share of GDP across all regions during 1995–2011, especially in ASEAN. Nonetheless, non-GVC related exports remain around two-thirds of world total exported DVA.

Our study can be seen in the context of previous work on how foreign intermediates affect the sensitivity of prices and quantities to exchange rate changes. Looking at prices, Amiti, Itskhoki, and Konings (2014) and Ollivaud, Rusticelli, and Schwellnus (2015) find that exchange rate pass through to export prices is weaker when exporters rely more intensively on imports. This result can be attributed to the fact that prices of imported intermediates are typically denominated in a currency other than the exporter's own, thereby cushioning the exporter's marginal cost (measured in foreign currency terms) from fluctuations in its own currency.

To the extent that export prices are shielded from exchange rate changes, the response of export quantities should also be dampened. Consistent with this, Fauceglia, Lassmann, Shingal, and Wermelinger (2014) and Powers and Riker (2013) observe that the decrease in gross exports in response to an appreciation is smaller when the share of imported intermediates is larger. Using a simulated partial equilibrium approach, Riad et al. (2012) find that position in the supply chain also matters, with exports and imports being cushioned from exchange rate changes in countries that are more downstream in the supply chain – and which, by definition, have a larger foreign content in their exports. Ahmed, Appendino, and Ruta (2015) observe that the exchange rate elasticity of manufacturing exports has declined during the past two decades, with the growing role of GVC trade accounting for about two-fifths of the decline. Focusing on China, Garcia-Herrero and Koivu (2009) find that appreciation of the renminbi *reduces* China's imports from other Asian countries, which they attribute to the high degree of vertical integration in Asia's exports. This result is consistent with Bems and Johnston (2012), who use national input–output tables to obtain country-specific real effective exchange rate (REER) weights, and find that negative weights are possible, consistent with situations where depreciation by one country *boosts* the exports of its supply chain partners.[2]

We add to this existing literature in several ways. First, we identify separately the impact of exchange rate changes on DVA and FVA, for both GVC- and non GVC-related trade. This allows us to isolate the response of DVA – the concept that determines GDP and competitiveness, and which is of ultimate interest to policymakers. Separating total trade into GVC and non-GVC components also reduces aggregation bias that is common in empirical studies that use gross exports and gross imports, and which are implicitly assuming a uniform exchange rate response across all categories of exports and imports.[3] Second, we use the empirical estimates and other country characteristics to obtain country-specific exchange rate elasticities. And third, we examine the effect of REER changes on the real trade balance.

The key findings of our paper are as follows. For GVC-related trade, a real appreciation not only reduces exports of DVA (a conventional result), but also lowers imports of FVA (contrary to traditional trade theory). This latter result is consistent with the notion that GVC-related DVA and FVA are complements in production, so producing and exporting less DVA also reduces the derived demand for imported FVA. In addition, the size of the response depends on the country's FVA share (that is, the import content) in its GVC-related exports, with a larger FVA share dampening the elasticity of GVC imports and exports to exchange rate changes. Where the foreign contribution reaches or exceeds 60%, import and export elasticities flip to a positive sign, indicating that the country's DVA (and FVA) actually *increases* in response to an appreciation.

---

[2] The FVA share in the total VA of exports is also relevant to the concept of effective protection, whereby a tariff is levied on the entire product, but the benefits accrue only to the DVA of the country that imposes the tariff. Thus, the effective protection rate (EPR) exceeds the nominal tariff rate whenever the FVA share is larger than zero, and the EPR escalates as the FVA share rises (Corden, 1966). When production is fragmented across countries, the concept of cumulative effective protection, which takes account of tariffs imposed along the entire production chain, is relevant (Rouzet & Miroudot, 2013).

[3] Aggregation bias that arises from using gross exports and gross imports may help account for the wide variation in real exchange rate elasticities obtained in empirical studies using different country samples and time periods, as documented in Tokarick (2010), and Auboin and Ruta (2011).

These empirical results are quite intuitive. When a country's own DVA contribution to the final GVC good is relatively small, a change in its REER will have only a modest effect on the competitiveness of the entire supply chain, therefore muting the DVA and FVA response from a change in its own REER. However, REER changes in countries with large DVA contributions affect the competitiveness of the entire supply chain, thereby generating spillovers to other participants in the chain. Thus, a country with a small DVA contribution will benefit when a supply-chain partner with a large DVA contribution depreciates, even if the REER of the small DVA-contributing country is itself appreciating. On the other hand, for non-GVC-related exports and imports, we confirm the existence of conventionally-signed REER elasticities. Using country-specific characteristics, we find that across the 57 countries in the sample, a depreciation always improves the real trade balance – but with considerable cross-country variation in the magnitude – indicating that the Marshall-Lerner condition applied to the real trade balance always holds in practice.

Our findings have a number of important policy-relevant implications. For products manufactured in GVCs, competitiveness is a concept that is defined over the entire supply chain, rather than at the level of individual participating countries. This is because each country's DVA is essential to the manufacture of the final product.[4] It then follows that size matters, with exchange rate changes by a small DVA contributor having little impact on its own or its GVC-partners' production and trade. On the other hand, exchange rate changes by a large DVA-contributing country will generate spillovers to its smaller GVC partners, inducing them to adjust their DVA and FVA. This result tends to obviate traditional 'beggar-thy-neighbor' concerns regarding depreciations by large DVA contributors within the same GVC. Thus, somewhat paradoxically, a high degree of trade interconnectedness through GVCs may actually dampen the sensitivity of trade and trade balances to changes in one's own real exchange rate. Nonetheless, with the Marshall-Lerner condition applied to the total real trade balance found to always hold in practice, real exchange rates remain an effective tool to influence real output.

The remainder of the paper proceeds as follows: Section 2 discusses the OECD-WTO TiVA dataset and the transformations and other data we use in the estimations. Section 3 discusses the empirical strategy and the findings. Section 4 concludes.

2. Data and Stylized Facts

This section discusses the trade and real exchange rate variables used in the subsequent empirical analysis.

Trade Data

We use the OECD-WTO TiVA database, which contains information on nominal US dollar-denominated imports and exports for GVC-related and other trade for the years 1995, 2000, 2005, 2008, 2009. The data cover 57 large and emerging market countries. In order to obtain annual time series through 2011, we interpolate the data during 1995 and 2009, and extrapolate thereafter, using an approach similar to the one detailed in

---

[4] However, over the long run, persistent country-specific REER changes may push out more expensive suppliers from the GVC in favor of lower-cost countries.

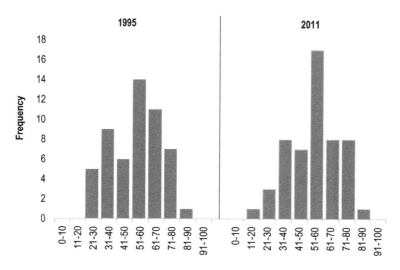

Figure 2. Frequency of distribution of FVA in GVC gross exports, 1995 and 2011 (in percent).
Source: authors' calculations.

Duval et al. (2014). Given our interest in real trade volumes, we convert the trade data into local currency using current exchange rates and deflate the resulting nominal DVA series using the consumer price index (CPI), while the nominal FVA series are deflated using the import price index, which is the trade-weighted index of partners' CPI.

At a conceptual level, a country's DVA contribution to the final good can be seen as influencing the size of the response of GVC trade to a change in its own real exchange rate. Given limitations in the data, we approximate this measure for country i by the share of FVA in its gross GVC-related exports, defined as follows:

$$S_i = \frac{FVA_i}{FVA_i + DVA_{GVCi}}$$

where FVA_i is the FVA in GVC exports of country i, and DVA_{GVCi} is the GVC-related DVA in GVC exports of country i.[5,6] In the GVC literature, this measure is referred to as a country's backward participation.[7] As shown in Figure 2, in 2011, the shares of FVA in gross GVC exports were distributed quite symmetrically across the 57 countries, were clustered around 50–60%, and lay within the range of 10–90%. Compared with 1995 (the first year of available data), countries have tended to move toward the center.

---

[5] Note that $(1-S_i)$ would express this share in terms of country i's own DVA contribution. The FVA formulation is easier to work with in the empirical estimations but, being a simple linear transformation, generates equivalent empirical estimates.

[6] The FVA share in a country's gross GVC exports is a proxy for the share of other countries' VA contributions in the total value added of the final product. This proxy is used because the OECD-TiVA data do not report trade along individual supply chains. Using instead the FVA share in a country's gross GVC exports tends to understate other countries' VA contribution to the final product for countries upstream in the production chain. On the other hand, exclusion of the final stage of GVC products from GVC trade data because it is not subsequently re-exported for further processing (and which TiVA records under other trade) tends to overstate other countries' VA contribution to the final product in the case of countries downstream in the production chain. It is assumed that these measurement issues neutralize one another, so that the FVA share is a good proxy for all other countries' VA contribution to the final product. Other empirical studies of the role of imported intermediates are subject to this same data limitation.

[7] See Fally (2011).

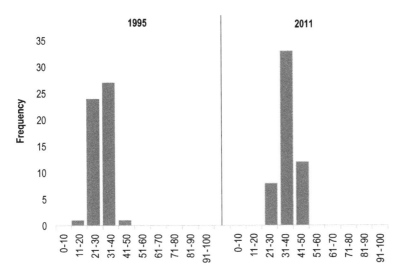

Figure 3. Frequency distribution of GVC-related DVA exports in gross exports, 1995 and 2011 (in percent).
Source: Authors' calculations.

To assess the impact of exchange rate changes on a country's total trade balance, the share of exported DVA associated with GVCs is a key parameter. We define W_i as the share of GVC-related exports of DVA in country i's total exports of DVA:

$$W_i = \frac{DVA_{GVC_i}}{DVA_{GVC_i} + DVA_{non-GVC_i}}$$

where DVA_{GVC_i} is the GVC-related DVA in country i's exports and $DVA_{non-GVC_i}$ is its exports of DVA in non-GVC products. As shown in Figure 3, for all countries in the sample, more than half of exported DVA is embodied in non-GVC goods, with most countries having 30–40% of their exports of DVA produced as part of a GVC. Since 1995, the share of GVC-related exports of DVA has risen modestly across the group of countries.

Exchange Rate Data

Following the methodology in Bayoumi et al. (2005), we construct real exchange rate indices using weights based on the DVA in exports. With DVA weights, bilateral exchange rates are weighted according to the country's pattern of exported DVA. Specifically, the REER index for country i is constructed as:

$$REER_i = \prod_{j \neq i} \left(\frac{P_i R_i}{P_j R_j} \right)^{W_{ij}}$$

where j refers to trade partners of country i, P_i (P_j) is the CPI of country i (j), R_i (R_j) is the bilateral nominal exchange rate of country i (j) relative to the US dollar (defined as units of local currency per US dollar, so that an increase is consistent with a depreciation of the local currency), and W_{ij} is the share of exported domestic value added of country i that is sent to country j.[8] Applying DVA weights generates a REER in terms of traded domestic value added. This differs from the conventional REER measure where weights are based on gross trade by excluding the FVA component of gross exports which, by definition, is produced elsewhere. This DVA-based REER is the appropriate concept for assessing the impact on own production in a world where GVC-related trade is common.

3. Empirical Strategy and Findings

Empirical Setup

A panel framework with time and country fixed effects is used to estimate the responsiveness of export and import volumes to changes in the REER using the following specification:

$$\log \left(\textit{export or import volume}\right)_{i,t} = \alpha_t + \alpha_i + \alpha_1 \log \left(REER\right)_{i,t-1} + \alpha_2 \log \left(REER\right)_{i,t-1}$$
$$\times S_{i,t-1} + \alpha_3 \log \left(Demand\right)_{i,t-1}$$
$$+ \alpha_4 \log \left(Controls\right)_{i,t} + \varepsilon_t$$

A term interacting the REER and S, the share of FVA in gross GVC-related exports, is included to capture the dampening effect on REER elasticities that occurs in the presence of a larger FVA share. The measure of demand varies with the dependent variable. In the GVC-related export and import equations, trade-weighted GDP of partner countries is used as a regressor, reflecting the fact that these exports and imports are intended for re-export, and hence depend on external demand conditions. In the case of non-GVC trade, partner trade-weighted demand is used in the export regression, while domestic demand is used in the import regression. The control variables included in each specification are the output gap, effective tariff rates, FVA share, and the log of the real stock of FDI.

In order to capture long-run relationships, the regressions are estimated using ordinary least squares. All variables are expressed in levels of natural logarithms. To mitigate endogeneity concerns, lagged values of the explanatory variables are added to the regressions.

Empirical Results

Three pairs of regressions, which differ in terms of the dependent variables, are estimated in order to capture the heterogeneous exchange rate responses of different types of trade: (i) total gross exports and total gross imports; (ii) GVC-related trade, where exports are defined as GVC–related DVA, and imports are GVC-related FVA; and (iii) other trade, where exports are non-GVC-related DVA and imports are non-GVC-related FVA. The results are presented in Table 1.

Columns 1 and 2 show the results when total gross exports and total gross imports are the dependent variables. Aggregating in this way across imports and exports without regard

---

[8] As a robustness check, we also use the DVA REER series constructed by Bems and Johnson (2012). This series differs from the one defined above mainly in that it uses the GDP deflator rather than CPI to derive the bilateral real exchange rates. The Bems and Johnson VA REER series is directly obtained from the following website: http://dl.dropbox.com/u/7512224/webdata4VAREERpaper_WIOD.zip.

Table 1. Response of trade to the real exchange rate

Variables	(1) Gross Imports	(2) Gross Exports	(3) Imports (FVA$_{DD}$)	(4) Exports (DVA$_{Non-GVC}$)	(5) Imports (FVA$_X$)	(6) Exports (DVA$_{GVC}$)
	Gross trade		Other trade		GVC-related exports	
Lagged log(REER-Value-added-based)	0.253	−0.604*	1.235**	−1.102**	−1.390***	−1.670***
	(0.663)	(−1.841)	(2.287)	(−2.378)	(−2.822)	(−3.527)
lagged log(REER) × lagged (FVA/DVA+FVA)	−0.003	0.013**			0.027***	0.026***
	(−0.443)	(2.150)			(3.166)	(3.330)
Lagged log(Demand)	0.709***	1.110***	0.884***	0.795***	1.108***	0.758***
	(4.716)	(9.257)	(3.089)	(6.446)	(5.961)	(4.470)
Time FE	Y	Y	Y	Y	Y	Y
Country FE	Y	Y	Y	Y	Y	Y
Additional controls	Y	Y	Y	Y	Y	Y
Clustering	Country level	Country level	Country level	Country level	Country level	Country level
Observations	690	690	690	690	699	699
R-squared	0.909	0.846	0.666	0.741	0.733	0.681

Source: IMF staff estimates.
Note: REER stands for real effective exchange rate. Specification log(Exports [Imports] volume)$c,t = \alpha t + \alpha c + \alpha_1 \log(REER)_{c,t-1} + \alpha_2$ interaction term $+ \alpha_3 \log(Demand)_{c[w],t-1} + \alpha_i \log(Controls)_{c,t+\epsilon t}$. Additional controls included in the specifications are log of real stock of FDI, FVA share, tariffs, output gap. Demand is proxied by GDP. Robust t-statistics in parentheses.
*** $p < 0.01$, ** $p < 0.05$, * $p < 0.1$

for whether they are single-country or multi-country goods has been the standard practice in the literature. The estimated signs of the coefficients on the REER terms, which denote trade elasticities, accord with traditional theory (positive for imports and negative for exports); however, the coefficients have low economic and statistical significance. This result is not surprising given that gross imports include a component intended for re-export, while gross exports include FVA.

The REER coefficients for non-GVC trade, shown in columns 3 and 4, accord with standard theory. The estimated REER elasticity for imports is positive, while the elasticity for exports is negative, consistent with the notion of trade in single-country goods. Both coefficients are strongly statistically significant.[9]

The results for GVC-related trade are shown in columns 5 and 6. Two results distinguish the response of GVC-related trade from traditional final goods trade:

- As can be seen in the first row of the table, a real appreciation not only reduces exports of DVA (a conventional result), but also lowers imports of FVA (contrary to traditional theory). This latter result is consistent with the notion that GVC-related DVA and FVA are complements in production, so producing and exporting less DVA also reduces the derived demand for imported FVA.[10]

---

[9] Moreover, and as expected, the FVA contribution in gross GVC exports is found to not significantly affect the response of non-GVC trade to REER changes. Coefficient values and their significance are little affected by omitting this variable from regressions 3 and 4.

[10] Also, the GVC-related export and import elasticities are fairly similar in magnitude, suggesting limited substitutability in production.

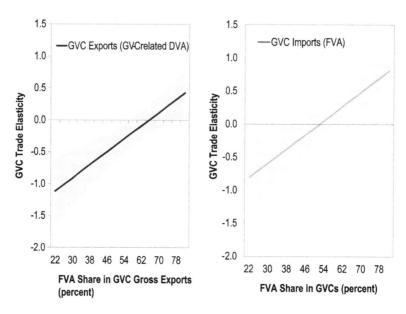

Figure 4. GVC trade elasticities (with 90% confidence intervals).
Source: Author's estimates.

- The response of DVA and FVA to REER changes tends to be dampened in the presence of a larger FVA share in gross GVC-related exports. This can be seen from the positive coefficients on the interaction between REER and the FVA share in line 2 of Table 1. Intuitively, this result is consistent with the notion that when a country's own DVA contribution in gross GVC exports is relatively small, a change in its REER will have only a modest effect on the competitiveness of the entire supply chain, therefore muting the DVA and FVA response from a change in its own REER.

REER Elasticities of GVC-related Trade

The dampening effect on GVC import and export elasticities that occurs in the presence of a larger FVA share is illustrated in Figure 4, which is calculated using the estimated coefficients shown in lines one and two. When the FVA share is very small (corresponding to a large DVA contribution), the spillover from an own depreciation to the competitiveness of the entire supply chain is correspondingly large. Therefore, the DVA and FVA elasticities are negative and close to the 'own effect' coefficients in line 1, and induce an increase in both GVC-related DVA and GVC-related FVA. Where the FVA share is larger – corresponding to a smaller own DVA contribution to the GVC – the spillover benefit from an own depreciation to the competitiveness of the entire supply chain (line 2) is weaker, resulting in smaller (i.e., less negative) GVC trade elasticities. When the FVA share rises to 50–60%, the competitiveness benefit for the entire supply chain from an own depreciation is neutralized by the corresponding relative appreciation of GVC partners' REERs, resulting in import and export elasticities of around zero.

Where the FVA share is larger still, import and export elasticities can switch to a positive sign. To understand this situation, note that the corollary to a very large FVA share (i.e., a

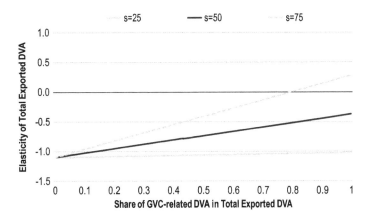

Figure 5. Elasticity of total exported DVA.
Sources: OECD-WTO TiVA database and authors' calculations; s denotes share of FVA in GVC gross exports.

very small DVA contributor) is a supply chain partner that contributes most of the value added to the final product. Appreciation by this large DVA contributor would then weaken the competitiveness of the entire chain, inducing the very small DVA contributor, whose own REER has depreciated, to contract both DVA and FVA. It is worth noting, however, that while positive REER elasticities remain a plausible theoretical result, their relevance appears to be limited in practice.[11]

REER Elasticity of Total Exported DVA

As observed above, while GVC-related exports have grown considerably in recent decades, conventional exports remains important – if not dominant – at the global level. Based on the empirical results presented here, it is apparent that country-specific REER elasticities for total exported DVA depend on two factors: (i) the share of GVC-related DVA in total exported DVA (namely W); and (ii) the FVA contribution to GVC-related exports (namely S).

Figure 5 shows how REER elasticities for total DVA exports vary with changes in S and W, calculated using the estimated coefficients in Table 1. As the proportion of GVC-related exports (W) increases, the elasticity of total exports becomes less negative (i.e., smaller in absolute terms), as shown by the positive slope of the lines. This elasticity declines more rapidly when the FVA share in GVC-related exports is larger, as illustrated by the successively steeper gradients as S increases. In addition, for any value of W, a larger FVA share in GVC-related exports is associated with a less negative REER elasticity (i.e., the line pivots upward as S increases). These results indicate that when exported DVA is derived mostly from GVCs, and the FVA share in GVC-related exports is large, the REER elasticity of total exported DVA is likely to be only weakly negative (or even positive).

---

[11] This is because: (I) the estimated export elasticities corresponding to FVA shares of 50–80% lie within the 90% confidence interval spanning zero, suggesting that the elasticities are not statistically distinguishable from zero. For import elasticities, the corresponding FVA share range is 38–62%, but above this range, a positive elasticity cannot be rejected. And (ii) the maximum FVA contribution to GVC–related gross exports for any country in the dataset is less than 80%, with the average FVA share around 50–60%. Thus, most countries tend to operate in the range where GVC elasticities are about zero.

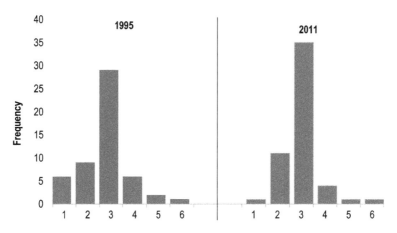

Figure 6. Frequency distribution of the effect of a 10% real depreciation on the real trade balance, 1995 and 2011 (in percent of real GDP).

REER Effect on the Real Trade Balance

Using the estimated results presented in columns 3–6 of Table 1 and the country-specific data, we then evaluate the response of real trade balances to a change in the REER. The results vary across countries and depend on: (i) the share of GVC-trade in total trade (W); (ii) the FVA contribution in GVC-related exports (S); and (iii) the initial real trade balance. Assuming a 10% real effective depreciation for all countries, we plot the distribution of the resulting changes in the real trade balance for 1995 and for 2011 (Figure 6). In all countries, a depreciation is found to improve the real trade balance, with non-GVC trade mainly driving the result. Therefore, the Marshall-Lerner condition (applied to real trade balances) is found to always hold in practice. However, cross-country variation is large, ranging from near zero to 6 percentage points of GDP, with a mode of 3 percentage points. Comparing the distributions over time, one can see that fewer countries were in the lower tail in 2011 than in 1995, suggesting that over time the REER has become a somewhat more effective tool for influencing the real trade balance and hence GDP.

4. Concluding Remarks and Policy Implications

Goods produced in GVCs are multi-country products and it is therefore not surprising that trade in these products responds differently to exchange rates than does trade in traditional single-country products. This is because within a GVC, foreign and domestic value-added are complements in production and therefore co-move in response to exchange rate changes. The strength of this exchange rate elasticity is found to depend on the foreign content in a country's GVC exports, with a larger foreign share working to dampen the response and, potentially, even turning it positive. In practice, however, many countries have foreign input shares that cause GVC-related export (and import) elasticities with respect to their own exchange rate to be less than – but close to – zero.

These findings have several important policy-relevant implications. First, for products manufactured within a GVC, competitiveness is defined at the level of the entire supply chain. This reflects that the price of the final product depends on the exchange-rate-adjusted prices of all the individual countries' inputs, weighted by their respective value-added contributions. Related to this is the second key message – that exchange rate changes by small DVA contributors have little effect on their own value added or the value added of others in the same supply chain. On the other hand, exchange rate changes in countries that are large contributors to the final product generate spillovers to their smaller GVC partners, tending to obviate traditional 'beggar-thy-neighbor' concerns among countries within the same GVC. Thus, somewhat paradoxically, a high degree of trade interconnectedness through GVCs may dampen the sensitivity of trade and trade balances to the real exchange rate. Therefore, larger exchange rate movements are needed to achieve a given change in the trade balance in a country whose exports are produced mainly in a GVC, especially if the country is a relatively small contributor to the total value added of the supply chain.

Acknowledgements

We would like to thank the editor, in addition to Tam Bayoumi, Daniel Leigh, participants at the Center on Asia and Globalization (CAG) conference on finance, trade and investment in Singapore as well as several IMF seminars in Washington, DC, for helpful comments. Any remaining errors and omissions are ours.

References

Ahmed, S., Appendino, M., & Ruta, M. (2015). Depreciations without Exports? Global value chains and the exchange rate elasticity of exports. World Bank Policy Research Working Paper 7390.

Amiti, M., Itskhoki, O., & Konings, J. (2014). Importers, exporters, and exchange rate disconnect. *American Economic Review*, *104*, 1942–1978. Retrieved from http://pubs.aeaweb.org/doi/pdfplus/10.1257/aer.104.7.1942

Auboin, M., & Ruta, M. (2011). The relationship between exchange rates and international trade: A review of economic literature. WTO Working Paper, Economic Research and Statistics Division, 2011–17.

Bayoumi, T., Faruqee, H., & Lee, J. (2005). A fair exchange? Theory and practice of calculating equilibrium exchange rates. IMF Working Paper Series. WP/05/229.

Bems, S., & Johnson, R. (2012). Value-Added exchange rates. NBER Working Paper Series w18498.

Corden, M. (1966). The structure of a tariff system and the effective protective rate. *Journal of Political Economy*, *74*, 221–237.

Duval, R., Cheng, K., Oh, K., Sarah, R., & Seneviratne, D. (2014). Trade integration and business cycle synchronization: A reappraisal with focus on Asia, IMf Working Paper Series, WP/14/52.

Fally, T. (2011). On the fragmentation of production in the US. University of Colorado-Boulder mimeo, October. Retrieved from http://sciie.ucsc.edu/14AIEC/Fragmentation_Fally.pdf

Fauceglia, D., Lassmann, A., Shingal, A., & Wermelinger, M. (2014). Backward participation in global value chains and exchange rate driven adjustments of Swiss Exports. Study on behalf of the State Secretariat for Economic Affair, SECO. Retrieved from http://www.seco.admin.ch/dokumentation/publikation/00004/05560/index.html?lang=en

Garcia-Herrero, A., & Koivu, T. (2009). China's exchange rate policy and Asian trade. BIS Working Papers No. 282. Retrieved from http://www.bis.org/publ/work282.htm

Ollivaud, P., Rusticelli, E., & Schwellnus, C. (2015). The changing role of the exchange rate for macroeconomic adjustment. OECD Economics Department Working Papers, No. 1190. Retrieved from http://www.oecd-ilibrary.org/economics/the-changing-role-of-the-exchange-rate-for-macroeconomic-adjustment_5js4rfhjf15l-en

Powers, W., & Riker, D. (2013), Exchange rate pass-through in global value chains: The effects of upstream suppliers. US International Trade Commission, Office of Economics Working Paper Series, No. 2013-02B. Retrieved from http://www.usitc.gov/publications/332/EC201302B.pdf

Riad, N., Errico, L., Henn, C., Saborowski, C., Saito, M., & Turunen, J. (2012). *Changing patterns of global trade*. Washington, DC: International Monetary Fund. Retrieved from http://www.imf.org/external/pubs/ft/dp/2012/dp1201.pdf

Rouzet, D., & Miroudout, S. (2013). The cumulative impact of trade barriers along the value chain: An empirical assessment using the OECD inter-country input-output model. Paper prepared for the 16th Annual Conference on Global Economic Analysis, OECD.

Tokarick, S. (2010). A method for calculating export supply and import demand elasticities, IMF Working Paper Series, WP/10/180.

Exchange Rates and Production Networks in Asia: A Twenty-first Century Perspective

Willem Thorbecke

Research Institute of Economy, Trade and Industry, Chiyoda-ku, Tokyo, Japan

ABSTRACT

China's surplus in processing trade, correctly measured, approaches half a trillion dollars year after year. Processed exports are final goods produced using parts and components imported from East Asia. Cointegration evidence indicates that processed exports depend, not only on the renminbi exchange rate, but also on exchange rates in East Asian supply chain countries. Results from out-of-sample forecasts indicate that exchange rates in supply chain countries remain important for explaining processed exports over the 2013–2015 period even as China's value-added has increased. While the renminbi has appreciated by 50% between 2005 and 2015, exchange rates in South Korea, Taiwan, and Japan have depreciated or stayed the same during this period, despite large current account surpluses. In order to switch expenditures away from China's processed exports and rebalance trade, it is necessary for exchange rates in Asian supply chain countries to also appreciate.

1. Introduction

Traditional models of international trade assume that a country's exports only contain domestic value added. An appreciation of the exporter's currency will raise prices in the importing country's currency and reduce exports. This response will be smaller, however, when exports contain significant foreign value-added. In this case, an appreciation in a country exporting final goods unaccompanied by appreciations in the countries providing intermediate inputs will only affect the foreign currency costs of the downstream country's value-added in exports. If significant value-added comes from imported inputs, the effect of a unilateral appreciation in the final exporting country on its exports will be attenuated (see Arndt, 2009; Koopman, Wang, & Wei, 2008).

An excellent laboratory to study these effects is China's processing trade. Imports for processing are parts and components that come into China duty free and that can only be used to produce goods for re-export. Processed exports are the final goods produced using imports for processing and domestic factors. As documented in the next section, significant value-added comes from East Asia and final processed exports go largely to the West.

Ahmed (2009), Thorbecke and Smith (2010) and others have investigated how exchange rates throughout the supply chain affect China's processed exports. Ahmed used quarterly data and an autoregressive distributed lag model to investigate China's exports over the 1996Q1–2009Q2 period. He reported that a 10% appreciation of the renminbi relative to non-Asian countries would reduce processed exports by 17% and that a 10% appreciation relative to Asian supply chain countries would increase China's processed exports by 15%. He interpreted these results to mean that a unilateral appreciation of the renminbi against non-Asian countries would have a much smaller effect on China's processed exports than if Asia's exchange rates appreciated together. Thorbecke and Smith (2010) constructed an integrated exchange rate to measure how exchange rates affect the relative foreign currency costs not just of China's value-added but of China's entire output of processed exports. Employing a panel dataset with China's exports to 31 countries over the 1994 to 2004 period and dynamic ordinary least squares techniques, they reported that a 10% appreciation across the supply chain would reduce China's processed exports by 10%.[1]

This paper extends the estimation to 2015 and investigates whether exchange rates in supply chain countries continue to matter as China's value-added in processing trade has increased. Results from out-of-sample forecasts indicate that, even over the 2013–2015 period, exchange rates in supply chain countries are important for explaining China's processed exports.

The next section provides data on China's processing and ordinary trade. Section 3 discusses the data and methodology. Section 4 presents the results and Section 5 concludes.

2. China's Processing and Ordinary Trade

Processed exports are produced through intricate production and distribution networks centered on East Asian countries while ordinary exports are produced primarily using domestic inputs (see Gaulier, Lemoine, & Unal-Kesenci, 2005). Processed exports therefore contain significant foreign value-added while ordinary exports contain primarily domestic value-added.

Imports for processing can only be used to produce goods for re-export while ordinary imports flow primarily to the domestic market.

Table 1 presents imports, exports, and the trade balance between China and its major trading over the 2002–2014 period. Table 1(a) presents data for processing trade and Table 1(b) presents data for ordinary trade.

The first panel of Table 1(a) shows the major sources of imports for processing. In 2014, about $100 billion dollars of imports for processing came from South Korea, $76 billion from Taiwan, $56 billion from Japan, $35 billion from ASEAN-4 (Indonesia, Malaysia, the Philippines, and Thailand), and $25 billion from the US. An additional $23 billion came from Germany and the rest of Europe. In 2008, both Korea and Japan provided $60 billion of imports for processing. Since then, imports for processing from Korea have increased by $40 billion and imports for processing from Japan have fallen.

Imports for processing in column (9) from countries not listed in the table equaled $205 billion in 2014. However, $76 billion of these goods were imports for processing into China from China. These are goods that are produced in China and round tripped out of China

---

[1] Thorbecke (2015) has also investigated how exchange rates throughout the supply chain affect China's exports.

and back in to take advantage of favorable tax treatment. Subtracting these, imports for processing from all other countries in 2014 equaled $129 billion.

The second panel of Table 1(a) reports processed exports. Almost $200 billion went to the US and about $120 billion went to Germany and the rest of Europe. $376.9 billion is recorded as going to other countries not listed in the table. However, of this $376.9 billion, $215 billion are recorded as going to Hong Kong. The vast majority of these goods are then transshipped to the West and to other countries. Subtracting exports to Hong Kong from column (9) implies that 24% of China's processed exports flowed to countries not

Table 1. (a) China's processing trade, 2002–2014.

	S. Korea (1)	Taiwan (2)	Japan (3)	ASEAN-4 (4)	US (5)	Germany (6)	Rest of Europe (7)	Australia & Brazil (8)	Rest of the World (9)	Total (10)
Imports for processing (billions of US dollars)										
2002	14.4	24.6	25	11.8	6.9	2	4.3	1.7	31.6	122.3
2003	20.7	32.5	32.8	17.9	8.1	2.1	4.9	2.2	41.8	163
2004	32	43.9	40.2	23.8	11	2.9	6.9	3.1	58	221.8
2005	42.8	52.1	45.2	29.6	12.8	3.6	8.6	3.6	75.8	274.1
2006	48.5	61.2	51.1	33.8	16.8	5.1	11	3.3	90.4	321.2
2007	56.2	69.1	59.4	39.2	18.2	5.9	12.6	3.2	104.6	368.4
2008	59.2	68.4	61.3	38.8	19.7	7.2	14.5	2.6	106.7	378.4
2009	54.7	54.7	50	31.4	15.5	5.6	12.2	2.4	95.8	322.2
2010	71.1	70	61.6	42.1	21.7	6.7	13.2	3.1	127.9	417.4
2011	79.6	71.9	64.9	44.7	21.9	7.3	15.6	3.9	160	469.8
2012	83.9	68.5	62.8	38.2	19.8	6.4	13.5	4.6	183.5	481.2
2013	87.1	72.5	56.4	36.2	21.6	7.4	14.9	4.8	196.1	497
2014	98.7	76.2	55.6	35.2	24.8	8.2	15.2	5.3	205.3	524.5
Processed exports (billions of US dollars)										
2002	7	4	28.1	5.9	46.8	6.9	19.2	2.4	59.7	180
2003	9.3	5.3	35.1	7.3	62.4	11	30.1	3.5	77.9	241.9
2004	13.7	7.2	43.5	10.1	83.7	15.4	41.8	5.4	107.5	328.3
2005	16.5	9.2	49.7	13.4	105.7	20.3	54.9	6.8	140.2	416.7
2006	20.2	11.2	52.9	16.4	128.8	25	66.2	8.9	181	510.6
2007	24.6	11.9	57.7	20.1	145.4	27.6	87.2	12.3	230.8	617.6
2008	32.1	12.7	62.3	22.1	149.9	31.8	94.5	15.2	254.6	675.2
2009	29.1	10.9	53.6	19.9	133.1	25.4	77.3	13.5	224.1	586.9
2010	34.9	15	65.5	25.2	162.6	33.2	94.1	18.1	291.7	740.3
2011	39.6	17.7	75.2	28.6	175.6	34.2	101.4	21.7	341.5	835.5
2012	46.1	16.2	78.6	32	184.6	29.7	93.8	22.8	359	862.8
2013	47.2	16.6	75.9	31.7	186.7	26.0	88.2	22.8	365.4	860.5
2014	47.8	18.3	73.5	31.8	194.8	27.6	91.6	22.0	376.9	884.3
Balance in processing trade (billions of US dollars)										
2002	−7.4	−20.6	3.1	−5.9	39.9	4.9	14.9	0.7	28.1	57.7
2003	−11.4	−27.2	2.3	−10.6	54.3	8.9	25.2	1.3	36.1	78.9
2004	−18.3	−36.7	3.3	−13.7	72.7	12.5	34.9	2.3	49.5	106.5
2005	−26.3	−42.9	4.5	−16.2	92.9	16.7	46.3	3.2	64.4	142.6
2006	−28.3	−50.0	1.8	−17.4	112.0	19.9	55.2	5.6	90.6	189.4
2007	−31.6	−57.2	−1.7	−19.1	127.2	21.7	74.6	9.1	126.2	249.2
2008	−27.1	−55.7	1.0	−16.7	130.2	24.6	80.0	12.6	147.9	296.8
2009	−25.6	−43.8	3.6	−11.5	117.6	19.8	65.1	11.1	128.3	264.7
2010	−36.2	−55.0	3.9	−16.9	140.9	26.5	80.9	15.0	163.8	322.9
2011	−40.0	−54.2	10.3	−16.1	153.7	26.9	85.8	17.8	181.5	365.7
2012	−37.8	52.3	15.8	−6.2	164.8	23.3	80.3	18.2	175.5	381.6
2013	−39.9	−55.9	19.5	−4.5	165.1	18.6	73.3	18	169.3	363.5
2014	−50.9	−57.9	17.9	−3.4	170.0	19.4	76.4	16.7	171.6	359.8

Notes: ASEAN 4 includes Indonesia, Malaysia, the Philippines, and Thailand. The rest of Europe includes Austria, Belgium, Denmark, Finland, France, Germany, Greece, Ireland, Luxembourg, Netherlands, Italy, Portugal, Spain, Sweden and United Kingdom.
Source: China Customs Statistics.

Table 1. (b) China's ordinary trade, 2002–2014.

	S. Korea (1)	Taiwan (2)	Japan (3)	ASEAN- 4 (4)	US (5)	Germany (6)	Rest of Europe (7)	Australia & Brazil (8)	Rest of the World (9)	Total (10)
Ordinary imports (billions of US dollars)										
2002	11.3	8.1	18.7	8.8	14.7	16.4	7.7	6.4	37.0	129.1
2003	16.7	10.9	27.8	12.7	18.9	24.3	10.4	10.3	55.9	187.9
2004	21	13	34.7	15.4	24.4	30.4	11.1	16	81.7	247.7
2005	23.5	14	35.9	15.8	25.9	30.7	11.4	21.1	101.4	279.7
2006	26.7	15.2	42.2	20	28.3	30.2	22.5	27.6	120.5	333.2
2007	30.2	18.3	50.5	27.6	36.1	45.4	22.3	39.1	159.2	428.7
2008	35.2	20.1	62.3	31.3	47	55.8	24.1	61.8	235.1	572.7
2009	34.6	20	62.8	33.2	50.2	41.6	43.6	62.1	186.2	534.3
2010	45.3	29.2	89.4	49	63.8	57.9	56.7	91	286.0	768.3
2011	55.9	34.2	100.5	67	81.4	73.5	70.8	122.4	401.9	1007.6
2012	56.8	36.1	88.7	68	90	72.3	70.4	122.6	416.9	1021.8
2013	62.6	42.2	82.9	71.8	94.9	73.5	75.5	139.5	467.0	1109.9
2014	63.6	48.8	83.8	68	96.4	81.9	81.3	134.6	451.5	1109.9
Ordinary exports (billions of US dollars)										
2002	8.3	2.5	19.8	7.3	21.5	4.4	16.9	3.5	52.0	136.2
2003	10.4	3.5	23.6	9.9	27.9	6.1	23.7	4.8	72.2	182.1
2004	13.4	5.9	29.1	13.8	38.1	8	32.9	6.9	95.6	243.7
2005	17.7	6.8	33.4	17.2	52.8	11.6	45.3	8.8	121.6	315.2
2006	22.8	8.8	37.4	21.1	69.1	14.6	59.9	11.6	171.1	416.4
2007	29.5	10.2	41.8	28	80.3	19.7	81	16.	248.1	538.6
2008	39.4	11.7	50.2	37.9	93.6	25.5	101.4	23.8	279.1	662.6
2009	22.5	8.2	41.3	32.8	78.6	22.4	77.1	19.1	227.7	529.7
2010	30.1	12.4	51.1	46.5	107.5	31.8	105.7	29.9	305.7	720.7
2011	38.6	15.2	66.5	61.3	135.6	39.4	127.4	39.6	393.4	917.0
2012	36	15.4	66.4	78.8	151.3	36.2	121.1	43.3	439.5	988.0
2013	38.4	17.2	67	92.7	162	37.4	128.2	45.7	498.9	1087.5
2014	46.1	20.1	69	97.4	179	40.7	145	46.6	559.9	1203.8
Balance in ordinary trade (billions of US dollars)										
2002	−3	−5.6	1.1	−1.5	6.8	−12	9.2	−2.9	15	7.1
2003	−6.3	−7.4	−4.2	−2.8	9	−18.2	13.3	−5.5	16.3	−5.8
2004	−7.6	−7.1	−5.6	−1.6	13.7	−22.4	21.8	−9.1	13.9	−4
2005	−5.8	−7.2	−2.5	1.4	26.9	−19.1	33.9	−12.3	20.2	35.5
2006	−3.9	−6.4	−4.8	1.1	40.8	−15.6	37.4	−16	50.6	83.2
2007	−0.7	−8.1	−8.7	0.4	44.2	−25.7	58.7	−23	88.9	109.9
2008	4.2	−8.4	−12.1	6.6	46.6	−30.3	77.3	−38	44	89.9
2009	−12.1	−11.8	−21.5	−0.4	28.4	−19.2	33.5	−43	41.5	−4.6
2010	−15.2	−16.8	−38.3	−2.5	43.7	−26.1	49	−61.1	19.7	−47.6
2011	−17.3	−19	−34	−5.7	54.2	−34.1	56.6	−82.8	−8.5	−90.6
2012	−20.8	−20.7	−22.3	10.8	61.3	−36.1	50.7	−79.3	22.6	−33.8
2013	−24.2	−25	−15.9	20.9	67.1	−36.1	52.7	−93.8	31.9	−22.4
2014	−17.5	−28.7	−14.8	29.4	82.6	−41.2	63.7	−88	108.4	93.9

Notes: ASEAN 4 includes Indonesia, Malaysia, the Philippines, and Thailand. The rest of Europe includes Austria, Belgium, Denmark, Finland, France, Germany, Greece, Ireland, Luxembourg, Netherlands, Italy, Portugal, Spain, Sweden and United Kingdom.
Source: China Customs Statistics.

included in columns (1) through (8). Thus the lion's share of China's processed exports flows to wealthy economies such as the US, Europe, Japan, South Korea, Taiwan, and Australia. Xing (2015) has presented econometric evidence indicating that process exports go disproportionately to high income countries.

The third panel of Table 1(a) reports China's balance in processing trade. In 2014, it recorded a deficit of more than $100 billion in processing trade with South Korea and Taiwan, balanced trade with Japan and ASEAN, and a surplus of $170 billion with the US and $100 billion with Europe. Taking account of goods flowing through Hong Kong to the US and Europe, China's surplus with Western countries is actually much larger.

Table 1(b) shows that China's ordinary imports from South Korea, Taiwan, and Japan exceed China's ordinary exports to these countries. Thus, China runs deficits with each of these Asian neighbors averaging about $20 billion per year. Up until 2010, China's ordinary trade with ASEAN-4 was balanced. In 2014, it ran a surplus of $30 billion in ordinary trade with ASEAN. It also ran surpluses of more than $80 billion with the US and more than $60 billion with Europe excluding Germany. With Germany, however, it ran a deficit of more than $40 billion and with Australia and Brazil deficits of more than $80 billion. Its deficit with Germany reflects imports of automobiles, capital goods and machinery and its deficits with Australia and Brazil reflects imports of natural resources.

If one subtracts China's ordinary exports to Hong Kong to try to correct for entrepôt trade, then 43% of China's ordinary exports flow to countries in column (9). This compares with 24% from China's processed exports. Thus, for ordinary exports, a smaller share flows to the wealthier economies listed in columns (1) through (8) and a larger share flows to emerging markets.

Figure 1(a) plots China's aggregate processed exports and imports for processing, Figure 1(b) plots China's aggregate ordinary exports and imports, and Figure 1(c) plots China's aggregate balances in processing and ordinary trade. Figure 1(a) indicates that China's processed exports accelerated after 2001. This was the year that China joined the World Trade Organization (WTO), and many have argued that China's WTO accession gave foreign investors confidence to shift production to China (see, for example, Chin, Yong, & Yew, 2015). Figure 1(c) indicates that China's surplus in processing trade began growing soon after China joined the WTO. The surplus kept increasing with only a minor interruption in 2009 during the global financial crisis. Between 2011 and 2015 the surplus averaged $90 billion per quarter ($360 billion per year) or more. The surplus is actually larger because about $80 billion per year represents imports into China from China. Correcting for this, China's surplus in 2014 was $440 billion and it has been close to half a trillion dollars per year over the last four years.

Figure 1(b) shows that, before the global financial crisis, ordinary exports exceeded ordinary imports. This resulted, as Figure 1(c) and Table 1 show, in surpluses in ordinary trade of about $100 billion per year in 2007 and 2008. Beginning in 2009, the growth of ordinary imports exceeded the growth of ordinary exports and China ran deficits in ordinary trade between 2009 and 2013. Only in 2014 and especially 2015, as the prices of commodity imports fell, did surpluses of $100 billion per year or more reappear in ordinary trade.

3. Data and Methodology

The imperfect substitutes model of Goldstein and Khan (1985) is used to specify export functions. In this framework, multilateral exports are a function of real income in the importing countries and of the real effective exchange rate:

$$ex_t = \alpha_{10} + \alpha_{11}y_t^* + \alpha_{12}reer_t + \varepsilon_t \qquad (1)$$

where ex_t represents the log of real exports, y_t* represents the log of foreign real income, and $reer_t$ represents the log of the real effective exchange rate.

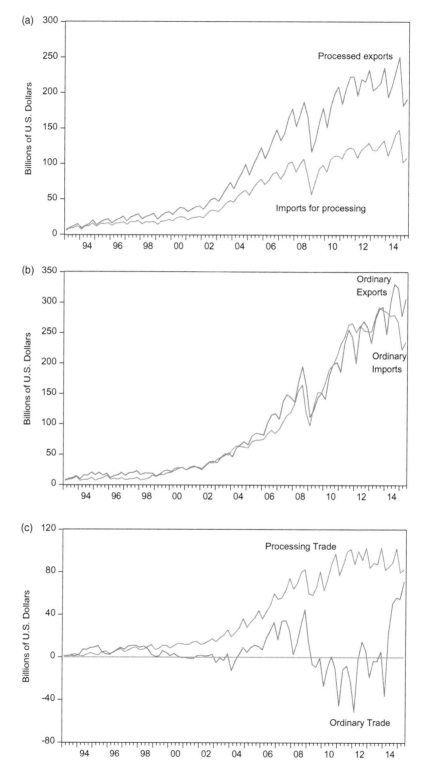

Figure 1. (a) China's processing trade with the world. (b) China's ordinary trade with the world. (c) China's balance in processing and ordinary trade with the world.
Source: China Customs Statistics.

To measure China's exports, its two major customs regimes – processed exports and ordinary exports – are used. As discussed above, foreign value added is higher in processed exports than in ordinary exports. In one specification, processed exports are also disaggregated into processing and assembly (PAA) exports and processing with imported materials (PWIM) exports. PAA refers to foreign firms importing inputs that belong to them and using these to produce goods for re-export (see Gaulier et al., 2005). PWIM refers to foreign suppliers importing inputs from other firms and using these to produce goods for re-export. Chinese firms play a more active role in PWIM trade than they do in PAA trade. They are more involved in sourcing materials and in deciding what to produce (see Freund, Hong, & Wei, 2012). Chinese firms thus contribute more to the value added of PWIM exports than they do to the value added of PAA exports (see also Thorbecke, 2013). Since foreign value-added is higher for processed exports than for ordinary exports and for PAA exports than for PWIM exports, one would expect processed exports in general and PAA exports specifically to be more sensitive to exchange rates in supply chain countries. One would also expect ordinary exports and PWIM exports to be more sensitive to the RMB exchange rate.

China's exports to the world in each category are used. These data are obtained from the CEIC database. Following Cheung, Chinn, and Qian (2012) and others, exports are deflated using the Hong Kong to US re-export unit value indices obtained from the Customs and Statistics Department of the Government of Hong Kong.

Since processed exports flow largely to higher income countries, quarterly data on the volume of real GDP in OECD countries are used to represent y_t^* in equation (1). These data are seasonally adjusted and obtained from the OECD.[2]

Data on the Chinese real effective exchange rate are taken from the IMF's *International Financial Statistics*.[3] This measure of the *reer* is CPI-deflated.

To take account of exchange rates in supply chain countries, data on the value of parts and components coming from the nine leading suppliers are used. These are South Korea, Taiwan, Japan, the United States, Singapore, Thailand, Malaysia, the Philippines, and Germany. Weights ($w_{i,t}$) are calculated for each of these countries by determining the value of imports for processing each country provided in each year divided by the value of parts and components coming from all nine countries together. These weights are converted to quarterly frequencies using linear interpolation. They are then employed to calculate a weighted exchange rate in supply chain countries (*ssreer$_t$*) by using the following formula:

$$ssreer_t = ssreer_{t-1} \prod_{i=1}^{9} (reer_{i,t}/reer_{i,t-1})^{w_{i,t}} \tag{2}$$

where $reer_{i,t}$ is the real effective exchange rate for supply chain country i at time t. An increase in $reer_{i,t}$ and $ssreer_t$ represent real exchange rate appreciations. $ssreer_t$ is set equal to 100 in the first quarter of 1993.

Data on real effective exchange rates are taken from *International Financial Statistics*, except for Korea and Taiwan. For these two economies data are obtained from the Bank for International Settlements.[4] These exchange rate data are again CPI-deflated.

---

[2] The website for these data is http://stats.oecd.org.
[3] The IMF data are obtained from the CEIC database.
[4] These data are obtained from the CEIC database.

Augmented Dickey–Fuller tests indicate that the series are integrated of order one. The trace statistic and the maximum eigenvalue statistic, reported in Table 2, permit rejection at the 5% level of the null of no cointegrating relations against the alternative of one cointegrating relation in most cases.

Since the evidence points to a cointegrating relationship between the variables, the parameters are estimated using Johansen maximum likelihood methods. The model can be written in vector error correction form as:

$$\Delta ex_t = \beta_{10} + \varphi_1(ex_{t-1} - \alpha_1 - \alpha_2 y^*_{t-1} - \alpha_3 rmbreer_{t-1} - \alpha_4 ssreer_{t-1})$$
$$+ \beta_{11}(L)\Delta ex_{t-1} + \beta_{12}(L)\Delta y_{t-1}* + \beta_{13}(L)\Delta rmbreer_{t-1}$$
$$+ \beta_{14}(L)\Delta ssreer_{t-1} + v_{1t} \tag{3a}$$

$$\Delta y^*_t = \beta_{20} + \varphi_2(ex_{t-1} - \alpha_1 - \alpha_2 y^*_{t-1} - \alpha_3 rmbreer_{t-1} - \alpha_4 ssreer_{t-1})$$
$$+ \beta_{21}(L)\Delta ex_{t-1} + \beta_{22}(L)\Delta y^*_{t-1} + \beta_{23}(L)\Delta rmbreer_{t-1}$$
$$+ \beta_{24}(L)\Delta ssreer_{t-1} + v_{2t} \tag{3b}$$

$$\Delta rmbreer_t = \beta_{30} + \varphi_3(ex_{t-1} - \alpha_1 - \alpha_2 y^*_{t-1} - \alpha_3 rmbreer_{t-1} - \alpha_4 ssreer_{t-1})$$
$$+ \beta_{31}(L)\Delta ex_{t-1} + \beta_{32}(L)\Delta y^*_{t-1} + \beta_{33}(L)\Delta rmbreer_{t-1}$$
$$+ \beta_{34}(L)\Delta ssreer_{t-1} + v_{3t} \tag{3c}$$

$$\Delta ssreer_t = \beta_{40} + \varphi_4(ex_{t-1} - \alpha_1 - \alpha_2 y^*_{t-1} - \alpha_3 rmbreer_{t-1} - \alpha_4 ssreer_{t-1})$$
$$+ \beta_{41}(L)\Delta ex_{t-1} + \beta_{42}(L)\Delta y^*_{t-1} + \beta_{43}(L)\Delta rmbreer_{t-1}$$
$$+ \beta_{44}(L)\Delta ssreer_{t-1} + v_{4t} \tag{3d}$$

Here, ex_t represents China's real exports to the world (either processed, ordinary, PAA, or PWIM), y_t* equals real income in the rest of the world, $rmbreer_t$ represents the renminbi real effective exchange rate, and $ssreer_t$ represents the weighted exchange rate in supply chain countries. φ_1, φ_2, φ_3 and φ_4 are error correction coefficients that measure how quickly exports, income, the renminbi real exchange rate, and the weighted exchange rate in supply chain countries, respectively, respond to disequilibria. If these variables move towards their equilibrium values, the corresponding correction coefficients will be negative and statistically significant. The Ls represent polynomials in the lag operator. x_t, y_t*, $rmbreer_t$, and $ssreer_t$ are measured in natural logs and seasonal dummies are also included.

Based on the Schwarz information criterion, one lag is included. The sample period extends from 1993Q3 to 2015Q1.

The model is also estimated using dynamic ordinary least squares (DOLS). DOLS involves regressing the left-hand-side variable on a constant, the right-hand side variables, and lags and leads of the right-hand side variables. The equation has the form:

$$ex_t = \beta_0 + \beta_1 y_t * + \beta_2 rmbreer_t + \beta_3 ssreer_t + \beta_4 Time + \sum_{j=-p}^{p} \alpha_{y*,j}\Delta y_{t-j}*$$
$$+ \sum_{j=-p}^{p} \alpha_{rmbreer,j}\Delta rmbreer_{i,t-j} + \sum_{j=-p}^{p} \alpha_{ssreer,j}\Delta ssreer_{t-j} + u_t, \tag{4}$$

Here, *Time* is a time trend and the other variables are defined above. Seasonal dummy variables are again included.

4. Results

Table 2 presents the results from the Johansen maximum likelihood estimation and Table 3 presents the results from the DOLS estimation. In Tables 2 and 3, a trend was selected for inclusion in every specification except for PAA exports. This is not surprising since the volume of PAA exports increased until 2007 and then decreased while the volume of exports for the other categories has continued to increase.

The first row of Table 2 and the first column of Table 3 present the results for processed exports. In both cases all of the coefficients are of the expected signs and they are all statistically significant except for the coefficient on rest of the world GDP in Table 2. The results in Table 2 imply that a 10% appreciation of the RMB will reduce processed exports to the world by 25% and a 10% appreciation in supply chain countries will reduce processed exports by 35%. The results in Table 3 imply that a 10% appreciation of the RMB will reduce processed exports to the world by 21% and a 10% appreciation in supply chain countries will reduce processed exports by 24%. The coefficient on rest of the world GDP in Table 2 implies that a 10% increase in foreign income would increase Chinese processed exports by 6% and the results in Table 3 imply a 10% increase in y_t* would increase processed exports by 19%. The DOLS estimates in Table 3 appear more plausible. Since Stock and Watson (1993) found that the distribution of the Johansen estimator has more outliers than the distribution of the DOLS estimator, more weight in this case should probably be attached to the elasticities in Table 3.

The error correction coefficient on exports in Table 2 indicates that there is a tight relationship between processed exports and the independent variables. Thirty-two percent of the gap between actual processed exports and their predicted values closes after one quarter. This implies that, *ceteris paribus*, more than 50% of the gap would close after two quarters and almost 80% would close after four quarters. Thus, exports are strongly influenced by exchange rates in China and throughout the supply chain and by rest of the world GDP.

The second row of Table 2 and the second column of Table 3 present the results for PAA exports. It is noteworthy that, while the coefficients on $rmbreer_t$ and $ssreer_t$ remain statistically significant, the elasticity for $rmbreer_t$ drops and the elasticity for $ssreer_t$ increases as compared with processed exports in general. This is what one would expect, since more of the value added of PAA exports comes from abroad than for processed exports in general. The coefficient on rest of the world GDP in Table 2 implies that a 10% increase in foreign income would increase PAA exports by 27% and the results in Table 3 imply a 10% increase in y_t* would increase PAA exports by 37%. The error correction coefficient on PAA exports in Table 2 again implies a tight relationship between exports and the independent variables, with 26% of the gap between PAA exports and their predicted values closing after one quarter.

The third row of Table 2 and the third column of Table 3 present the results for PWIM exports. In both tables the coefficients on $rmbreer_t$ and $ssreer_t$ are again statistically significant. As compared with the results for PAA exports, in absolute value terms the elasticity for $rmbreer_t$ is higher and the elasticity for $ssreer_t$ is lower than for PWIM exports. This is

Table 2. Johansen MLE estimates for Chinese exports to the World.[a]

	Number of Cointe-grating Vectors	Number of Obser-vations	RMB REER	SSREER	Rest of the World GDP	Error Correction Coefficients:			
						Exports	RMB REER	SSREER	Rest of the World GDP
Processed exports (Lags: 1; Sample: 1993:III–2015:I; Trend in cointegrating equation; Seasonal dummies for the first, second, and third quarters included)	1,1	87	-2.51*** (0.26)	-3.47*** (0.61)	0.58 (0.83)	-0.32*** (0.06)	-0.07 (0.04)	-0.03** (0.01)	-0.01** (0.00)
Processing & assembly exports (Lags: 1; Sample: 1993:III–2015:I; Seasonal dummies for the first, second, and third quarters included)	1,1	87	-1.93*** (0.28)	-4.99*** (0.77)	2.72*** (0.41)	-0.26*** (0.06)	-0.03 (0.04)	-0.03** (0.04)	-0.00 (0.00)
Processing with imported materials exports (Lags: 1; Sample: 1993:III–2015:I; Trend in cointegrating equation; Seasonal dummies for the first, second, and third quarters included)	1,1	87	-2.85*** (0.28)	-3.50*** (0.64)	-0.16 (0.87)	-0.31*** (0.06)	-0.07 (0.04)	-0.03** (0.01)	-0.01** (0.00)
Ordinary exports (Lags: 1; Sample: 1993:III–2015:I; Trend in cointegrating equation; Seasonal dummies for the first, second, and third quarters included)	0,0	87	-2.85*** (0.36)	-0.83 (0.85)	-3.08** (1.17)	-0.19*** (0.07)	0.07** (0.03)	-0.01 (0.01)	-0.01*** (0.00)
Ordinary exports (Lags: 1; Sample: 1993:III–2015:I; Trend in cointegrating equation; Seasonal dummies for the first, second, and third quarters included)	0,1	87	-2.82*** (0.35)		-2.13** (0.92)	-0.20*** (0.07)	-0.08** (0.03)		-0.01*** (0.00)

[a]Number of cointegrating vectors indicates the number of cointegrating relations according to the trace and maximum eigenvalue test using 5% asymptotic critical values. RMB REER is the Chinese real effective exchange rate. SSREER is a weighted average of real effective exchange rates in supply chain countries. Rest of the World GDP is real, seasonally adjusted GDP in OECD countries.
*** (**) denotes significance at the 1% (5%) level.

Table 3. DOLS Estimates of China's exports to the world.

Independent variables	(1) Processed exports	(2) Processing and assembly exports	(3) Processed with imported materials exports	(4) Ordinary exports	(5) Ordinary exports	(6) Processed exports	(7) Processed exports
RMB REER	−2.05***	−1.72***	−2.35***	−2.42***	−2.39***	−1.87***	−1.58***
	(0.23)	(0.22)	(0.24)	(0.32)	(0.30)	(0.24)	(0.29)
SSREER	−2.37***	−3.17***	−2.53***	0.07		−1.95***	
	(0.58)	(0.64)	(0.62)	(0.80)		(0.61)	
Rest of the world GDP	1.88**	3.68***	1.13	−1.06	−0.99	1.81**	3.42***
	(0.77)	(0.35)	(0.82)	(1.07)	(0.77)	(0.76)	(0.76)
Time	0.03***		0.04***	0.05***	0.05***	0.03***	0.02***
	(0.00)		(0.00)	(0.01)	(0.01)	(0.00)	(0.01)
Adjusted R-squared	0.991	0.97	0.991	0.986	0.993	0.991	0.988
Sample Period	1993:III–2014:IV	1993:III–2014:IV	1993:III–2014:IV	1993:III–2014:IV	1993:III–2014:IV	1993:III–2013:I	1993:III–2013:I
No. of observations	86	86	86	86	86	79	79
RMSE						0.114	0.216

Notes: DOLS (1,1) estimates. Heteroskedasticity-consistent standard errors are in parentheses.
*** (**) denotes significance at the 1% (5%) level. RMB REER is the Chinese real effective exchange rate. SSREER is a weighted average of real effective exchange rates in supply chain countries. Rest of the World GDP is real, seasonally adjusted GDP in OECD countries. RMSE represents the root mean squared error measure of the model's forecast error for the 2013:II–2015:1 period using actual out-of-sample observations.

what one would expect, since more of the value added of PWIM exports comes from China than for PAA exports. The coefficient on rest of the world GDP in Table 2 is of the wrong sign and equals 1.12 but is not statistically significant in Table 3. The puzzling results for ROW GDP could be due to the presence of a trend term in the estimation. Since GDP in the rest of the world increased steadily over the sample period, there is a lot of multicollinearity between ROW GDP and the trend term. The error correction coefficient again indicates that there is a tight relationship between exports and the right hand side variables, with 31% of the gap between actual and predicted values closing after one quarter.

The fourth and fifth rows of Table 2 and the third and fourth columns of Table 3 present the results for ordinary exports. In both tables the coefficients on $rmbreer_t$ are large and of the expected sign and the coefficients on $ssreer_t$ are not statistically significant. This suggests that the renminbi exchange rate matters for ordinary exports but that exchange rates in supply chain countries do not.

Many have reported that China's value-added in processing trade has increased in recent years (see Xing, 2014). It is thus possible that exchange rates in supply chain countries mattered in earlier years but do not matter now. To test for this, the model is estimated up until 2013Q1 and then out of sample forecasts are obtained using actual values of the independent variables over the next eight quarters. The model is estimated both including and excluding $ssreer_t$; Column 6 reports the results including $ssreer_t$ and column 7 excluding $ssreer_t$ The root mean squared error measure of the model's forecast error for the 2013Q2–2015Q1 period equals 0.114 when $ssreer_t$ is included and 0.216 when $ssreer_t$ is excluded. This indicates that, even in the most recent years, the specification with exchange rates in supply chain countries included far outperforms the specification with the renminbi included as the only exchange rate measure.

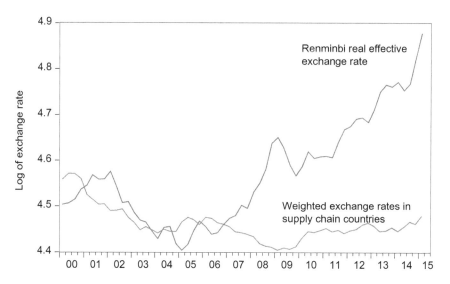

Figure 2. Renminbi real effective exchange rate and weighted exchange rates in countries providing parts and components to China.
Note: The weighted exchange rate in supply chain countries represents the geometrically weighted average of exchange rate changes in the nine leading suppliers of parts and components (P&C) to China, with weights determined by the value of P&C coming from each of the nine suppliers individually relative to the value coming from all nine together. The nine leading suppliers are Germany, Japan, Malaysia, the Philippines, Singapore, South Korea, Thailand, Taiwan, and the United States.
Source: International Monetary Fund, Bank for International Settlements, China Customs Statistics, and calculations by the author.

5. Conclusion

The results in this paper indicate that exchange rates in supply chain countries remain important for explaining Chinese processed exports. Figure 2 shows how $ssreer_t$ and $rmbreer_t$ have evolved. It is notable that, while the renminbi has appreciated by 50% in real effective terms between 2005Q1 and 2015Q1, weighted exchange rates in supply chain countries have not appreciated at all. This helps explain why, as Section 2 documents, the surplus in ordinary trade disappeared between 2008 and 2013 while the surplus in processing trade remains close to half a trillion dollars year after year.

Table 1 shows that the primary supply chain economies are Taiwan, South Korea, and Japan. Taiwan has run current account surpluses averaging 9% of GDP since 2006 and 10% of GDP since 2011. South Korea has run current account surpluses averaging 3% of GDP since 2006 and 5% of GDP since 2011. Japan has run current account surpluses averaging 3% of GDP since 2006 and 1% of GDP since 2011. Nevertheless, between January 2006 and July 2015, the New Taiwan dollar has only appreciated by 1% while the Korean won has depreciated by 17% and the Japanese yen by 8%. As a result, $ssreer_t$ has not appreciated at all.[5]

---

[5] Data on current account surpluses relative to GDP come from Trading Economics (www.tradingeconomics.com). The exchange rate data are the real effective exchange rate (broad index) obtained from the Bank for International Settlements (www.bis.org).

In the twentieth century, economists focused on the effect of exchange rates in an individual country on a country's trade. In Asian trade in the twenty-first century, however, cross border production networks are paramount. To understand the effect of exchange rates on the price competitiveness of goods produced within these value chains, it is necessary to take account of exchange rates throughout the supply chain. Huge trade surpluses throughout the supply chain combined with huge current account surpluses should cause exchange rates in these countries to increase. The problem in East Asia, however, is that not only do firms from different countries cooperate extensively through production fragmentation, they also compete in selling goods to third markets. For this reason, a country such as South Korea in 2015 resists currency appreciation even when its current account surplus is approaching 9% of GDP because it does not want to lose price competitiveness relative to Japan.[6] When upstream countries do not let their currencies appreciate in the face of enormous current account surpluses, as has happened over the last 10 years, no amount of renminbi appreciation will rebalance China's half a trillion dollar surplus in processing trade.

One way out of this impasse is for East Asian countries to allow their currencies to appreciate together in response to market forces. If they appreciated in concert against currencies such as the US dollar, then any loss of competitiveness relative to other East Asian countries would be small. The effect on real effective exchange rates in East Asia countries would also be attenuated because the currencies of neighboring countries with whom they trade intensively would also be appreciating. Strengthening currencies would also increase the purchasing power of Asian consumers and allow them to import more.

Asian governments have often resisted appreciation pressure by accumulating reserves or by encouraging capital to flow abroad. The counterpart of these capital outflows are current account surpluses. While growth driven by net exports has served the region well up until now, the rest of the world in the long run cannot continue absorbing massive surpluses coming out of Asia. In addition, private and social rates of return on Asia's investments abroad are less than the returns available from channeling funds into domestic investments such as health, education, and pollution abatement. Rather than encouraging more capital to flow abroad, Asian governments should invest in their own people. Doing so would provide a stimulus to offset any decrease in net exports. Investing in Asian citizens beginning in the first 1000 days of their lives would also help them to develop into workers who are productive and innovative and able to compete and lead in the twenty-first century.

Acknowledgements

This paper was prepared for the conference entitled 'Evolving Finance, Trade and Investment in Asia' at the National University of Singapore on 16–17 September 2015. I thank conference participants and colleagues at RIETI for valuable comments. Any errors are my own responsibility.

References

Ahmed, S. (2009). Are Chinese exports sensitive to changes in the exchange rate? International Finance Discussion Papers No. 987, Federal Reserve Board.
Arndt, S. (2009). Production networks, exchange rates, and macroeconomic stability. In S. Arndt, (Ed.), *Evolving patterns in global trade and finance* (pp. 137–148). Singapore: World Scientific.

---

[6] Schott (2015) documents the rise in Korea's current account surplus.

Cheung, Y. W., Chinn, M., & Qian, X. (2012). Are Chinese trade flows different? *Journal of International Money and Finance*, 31, 2127–2146. doi:10.1016/j.jimonfin.2012.05.004

Chin, M. Y., Yong, C. C., & and Yew, S. Y. (2015). The determinants of vertical intraindustry trade in SITC 8: The case of ASEAN-5 and China. *The Journal of Developing Areas*, 49, 257–270.

Freund, C., Hong, C., & Wei, S.-J. (2012). China's trade response to exchange rate. Paper presented at the American Economic Association Annual Meeting, Chicago.

Gaulier, G., Lemoine, F., & Unal-Kesenci, D. (2005). China's integration in East Asia: Production sharing, FDI, and high-tech trade. CEPII Working Paper No. 2005-09, Centre D'Etudes Prospectives et D'Information Internationales.

Goldstein, M., & Khan, M. (1985). Income and price effects in foreign trade. In S. R. Jones & P. Kenen, (Eds.), *Handbook of international economics* (vol. 2, pp. 1041–1105). Amsterdam: North-Holland.

Koopman, R., Wang, Z., & Wei, S. J. (2008). How much of Chinese exports is really made in China? Assessing domestic value-added when processing trade is pervasive. NBER Working Paper 14109, National Bureau of Economic Research.

Schott, J. (2015). PIIE chart: Korean currency policies and TPP entry [Peterson Institute Weblog]. Retrieved from www.iie.com

Stock, J., & Watson, M. (1993). A simple estimator of cointegrated vectors in higher order integrated systems. *Econometrica*, 61, 783–820.

Thorbecke, W. (2013). Investigating China's disaggregated processed exports: Evidence that both the RMB and exchange rates in supply chain countries matter. *The World Economy*, 36, 1245–1260. doi:10.1111/twec.12096

Thorbecke, W. (2015). Measuring the competitiveness of China's processed exports. *China & World Economy*, 23, 78–100. doi:10.1111/cwe.12100

Thorbecke, W., & Smith, G. (2010). How would an appreciation of the RMB and other East. Asian currencies affect China's exports? *Review of International Economics*, 18, 95–108. doi:10.1111/j.1467-9396.2008.00799

Xing, Y. (2014). Measuring value added in the People's Republic of China's exports: A direct Approach. ADBI Working Paper 493, Asian Development Bank Institute.

Xing, Y. (2015). Global value chains and China's exports to high income countries. GRIPS. Discussion Paper No. 15-06, Graduate Research Institute for Policy Studies.

Mega-FTAs and the WTO: Competing or Complementary?

Shujiro Urata

Waseda University, Shinjuku, Tokyo, Japan

ABSTRACT

Mega-FTAs involving many countries and encompassing bilateral and mini-lateral FTAs have begun to be negotiated, while the Doha Round of multinational trade negotiations under the WTO have been at a stalemate. Mega-FTAs, which are discriminatory, and the WTO, which is non-discriminatory, are not consistent, thereby leading to a view that they are competing. This article argues that mega-FTAs and the WTO can be complementary, as mega-FTAs could facilitate negotiations with a smaller number of negotiating members. It further stresses the importance of extending mega-FTAs to a global level by merging with other mega-FTAs and by accepting new members.

1. Introduction

The year 2015 marked the 20th anniversary of the establishment of the World Trade Organization (WTO). The WTO succeeded the General Agreement on Tariff and Trade (GATT) with more comprehensive issue coverage and a strengthened dispute settlement mechanism, and its main mission is to promote trade liberalization and to manage the world trading system. The Doha Development Agenda (Doha Round), the first multilateral trade negotiation under the auspices of the WTO, began in 2001, but the negotiations are not making much progress because of the differences in the opinions toward trade liberalization among the WTO members.

While the WTO is faced with problems in its trade negotiations, the number of free trade agreements (FTAs), which liberalize trade regimes between like-minded FTA members and discriminate against non-members, began to increase rapidly. Recent years have witnessed the emergence of mega-FTAs, which involve many countries and encompass bilateral and mini-lateral FTAs. Notable mega-FTAs are the Trans-Pacific Partnership (TPP) involving 12 countries from East Asia and the Americas, the Regional Comprehensive Economic Partnership (RCEP) involving 16 East Asian countries, and the Transatlantic Trade and Investment Partnership (TTIP) involving the United States (US) and the European Union (EU). Some observers argue that the mega-FTAs damage the world trading system managed by the WTO, because they violate one of the WTO's basic principles of non-discrimination among WTO members. By contrast, some observers argue that the mega-FTAs complement and strengthen the WTO trading system by complementing its deficiency and strengthening its weaknesses.

In light of these discussions, this paper examines the relationship between the mega-FTAs and the WTO. The main conclusion is that mega-FTAs can contribute to the improvement and strengthening of the WTO by enlarging the mega-FTAs by accepting new members and by merging with other mega-FTAs. The remainder of the paper is structured as follows. Section 2 discusses the experiences of multilateral trade liberalization under the GATT and the WTO, and Section 3 examines the proliferation of the FTAs in recent decades and the emergence of the mega-FTAs in recent years. Based on these discussions in Sections 2 and 3, the relationship between the mega-FTAs and the WTO is analyzed in Section 4. Section 5 presents some concluding remarks.

2. Multilateral Trade Liberalization

2.1. Multilateral Trade Liberalization under the GATT

Eight rounds of multilateral trade liberalization negotiation were conducted from 1947 to 1994 under the auspices of the General Agreement on Tariffs and Trade (GATT), whose basic principles were free (elimination of quantity restrictions and tariff reduction) and non-discrimination (most favored-nation and national treatment) (Table 1). From the first to the fifth rounds, the negotiations were conducted on tariff reduction of manufactured products. The sixth Round, that is the Kennedy Round, which began in 1962, negotiated non-tariff measures, although anti-dumping measures only, in addition to tariffs on manufactured products. In the seventh Round, the Tokyo Round, agreements on government procurement, technical barriers, subsidies and others, were concluded. These new trade rules were agreed upon by a subset of the GATT members and they are called 'codes.' Many of the codes concluded in the Tokyo Round became international treaties as a result of the eighth and the last round under the GATT, the Uruguay Round. A number of notable achievements were made in the Uruguay Round. They include the establishment of the World Trade Organization (WTO), liberalization in goods trade, establishment of the rules on service trade, intellectual property rights, investment, and the improvement and strengthening of the dispute settlement mechanism.

The GATT contributed to a large expansion of world trade. During the 44 years from 1950 to 1994, world trade expanded 14 times. During the same period, world production of goods increased five times. These figures indicate remarkable expansion of world trade. Various factors may be identified for the rapid expansion of the world trade. The reduction in transportation cost, which resulted from technological progress and deregulation in transportation services, promoted foreign trade. The reduction in tariff rates as a result of a series of multilateral trade negotiations under the GATT also played an important role in expanding foreign trade. Indeed, the average tariff rates for advanced countries declined to around 4%, which is about one-tenth of the rates before the GATT. Furthermore, the open and stable trading environment provided by the GATT backed by the free and non-discrimination principles also contributed significantly to the expansion of the world trade. The fact that the number of the GATT members rose sharply over the period indicates the benefits from the GATT membership.

For the trade negotiation, the GATT adopted the multilateral framework, where all the GATT members participate to discuss tariff reduction in a large number of products. The package approach, which includes a number of products and issues, may be easier for an

Table 1. Trade rounds: GATT and WTO.

Period	Name (Place)	No. of Countries	Areas of Trade liberalization	No. of tariff items	Rules
1947.4–1947.10	1st (Geneva)	23	Mining and manufacturing	45,000	
1948 GATT					
1949.8–1949.10	2nd (Annecy)	13	Mining and manufacturing	5,000	
1950.9–1951.4	3rd (Torquay)	38	Mining and manufacturing	8,700	
1956.1–1956.5	4th (Geneva)	26	Mining and manufacturing	3,000	
1961.5–1962.7	Dillon Round	26	Mining and manufacturing	4,400	
1964.5–1967.6	Kennedy Round	62	Mining and manufacturing	30,300	AD
1973.9–1979.7	Tokyo Round	102	Mining and manufacturing	33,000	AD, TBT, Gov. Procurement, Subsidies
1986.9–1994.4	Uruguay Round	123	Mining and manufacturing. Service, Agriculture	305,000	IPR, Investment, DS
1995 WTO					
2001.11-	Doha Development Agenda	161	Mining and manufacturing. Service, Agriculture		Trade rules, Trade facilitation, Development

Note: The number of participating countries for the DDA is as of April 26, 2015 (WTO website).
Source: METI (2015), WTO website.

agreement to be reached, because trade-offs can be made between the benefits and costs arising from the deal. On the other hand, it may be easier to reach an agreement for a single issue because of the simplicity in the content of the negotiation. As for the number of countries in the negotiation, the multilateral approach involving a large number of countries is beneficial for those developing countries with limited negotiating power. However, as the number of negotiating countries increases, reaching an agreement becomes difficult.

2.2. The Establishment of the WTO and the Doha Round

The World Trade Organization (WTO), which succeeded the GATT and included a number of new features, was established on 1 January 1995. Multilateral trade negotiations did not get started, mainly because of the differences between developed and developing countries in their opinions on new trade negotiations. It was at the fourth WTO Ministerial Conference in November 2001 that the first multilateral trade negotiations, named the Doha Development Agenda (DDA), or the Doha Round, were launched. In the Doha Round, the negotiations on eight areas – agriculture, non-agriculture market access, services, trade rules (anti-dumping, subsidy), trade facilitation, intellectual property, environment and development – proceeded with a target of reaching an agreement in all the areas in the form of a single undertaking. However, the negotiations fell into stalemate because of conflicts between the emerging countries such as China and India on the one hand and the developed countries such as the US on the other. Faced with the deadlock in the Doha Round negotiations, at the eighth Ministerial Conference in November 2011, the WTO members agreed on adopting new approaches to advance negotiations, where progress can be achieved, including focusing on the elements of the Doha Declaration that allow Members to reach provisional or definitive agreements based on consensus earlier than the full conclusion of the single undertaking.[1]

At the ninth Ministerial Conference in Bali, Indonesia in September 2013, the Bali Package was concluded by following the new approach adopted in the eighth Ministerial Conference. The Bali Package covered four areas: trade facilitation, agriculture, cotton, and development.[2] The Bali Package included the agreement on trade facilitation, which became the first multilateral agreement in the WTO in November 2014.[3] The Trade Facilitation Agreement (TFA) contains provisions for expediting the movement and release and clearance of goods.[4] It also sets out measures for effective cooperation between customs and other appropriate authorities on trade facilitation and customs compliance issues. It further contains provisions for technical assistance and capacity building in this area. Agriculture included provisions on public stockholding for food security purposes for the poor, improvement in the administration of tariff-quota system, and restraining export subsidies.[5] As for cotton, market access and reduction in domestic support and export subsidy were agreed to be examined. On development, the Bali package advances special and differential (S&D) treatment provisions for the least developed countries in the area of market access, services, and rules of origin.

In the midst of the stalled Doha Round negotiations, like-minded WTO members began several plurilateral trade negotiations, adopting new approaches agreed upon at the eighth Ministerial Conference in 2011. As of November 2015, the following plurilateral negotiations are under way, Information Technology Agreement (ITA), Trade in Service Agreement (TiSA) and Environmental Goods Agreement.

The Doha Round has been more or less in deadlock. Several reasons may be identified for the situation. First, the number of WTO members increased to reach 162 (as of the end of November 2015), a large increase from the 123 members during the Uruguay Round. The increase in the number of WTO members raises the probability of giving rise to a controversy, making it difficult to reach an agreement. Such a situation is likely to arise when one member has one vote and when the decision is made by consensus. Until the Uruguay Round, developed countries led the negotiations and, as such, the negotiations were concluded when an agreement was reached among developed countries, particularly among the Quad countries of the US, Canada, the European Community (EC), and Japan. However, the situation changed dramatically in the Doha Round. Emerging countries such as China, India, and Brazil, supported by high economic growth, increased negotiating power, resulting in an increase in conflicts and thereby reducing the chances of reaching an agreement.

One should also note that in the areas of market access in agricultural as well as manufactured products, trade liberalization has been pursued through a series of trade negotiations, and tariffs have declined substantially. As a consequence, only difficult areas for trade liberalization remain to be negotiated. As for the new areas, such as the environment, opinions

---

[1] WTO, 'Elements for Political Guidance,' Eighth Ministerial Conference, WT/MIN(11)/W/2 1 December 2011.
[2] WTO, 'Bali Ministerial Declaration' 11 December, 2013. https://www.wto.org/english/thewto_e/minist_e/mc9_e/balidec laration_e.htm.
[3] The Trade Facilitation Agreement (TFA) will enter into force when two-thirds of WTO members ratify the TFA.
[4] WTO, https://www.wto.org/english/tratop_e/tradfa_e/tradfa_e.htm.
[5] See Schnepf (2014) for details.

vary widely, not only between developed and developing countries, but also among developed as well as developing countries. These are some of the reasons why the Doha Round is making little progress.

We noted that the dispute settlement mechanism was improved and strengthened in the WTO compared with the situation in the GATT. Indeed, the number of disputes brought to the WTO increased substantially compared with those brought to the GATT. For 47 years from 1947 to 1994, the total number of disputes brought to the GATT was 314, or 6.5 per year, while the corresponding number brought to the WTO for 19 years from 1995 to 2014 was significantly higher at 488, or 24.4 per year.[6] The increase in the number of disputes is partly due to increased international activities by firms but it is also attributable to the improved and strengthened dispute settlement mechanism under the WTO.

3. From Multilateral Trading System to Regional Economic Integration

3.1. Proliferation of Free Trade Agreements

One of the notable recent developments in the world economy is proliferation of regional integration frameworks in the form of regional trade agreements (RTAs), which includes free trade agreements (FTAs) and customs unions.[7] This trend became particularly notable in the 1990s (Figure 1).[8] The cumulative number of RTAs reported to the GATT from 1949 to 1990 was 86. The number increased to 179 in 1995, and the rapid pace of the increase continued, reaching 615 as of 6 April 2015. It should be noted that many RTAs became inactive and the number of active RTAs stood at 406.

RTAs remove tariffs on trade among RTA members and, as such, they violate the most-favored-nation principle, one of the fundamental principles of the GATT/WTO. However, RTAs are accepted in the GATT/WTO with several conditions. The important conditions include the following: (1) tariff barriers vis-à-vis non-members shall not be raised from the pre-RTA levels; (2) tariffs should be eliminated with respect to substantially all the trade between the members; and (3) RTAs should be formed within a reasonable amount of time.[9] The definitions of the expressions 'substantially all the trade,' or 'reasonable amount of time' have not been defined. But there is understanding that the reasonable amount of time is 10 years, while understanding is not yet established concerning 'substantially all the trade.' It should be noted that these conditions are applied to RTAs involving developed countries. For those RTAs involving only developing countries, these conditions are not applied (the Enabling Clause). Having noted this, there are RTAs involving developed countries that do not satisfy these conditions.

Various factors may be found to result in rapid expansion of FTAs.[10] First, stalled multilateral trade negotiations under the GATT and the WTO prompted the countries interested in expanding exports to turn to FTAs with like-minded countries. As we saw earlier, the

---

[6] METI (2015).

[7] Both FTAs and customs unions remove tariffs on trade between the members. The difference is that for FTAs members apply their own tariff rates on imports from non-members, while the common tariffs are applied in the case of customs unions.

[8] WTO website, https://www.wto.org/english/tratop_e/region_e/regfac_e.htm.

[9] GATT Article XXIV, WTO website, https://www.wto.org/english/tratop_e/region_e/regatt_e.htm.

[10] Because a large number of RTAs are FTAs and because the expression 'FTA' is more commonly used than 'RTA', we use the expression FTAs instead of RTAs, unless otherwise indicated.

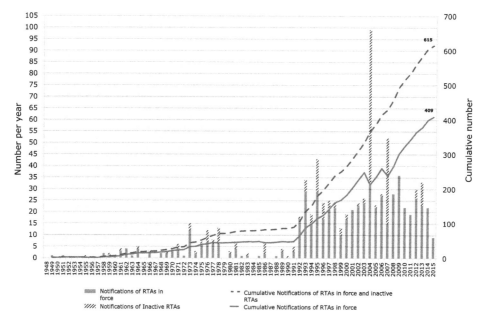

Figure 1. Evolution of regional trade agreements in the world, 1948–2015.
Notes: Notifications of RTAs: goods, services & accessions to an RTA are counted separately. Physical RTAs: goods, services & accessions to an RTA are counted together.
Source: WTO Secretariat.

number of FTAs began to rise sharply in the 1990s, when the Uruguay Round was in deadlock. The pace of the increase was maintained despite the establishment of the WTO, mainly because the first multilateral trade negotiations did not get started and even after they got started under the name of the Doha Round, progress was very limited.

Another factor is the discriminatory nature of the FTAs that led to the expansion of FTAs. Those countries that are excluded from an FTA suffer from the reduction in exports as their exports are treated less favorably vis-à-vis those exports from FTA members in the markets of the FTA members. In order to deal with the disadvantageous situation, these countries either join the existing FTAs or establish their own FTAs. As can be seen from this example, an FTA triggers the 'domino effect,' resulting in the proliferation of FTAs.

There are reasons that may make the countries interested in the establishment of FTAs even if the Doha Round is making progress. In recent decades, the world has witnessed active cross-border movement of goods, services, capital, people, and information globally, largely because of the reduction in the cost of transportation and communication, which in turn is due to deregulation and technological progress. Despite active movements of these factors, there still exist a variety of obstacles that impede freer movement. Since the WTO has basically to deal with free trade in goods, the WTO cannot provide the environment that is desired by the firms and the people. To cope with the unsatisfactory situation, some countries choose FTAs in order to set up the rules on investment, intellectual property rights, competition policy, etc.

So far, we have discussed economic motives behind the establishment of FTAs. There are non-economic motives as well. Many FTAs appear to have been established to construct good international political relations. A case in point is the US–Israel FTA, the first FTA for the US. For the US, Israel is not a large trading partner but it is a very important country for political and security reasons. It may not be an overstatement to say that a large number of FTAs have non-economic implications.

3.2. The Emergence of Mega-FTAs

Many of the FTAs that had been established in the Asia-Pacific region until the early twenty-first century were mostly bilateral or mini-lateral FTAs except for the ASEAN Free Trade Area (AFTA),[11] which consisted of the ten ASEAN Member States, and the North American Free Trade Agreement (NAFTA), which involved Canada, Mexico, and the United States. It should also be noted that Europe made substantial progress in forming a regional framework and established the European Union (EU).[12]

Entering the twenty-first century, East Asia began to witness the active formation of region-wide FTAs. In that process, ASEAN became the hub, resulting in five ASEAN + 1 FTAs, that is, ASEAN's FTAs each with China, Japan, Korea, India, and Australia-New Zealand, respectively. While East Asia was searching for ways to consolidate ASEAN + 1 FTAs into a single truly region-wide FTA, the US became active in forming an APEC-wide FTA encompassing both East Asia and North-South Americas. These developments turned into the negotiations of the Trans-Pacific Partnership (TPP), involving 12 APEC member countries[13] in March 2010, and the Regional Comprehensive Economic Partnership (RCEP) involving 16 East Asian countries in April 2013. Trying to avoid being left behind in the formation of region-wide or inter-regional FTAs, the EU and the US began to negotiate the Trans-Atlantic Trade and Investment Partnership (TTIP) in August 2013. The TPP, RCEP, and TTIP are characterized as mega-FTAs, which involve a large number of countries, with several major countries.[14] One of the common objectives of forming mega-FTAs is to consolidate a number of bilateral and mini-lateral FTAs with different rules into a single economic area, where open and free trade and investment business environment is established. The establishment of such an area would promote economic growth and economic prosperity.

The TPP negotiations reached an agreement on 5 October 2015, while RCEP, and TTIP are still under negotiation. The contents of TPP can be found, as the text of the TPP was released by TPP Parties on 5 November 2015 and can be accessed from the New Zealand Government's website. However, the text is not final as legal verification of the it is still under way.[15] For the RCEP and TTIP, the contents have not been decided. Given these constraints, we discuss some notable features of these mega-FTAs. For the RCEP and TTIP, we rely on the limited information obtained from various sources including the official documents and press reports.

The TPP attempts to establish a high-level and comprehensive FTA by essentially eliminating all the tariffs and establishing the rules in areas such as investment, competition,

---

[11] AFTA has been a core of regional economic framework for ASEAN and it became an important component of the ASEAN Economic Community (AEC), which was established at the end of 2015. AEC also consists of the ASEAN Framework Agreement on Services (AFAS) and ASEAN Comprehensive Investment Agreement (ACIA) and other components.

[12] The EU is a customs union and not an FTA.

[13] Urata (2014a) discusses the origins, evolution and significance of the TPP.

[14] The definition of mega-FTA does not seem to exist and some researchers include the Japan–EU FTA (EPA) and China–Japan–Korea FTA in mega-FTAs.

[15] http://tpp.mfat.govt.nz/text.

state-owned enterprises, intellectual property rights, and government procurement. In addition, it includes new areas including environment, labor, and regulatory coherence.[16] One of the motives behind the establishment of the TPP is the recognition that new rules are needed to deal with twenty-first century issues such as growing supply chains, which are not covered by the WTO, and that high levels of liberalization is needed in such areas as trade and investment, which are not dealt with sufficiently by the WTO. The fact that the TPP seeks a high-level and comprehensive framework made the negotiations difficult. In the area of setting new rules, which were led by developed countries, developed countries and developing countries had tough negotiations as developing countries tried to obtain special and differential treatment. In the area of trade liberalization, the debates took place mostly between the developed countries over agricultural products, such as dairy products and automobiles. It is ironic to observe that the negotiating countries were stuck with twentieth-century issues, i.e. trade liberalization, in their pursuit of establishing twenty-first century agreement.

The objective of the RCEP is to achieve a modern, comprehensive, high-quality and mutually beneficial economic partnership agreement among the ASEAN Member States and ASEAN's FTA Partners.[17] The RCEP is likely to cover trade in goods, trade in services, investment, economic and technical cooperation, intellectual property, competition, dispute settlement and other issues. Compared with the TPP, the RCEP is likely to be not as high level in terms of liberalization and less comprehensive in issue coverage. Having noted these differences between the RCEP and TPP, similar to the TPP, the RCEP recognizes the importance of establishing a business environment, under which supply chains can be constructed and utilized effectively. One of the special characteristics of the RCEP is its emphasis on economic cooperation. This is quite natural once one realizes that less developed countries including Cambodia, Lao PDR, and Myanmar are RCEP negotiating members. The RCEP is considered to be an extension and expansion of the ASEAN Economic Community, which is scheduled to be established by the end of 2015. As such, the ASEAN is expected to play a central role in the establishment of the RCEP.

The TTIP is expected to activate and increase the two largest economies in the world, the US and the EU by connecting these economies through high-level and comprehensive agreement. With a successful establishment of the TTIP, employment opportunities will be created and the consumers would enjoy the benefits. In order to achieve these objectives, the US and the EU are negotiating the TTIP in three areas, market access, regulatory matters, and rules.[18] In the area of market access they are trying to achieve a higher level of market opening by eliminating virtually all tariffs. Concerning regulatory matters, they are trying to eliminate unnecessary regulations and promote cooperation to achieve the rules that are compatible to each other. In the area of rules, they are eager to set up model rules, which eventually become the global rules. Although the EU and the US have a long history of economic interactions and thus developed very close economic relations, there are many areas where they have firmly established different regulations and rules. Because

---

[16] Ibid.

[17] ASEAN Secretariat, Guiding Principles and Objectives for Negotiating the Regional Comprehensive Economic Partnership, August 2012. http://www.asean.org/images/2012/documents/Guiding%20Principles%20and%20Objectives%20for%20Negotiating%20the%20Regional%20Comprehensive%20Economic%20Partnership.pdf.

[18] The EU website http://ec.europa.eu/trade/policy/in-focus/ttip/.

of this, there are views that it is not easy for the EU and the US to establish rules and regulations that may be acceptable to both of them.

4. Mega-FTAs and the WTO

Mega-FTA negotiations have been under way while the Doha Round negotiations have stalled. For the countries of the world, it is desirable that common rules on trade and investment are established and a free and open business environment is created under these rules. At present, the WTO is the organization that governs the trading system, as such this section examines the impacts of the mega-FTAs on the WTO, specifically their impacts on the WTO trading system and the Doha Round negotiations. Let me begin with the favorable impacts of the mega-FTAs on the WTO, and then turn to the unfavorable ones. Favorable impacts mean that the mega-FTAs would contribute to the improvement of the WTO system and to facilitate the Doha Round, while unfavorable impacts mean that the mega-FTAs would do damage to the WTO system and detract/hinder the Doha Round. To put it differently, the favorable impacts mean that the mega-FTAs would become build-ing block for the WTO, while the unfavorable impacts mean that the mega-FTAs would become stumbling block to the WTO.

One of the favorable impacts of the mega-FTAs on the WTO is their possible contribu-tion to facilitating the WTO negotiations in terms of trade liberalization. FTAs generally eliminate tariffs and thus attempt to reach higher levels of tariff liberalization than the WTO's trade liberalization negotiations, which attempt to lower tariff rates. The countries that have achieved a high level of trade liberalization under the mega-FTAs, albeit with a limited number of FTA members, may find less opposition against committing to the reduction in tariffs vis-à-vis the rest of the world. For example, if a country is commit-ted to eliminating a tariff on a product under the FTA, that country may find it easier to reduce the tariff rate on the same product imported from the rest of the world under the WTO trade liberalization negotiation. The mega-FTAs, particularly the TPP and TTIP, are eager to establish the new rules in a number of areas including investment and competi-tion policy, and regulatory coherence, which are not covered by the WTO. If these rules and regulatory frameworks were established under the mega-FTAs, then they could contribute to the future discussions/negotiations under the WTO.

Another favorable impact of the mega-FTAs on the WTO is to become a basis/base, from which the WTO can achieve trade liberalization as well as broaden its coverage in the areas of rulemaking. This impact can be realized if the mega-FTAs can increase their membership by accepting new members. The establishment of the mega-FTA would bene-fit its members by expanding their exports, while it has negative impacts on non-members by reducing their exports to mega-FTA members. To deal with the negative impacts, non-members desire to join the mega-FTA. If this kind of behavior on the part of non-members takes place and spreads to many non-members, the mega-FTA would become the 'WTO,' under which a free and open trade environment with new trade rules and regulatory regimes is established. In order for this kind of process to function, the mega-FTAs need to establish the rules and procedures regarding the accession of new members, and accept new members when the applicants satisfy the conditions for the accession.

In the transition from the mega-FTAs to the WTO, mega-FTAs have to be merged. In order for the mega-FTAs to be merged, the mega-FTAs need to have consistent rules and regulations and/or complementary relationship. There is a high probability that this issue becomes a serious problem between the TTP and the TTIP, both of which are attempting to set up comprehensive FTAs with new rules and regulations. We will return to this issue later in this section. Unlike the TTP or the TTIP, the RCEP is an FTA with relatively limited coverage and with an emphasis on economic cooperation, in order to deal with the problems of developing member countries. As such, the RCEP on the one hand and the TPP and the TTIP on the other hand are likely to form a complementary relationship.

Let us turn to the unfavorable impacts of the mega-FTAs on the WTO. One such impact is to slow down the WTO negotiations. This problem may arise from several reasons. The number of government officials that can get engaged in the trade negotiations is more or less fixed for many countries, especially for developing countries, where the availability of human resources is very limited. Under such circumstances, the number of officials that can participate in the WTO negotiations decreases if the number of officials involved in the FTA or mega-FTA negotiations increases. Because of this kind of relationship, the emergence of mega-FTA negotiations is likely to slow the WTO negotiations. It should also be noted that the increasing interest and attention of the business community on the mega-FTAs would reduce their interest and attention on the WTO, which in turn would slow the WTO negotiations. This problem is very plausible, but one may argue quite differently as follows. The WTO member countries may realize the importance of a multilateral trading system and multilateral trade negotiations, when FTAs and mega-FTAs are likely to become closed blocs. Indeed, Bergsten (1996) argues that it was a move toward regionalism in the Asia-Pacific region that induced the European Community to finally agree on the agricultural subsidy issues with the US to conclude the Uruguay Round.

Another negative impact of the mega-FTAs on the world trading system is argued to complicate the trading systems and rules, to result in the reduction of trade. This is possible but this problem can be overcome by combining and merging mega-FTAs to become the global FTA or the WTO. As was mentioned above, the merger of mega-FTAs with different rules and regulations is very difficult. A case in point may be the TPP and TTIP, which may have different rules and regulations. One possible solution may be that the US plays a dominant role in both mega-FTAs in that the rules and regulations adopted by the TPP and the TTIP are basically those practiced in the US. Although the discussion is on the merger of the TPP and TTIP, the problem that needs to be addressed first is the conclusion of the TTIP, as the US and the EU have different rules and regulations. On this point, Messerlin (2014) proposes an interesting idea of 'mutual equivalence' to reach an agreement. Under mutual equivalence, two countries decide, after a joint evaluation by their relevant regulatory bodies of their existing norms for a given good or regulations for a given service, that these norms or regulations are 'different but equivalent.' In such cases, producers are allowed to produce the good or service under the regulations of their own country and to sell it to the consumers of the other country without any other formality.

So far, we have discussed the impacts of the mega-FTAs on the WTO. We now examine the role of the WTO in the presence of the mega-FTAs. It was mentioned above that faced with the stalled Doha Round, several plurilateral frameworks, including the Information Technology Agreement (ITA), Trade in Service Agreement (TiSA) and Environmental Goods Agreement, with like-minded WTO members have been negotiated. It is now important to start the negotiations of plurilateral agreements in the area of competition policy, regulatory coherence and others, which are important areas for the construction and effective functioning of the global value chains, as the global value chains have their importance for the promotion of economic growth. It has to be emphasized that for pluri-taleral agreements the benefits of the agreements should be equally given to all the WTO members, similar to the case of the ITA. Finally, the dispute settlement mechanism of the WTO, which has improved tremendously from the GATT, needs to be further improved, and the monitoring mechanism of the trade policies needs to be strengthened.

5. Concluding Remarks

In the post-Second World War period, free and open trade systems established under the GATT contributed substantially to the rapid expansion of world trade, which in turn played an important role in achieving high economic growth. Specifically, trade liberalization or tariff reduction through a series of multilateral trade negotiations and the application of the MFN treatment in implementing the tariff reduction resulting from the negotiations were instrumental in the expansion of world trade. The WTO succeeded the GATT and the Doha Round of multilateral trade negotiations began in 2001, but there has been limited progress because of the differences in the views on trade liberalization among the WTO members.

In the midst of the stalemate in the Doha Round, the number of FTAs, which elim-inate tariffs on the trade with a small number of like-minded FTA members and thus are discriminatory, began to rise. In recent years, mega-FTAs, which encompass bilat-eral and mini-lateral FTAs and include many countries, began to be negotiated. While FTA negotiations covering a wide variety of areas, such as goods and service trade, invest-ment, intellectual property, competition policy, etc. with a limited number of countries, are being negotiated, plurilateral negotiations in selected areas such as information technology, services, and the environment are under way on single-issue basis.

Mega-FTAs and plurilateral agreements may be considered inappropriate, because they are not consistent with the principles of the GATT/WTO. However, it is possible to con-sider mega-FTAs and plurilateral agreements as the means to achieve a free and open world trade environment under the WTO by taking alternative approaches, which limit the number of countries and the number of issues/areas, respectively. Seeing the recent developments of mega-FTAs and plurilateral agreements from this angle, one realizes the importance of formulating the ways of expanding and extending mega-FTAs to a global level FTA[19] and plurilateral agreements to a comprehensive agreement covering a large number of areas. To achieve these objectives, it is important for the mega-FTAs to accept new members and for the plurilateral agreements to share the benefits with the non-negotiating members on the MFN basis.

For both the Doha Round and mega-FTAs with an objective of establishing twenty-first century trade rules, one of the more serious obstacles in reaching an agreement is liberalization of goods' trade, which is a twentieth-century issue. Under such situations, policy makers remind themselves of the beneficial impacts of trade liberalization for eco-nomic growth and economic welfare. Trade liberalization contributes to economic growth by enabling productive resources such as labor and capital to move from low productive to

---

[19] See Baldwin and Low (2009) and Urata (2014b) for the discussions on multilateralizing regionalism such as mega-FTAs.

high productive sectors, and by promoting innovation. Trade liberalization benefits consumers, both consumers of final products and consumers of raw materials and intermediate goods – that is, companies – as it lowers the price of imports. One important issue that needs to be addressed is the problem of adjustment for the workers, who need to move from low productive to high productive sectors. The government needs to provide assistance to these workers to ameliorate the problem of transition in the form of provision of temporary income compensation, technical training, and job search.

Finally, it needs be stressed that strong political leadership and formulation and implementation of appropriate policy are of crucial importance for achieving high economic growth by building a free and open economic environment through mega-FTAs and plurilateral agreements.

Acknowledgements

This article was presented at the Inaugural International Conference 'Evolving Finance, Trade and Investment in Asia,' Lee Kuan Yew School of Public Policy, 16–17 September 2015. The author is thankful to the participants for useful comments and suggestions.

References

Baldwin, R., & Low, P. (Eds.). (2009). *Multilateralizing regionalism: Challenges for the global trading system*. Cambridge, UK: Cambridge University Press.

Bergsten, C. F. (1996). Competitive liberalization and global free trade: A vision for the 21st century. Working Paper 96–12, Institute for International Economics, Washington, DC. Retrieved from http://www.iie.com/publications/wp/wp.cfm?ResearchID = 171

Messerlin, P. (2014). The transatlantic trade and investment partnership: Ambiguities, opportunities, challenges. Kokusai Mondai [International Affairs], No. 632, Japan Institute of International Affairs. Retrieved from http://www2.jiia.or.jp/en/pdf/publication/2014-06_005-kokusaimondai.pdf

Ministry of Economy, Trade and Industry (METI). (2015). *Fukosei Boeki Hokokusho* (2015 Report on Compliance by Major Trading Partners with Trade Agreements -WTO, EPA/FTA and IIA).

Schnepf, R. (2014). *Agriculture in the WTO Bali Ministerial Agreement*. Washington, DC: Congressional Research Service.

Urata, S. (2014a). The Trans-Pacific Partnership: Origins, evolution, and significance. Presented at the Conference on Mega-FTAs at University of California, Berkeley, on 10–11 October.

Urata, S. (2014b). Constructing and multilateralizing the regional comprehensive economic partnership: An Asian perspective. In R. Baldwin, M. Kawai, & G. Wignaraja (Eds.), *A world trade organization for the 21st century: The Asian perspective* (pp. 239–268). Cheltenham, UK: Edward Elgar.

Heterogeneous Patterns of Financial Development: Implications for Asian Financial Integration

Linh Bun & Nirvikar Singh

Department of Economics, University of California, Santa Cruz, CA, USA

ABSTRACT

This paper analyzes detailed differences in patterns of financial development across the major Asian economies, including three of the region's largest economies (China, Japan and South Korea), to understand how these differences might affect possibilities for greater regional financial integration. In particular, the paper argues that heterogeneous patterns of financial development, and not just differences in levels of financial development, may present an economic challenge to regional financial integration efforts, aside from possible political challenges. The paper provides background on the case for financial openness, Asian experiences with financial integration, and regional economic responses to external shocks. It also discusses policy options, including regulatory reform and coordination, and possible risk management policies and institutions, in the context of heterogeneous patterns of financial development.

1. Introduction

The rapid post-war rise of Japan to developed country status, followed by economies such as South Korea, Taiwan, Hong Kong and Singapore, began a process of making East (and Southeast) Asia a significant contributor to global economic activity. Even as Japanese growth slowed, the regional process has been accelerated by the growth of China, and the creation of regional production networks that include many smaller economies such as Malaysia and Vietnam in essential ways. These production networks have been an important aspect of openness to trade that characterized much of the region and contributed to economic growth.[1]

Strong real growth has not been immune to normal business cycle fluctuations, as well as to the negative impacts of international financial crises. The Asian financial crisis of 1997–1998 called attention to the differences between openness to trade and openness to capital, and produced a particular set of policy responses in the region, including 'self-insurance' through international reserve accumulation.[2] The global financial crisis of

---

[1] On regional production networks, trade, and growth, see Athukorala (2014) and Kaur (2014), as two examples of a large and growing literature.

[2] See Aizenman, Chinn and Ito (2013) as one of several articles by those authors that document and analyze this reserve accumulation.

2007–2009 had an unavoidable negative impact on East Asia as well, but it is arguable that the lessons of 1997–1998 permitted the region to be better prepared for this second, larger shock.

One of the issues brought to the fore by the global crisis was the benefits and costs of financial openness and financial integration. Openness and integration can cover several different aspects of economic interaction. The obvious example of financial openness is liberalization of capital flows between countries. Integration has several connotations beyond openness, including harmonization of institutions such as financial market trading rules, and policy coordination for managing risks and instabilities that are potentially associated with financial openness. The theoretical justification for financial openness has been questioned much more than in the case of openness to trade, but it remains a reality that has to be analyzed and managed. The last decade, before and after the global financial crisis, has seen continued academic and policy engagement with these questions.

A key complement to financial integration is the nature of domestic financial development. It has been argued that financial openness and integration are more likely to have positive outcomes in cases where the economies involved have adequate levels of financial development.[3] However, financial development is itself a multi-dimensional concept. For example, it can include various kinds of financial market institutions such as banks and stock markets, but also broader legal and regulatory frameworks that create the environment for financial decision-making by firms and households. This paper is motivated by debates about financial integration and policy coordination in East Asia, but focuses on financial development as a precondition for financial integration. In particular, it analyzes differences in patterns of financial development across the major East Asian economies, including three of the largest economies of the region (China, Japan and South Korea). In addition to differences in levels of financial development, differences in patterns of financial development may present an economic challenge to regional financial integration efforts.

The next section briefly reviews arguments for and against financial openness, the East Asian experience with financial crises and with financial integration, and how economies in the region have responded to external shocks. It also considers the possible connection between financial integration and financial development. Section 3 discusses data and measurement of patterns of financial development, as well as overall levels. A key idea here is that differences in various dimensions of financial development can be relevant for financial integration, as well as differences in overall levels of financial development. Section 4 presents the results of the paper, analyzing levels and patterns for 14 economies in the region. A key finding is that comparisons of overall levels of financial development convey somewhat different information than comparisons of patterns of financial development. This is borne out in a cluster analysis, which also provides some direct insights on possibilities for future financial integration. Section 5 concludes, offering some possible implications of the analysis for future thinking about financial integration in the region.

2. Financial Integration and Financial Development

The core aspect of financial integration is openness on the capital account, so that international capital flows are unrestricted. In practice, a completely open capital account does not

---

[3] Arguments for this view are taken up in the next section, where references are provided.

lead to perfect financial integration, in the sense of unified financial markets. An important reason for this imperfection is home bias in investment, reflected in a positive correlation between domestic savings and investment (Feldstein & Horioka, 1980). Investors do not view foreign and domestic assets as perfect substitutes, even when they have the same objective characteristics. This can be due to regulatory differences, tax treatment, asymmetries of information, and other kinds of market or institutional imperfections. Nevertheless, despite these perceptual and institutional barriers to complete financial integration, the main defining feature of modern-day globalization has been liberalization of restrictions on capital flows, allowing large amounts of capital to move swiftly between different countries. Furthermore, these capital flows now mainly consist of private capital, rather than official government flows. Large flows of capital, whether inward or outward, create challenges for the conduct of domestic macroeconomic policies,[4] and these are compounded by the volatility of these flows.

The post-Second World War global economy was initially one of fixed exchange rates, capital controls and monetary policy autonomy. This regime broke down in the 1970 s, and since then theory and practice have swung back and forth between different policy combinations. At one stage, the orthodoxy had coalesced on the desirability of flexible exchange rates and openness of the capital account, the idea being that markets would equilibrate to allocate resources efficiently around the globe. Few countries adopted this policy mix, however, instead pursuing various combinations of partial capital controls, partial exchange rate flexibility and partial monetary autonomy. The latest financial crisis finally pushed the weight of expert opinion away from full capital account openness.[5] One of the most striking examples of this change was the near reversal of the International Monetary Fund's position on capital account liberalization, after the global financial crisis.

Even before the global financial crisis of 2007–2009, there was evidence that full capital account openness did not have identifiable positive effects on economic performance. While the earlier 1997–1998 financial crisis was still unfolding, Dani Rodrik (1998) argued against full capital account convertibility, pointing out that financial markets are far from the textbook model of perfection, and subject to bubbles, panics and herd behavior in general, so that the theoretical case for capital account openness is difficult to make convincingly.[6] Looking at empirical evidence, Rodrik concluded, 'There is no evidence

---

[4] The main challenge for macroeconomic policy is encapsulated in the idea of the policy 'trilemma,' or 'impossible trinity,' based on the Mundell-Fleming model of an open economy macroeconomic framework. In the model, it is impossible for a government to simultaneously have monetary policy autonomy (and hence the ability to control the domestic inflation rate) and a fixed exchange rate when the capital account is completely unrestricted. Attempts to conduct an independent monetary policy will drive a wedge between foreign and domestic interest rates, leading to continued capital inflows or outflows (depending on the direction of the interest differential) in the absence of an equilibrating mechanism such as exchange rate adjustment. Rey (2013) has advanced the proposition that the weight of capital flows in the context of non-conventional monetary policies (essentially, what is known as QE or Quantitative Easing) makes exchange rate flexibility insufficient for domestic inflation control unless there are also controls on international capital flows. The theory and empirics of this view are still being debated. Aizenman, Chinn and Ito (2013) have been among the originators of quantitative approaches to measuring policy stances with respect to the trilemma.

[5] For an academic statement of the changed thinking, see Ostry, Ghosh, Chamon, and Qureshi (2012). Ghosh et al. (2008) provide an earlier, more policy-focused take with the same perspective, also from the IMF.

[6] Other prominent arguments against full capital account liberalization include Bhagwati (1998), Cooper (1999), Obstfeld (2009), and Stiglitz (2003).

in the data that countries without capital controls have grown faster, invested more, or experienced lower inflation.'[7]

More recently, Obstfeld (2009, pp. 104–105) offered a similarly cautious assessment, after an extensive literature review, 'Financial openness is not a panacea – and it could be poison. The empirical record suggests that its benefits are most likely to be realized when implemented in a phased manner, when external balances and reserve positions are strong, and when complementing a range of domestic policies and reforms to enhance stability and growth.'[8] Addressing the obverse of the issue, Aizenman, Pinto and Radziwill (2007) found evidence that domestic financial development might be more important for higher growth than foreign capital. They constructed a self-financing measure, which was positively correlated with growth, after controlling for the quality of domestic institutions. Even earlier, Eichengreen (2003) had emphasized the importance of domestic financial development, making that case in the context of criticizing the Chiang Mai Initiative (CMI) – designed in 2000 to provide regional swap lines – as a means of preserving fixed exchange rates among the CMI group.

Despite the cautions emerging from work such as discussed above, financial integration, especially in East Asia as an economically dynamic region of growing importance, has continued to receive considerable attention. Borensztein and Loungani (2011) used cross-border equity and bond holdings, as well as equity returns and interest rates, to argue that Asian (chiefly East Asian) financial integration had increased, but that extra-regional connections remained stronger than intra-regional measures of integration. These results echoed earlier, similar studies (Fung, Tam, & Yu, 2008; Garcia-Herrero, Yang, & Wooldridge, 2008), with the latter paper providing an explanation of limited Asian financial integration in terms of low liquidity in the region's financial markets. Another recent study (Lee, Park, & Yi, 2013) found no evidence for increased Asian financial integration after the global crisis, but an up-to-date survey (Financial Services Institute of Australasia, 2015) suggested that regional financial integration has increased. This is also the conclusion of a recent IMF study (IMF, 2015), which measures this increase in terms of intraregional financial flows, but nevertheless also concludes that 'Home bias … is particularly strong in Asia, limiting cross-border financial transactions within the region' (IMF, 2015, p. 94).

Aside from measuring trends in financial integration, various studies have also tried to estimate the potential costs and benefits. Hoxha, Kalemli-Ozcan, and Vollrath (2009) analyzed international financial integration, measured as foreign capital flows, and estimated that these flows had had significant positive impacts on consumption and welfare. Unfortunately, this analysis was performed before the global financial crisis. From a somewhat different welfare perspective, Pongsaparn and Unteroberdoerster (2011) estimated that greater financial integration in Asia would support global rebalancing, and hence financial stability. Park and Lee (2011) also implicitly assumed benefits from greater financial integration in 'emerging Asia,' through greater allocative efficiency, but emphasized

---

[7] Kaur and Singh (2014) provide a detailed review of the empirical evidence on how different East Asian economies reacted to the financial crises of 1997–1998 and 2007–2009, and the impacts of different policy mixes with respect to financial openness.

[8] There is also evidence that the specific nature of capital flows matters. For example, equity flows have a positive short-run impact on the host economy (Henry, 2007; Kose, Prasad, & Terrones, 2009), as does foreign direct investment (e.g., Kose et al, 2009).

the need for 'more effective financial supervisory and regulatory mechanisms,' as well as improvements in various dimensions of financial development.

There is a large empirical literature on the impacts of financial development, with the recent focus, post-global-crisis, being on the possibility that 'too much finance' is inimical to economic growth. A common approach in this literature is to use a quadratic term for the measure of financial development: Arcand, Berkes, and Panizza (2015a) provide the most recent example of this specification. On the other hand, Law and Singh (2014) used an endogenous threshold model to allow for negative effects of financial development on growth.[9] The typical conceptualization of financial development is in terms of financial depth, measured as a credit-to-GDP ratio, and the presumed channel of negative impacts of financial depth on growth is volatility or financial crises (Schularick & Taylor, 2012).[10] Arcand et al. (2015a) used the ratio of total private sector credit to GDP as the measure of financial depth, but their results are robust to using bank credit or household credit instead. Law and Singh used private sector credit, liquid liabilities and domestic credit as three possible measures of financial depth, with similar results.

Law, Azman-Saini, and Ibrahim (2013) examined the possibility that the finance-growth nexus depends on institutional quality, and find that this is the case using a threshold model. The institutional quality measures are generic – capturing control of corruption, rule of law and government effectiveness – and not specific to the financial sector. Earlier, Demetriades and Law (2006) had explored a similar connection between financial depth and institutional quality, using a specification with interactions, and a similar exercise is carried out by Arcand et al. (2015a).

Most relevant to the current context, Herwartz and Walle (2014) examined the impacts of trade openness and financial openness on the finance-growth linkage. They found that greater trade openness strengthened this linkage, whereas greater financial openness eroded it. Their result is interpreted as providing a caution to the Rajan and Zingales (2003) analysis that openness would promote financial development by overcoming the resistance of domestic interest groups, since the financial development achieved would come at the cost of a weaker finance-growth relationship. As in most other studies, Herwartz and Walle (2014) measure financial development as financial depth, specifically, the private-sector credit-to-GDP ratio.

Outside this large literature on financial integration and financial development, and their economic impacts, there has been some attention paid to the issue that financial development is broader than just financial depth. From 2009–2012, the World Economic Forum (WEF) produced a Financial Development Index with seven components, as the basis for its annual Financial Development Reports (FDRs), and the approach in that exercise will be the starting point for the analysis of the current paper. Since 2013, the World BankF has published annual Financial Development Reports, which are quite different from the WEF's documents, being focused on specific themes such as the role of the State in finance (World Bank, 2013) and financial inclusion (World Bank, 2014). These FDRs do not have

---

[9] Arcand et al. (2015a) also test a piecewise linear model with exogenous thresholds of financial depth.

[10] Law and Singh (2014) survey other possible explanations for the negative impact of financial depth on growth. Cline (2015) argues that all these results are merely a statistical artifact, and claims that the results are explained by slower growth at higher per capita income levels, but this claim seems to have been answered effectively by Arcand, Berkes, and Panizza (2015b).

an index of financial development, but they identify and provide data for four components or dimensions of overall financial development: depth, access, efficiency and stability.

Adnan (2011), building on the work of Saci and Holden (2008), constructed an index of financial development based on data for the banking and insurance sectors, as well as stock and bond markets. Thirteen variables were used, capturing depth and efficiency, with more in the former category. However, the index itself was derived using principal components analysis. No further analysis was performed, beyond the construction of the index.

More recently, Sahay et al. (2015) constructed an index of financial development that captured financial markets as well as financial institutions, and access and efficiency as well as depth. The authors used six indicators, with weights derived from principal components analysis, to construct the index. They confirmed the non-linear, sign-changing relationship between finance and growth, earlier found just for financial depth, but now extended to this broader measure of financial development. However, their results suggested that the 'too much finance' result is driven by financial deepening rather than greater efficiency or access, which is a plausible conclusion.

Another significant recent paper is by Aizenman, Jinjarak, and Park (2015), who distinguished between quantity and quality of financial intermediation, measuring the former by financial depth (private bank credit to GDP ratio) and the latter by the lending-deposit interest rate spread. They examined sectoral growth impacts, and found that quantity and quality each had positive, negative or non-linear impacts, depending on the sector and region considered. Their results, unlike Sahay et al. (2015), suggested that even 'quality' might have a non-linear impact in some circumstances.

The approach taken in the current paper also tries to decompose financial development into its different aspects, but in a different manner than the Sahay et al. and Aizenman et al. papers. In particular, it tries to isolate differences in patterns of financial development across countries. The methodology and results are described in the next two sections.

3. Measuring Financial Development: Levels and Patterns

The motivation for the analysis in this section and the next is the idea that possibilities for successful financial integration are a function of similarities in financial development among the countries that are integrating. This is not the only way to think about pre-conditions for successful financial integration. For example, dissimilarities in financial development may also be positive in some circumstances: if one country in a region has strong stock markets, they may serve the whole region better as financial integration progresses. Nevertheless, proceeding with the idea of comparing financial development across countries in a region such as East Asia, which is contemplating or pursuing greater financial integration, it is straightforward to use a single measure or an index of financial development as a basis for comparison.

As first suggested in Kaur and Singh (2014), however, comparing levels of financial development via a single index misses possible differences across countries in the various components of the index. One can compare levels of different components as well, but this just generates additional information on level differences. Kaur and Singh (2014) suggested a summary measure of differences in patterns of financial development. The idea in this case is that financial development is inherently multidimensional, and comparing a vector of indicators of financial development across countries can tell one something about how similar or different the patterns of financial development are.

To illustrate, we use some of the calculations in Kaur and Singh (2014). They used indices constructed from the WEF FDR of 2012. In the WEF methodology, the Financial Development Index (FDIndex) was constructed from seven underlying indicators, each of which was itself built up from numerous base measures. The seven dimensions of financial development in this framework were institutional environment, business environment, banking financial services, non-banking financial services, financial stability, financial markets and financial access. Each dimension was scaled from 1 to 7, and the overall index was an average of these seven numbers. Thus, the FDIndex was 5.10 for Singapore, 5.01 for Australia, 4.90 for Japan and 4.42 for South Korea, providing a numerical scaling as well as a ranking of levels of overall financial development.

Kaur and Singh proposed complementing this comparison of levels with a comparison of patterns of financial development, as follows. Each country could be thought of as characterized by a seven-dimensional vector of different aspects of financial development. Calculating a correlation coefficient between these vectors for two countries could then be a measure of how similar the two vectors were, and therefore a measure of similarity in patterns of financial development.[11] The correlation coefficient uses deviations from the mean (the overall FDIndex for that country), so it would not be affected by the similarity or difference of overall levels. For example, Singapore and Japan had a correlation coefficient of 0.64, while Australia and Japan, slightly closer in level terms than Singapore and Japan, had a correlation of 0.54. Korea had a correlation coefficient of 0.13 with Japan, but a higher correlation of 0.22 with Australia, which was slightly further away than Japan in level terms. In fact, Korea and China stood out among the 11 countries considered, for having patterns of financial development relatively different from other countries in the group. This idea of comparing patterns as well as levels is taken further in the analysis of this paper. The data are described next, followed by a mathematical statement of the concepts used.

3.1. Data

The WEF did not publish a FDR after 2012. Instead, we use data from the WEF Global Competitiveness Report, which calculates a Global Competitiveness Index. This index includes a FDIndex as one of its components,[12] but it is quite different from the one used in the FDR. There are eight components, listed in Table 1. As in the FDR, each component is scaled from 1 to 7. Besides being narrower than the index constructed in the FDR (something we address in our calculations), the indicators in Table 1 rely heavily on survey evaluations, rather than being constructed primarily from quantitative measures (e.g., the percentage of households with bank accounts for measuring the availability of financial services). Reported numbers are averages across a range of respondents. In terms of the Aizenman et al. (2015) dichotomy between 'quality' and 'quantity' of financial services, all the components in Table 1 are primarily quality indicators, although factors such as availability of financial services could be viewed as being closer to measures of 'quantity.'

---

[11] The interpretation of this calculation is discussed in more detail later in this section.
[12] More specifically, the term used is Financial Market Development, and it is one of 12 'pillars' of the GCI.

Table 1. Components of FDIndex, WEF global competitiveness report.

Category	Indicator
Efficiency	Affordability of financial services
	Availability of financial services
	Financing through local equity market
	Ease of access to loans
	Venture capital availability
Trustworthiness and confidence	Soundness of banks
	Regulation of securities exchanges
	Legal rights of investors

Table 2. Economies in the analysis.

Australia	New Zealand
Cambodia	Philippines
China	Singapore
Hong Kong	South Korea
Indonesia	Taiwan
Japan	Thailand
Malaysia	Vietnam

The GCI data is available from 2006–2007 to 2014–2015, but the earliest year with all eight of the components that are listed in Table 1 is 2010–2011. Henceforth, we refer to years by their first year. Hence, 2010–1011 is termed 2010. Since there is no discernible trend in the data over the period 2010 to 2014, we report calculations only for the first and last years for which there is complete comparable data, 2010 and 2014.

While the index constructed from the eight components listed in Table 1 has a much narrower scope than the FDR index, the GCI database includes several variables that are the same as, or close to, those used in the FDR index. We therefore constructed two additional potential components for the FDIndex, capturing institutional environment and business environment. The underlying variables for these two additional components are provided in the Appendix. The GCI data did not provide variables to capture financial stability, or enable distinguishing of banking and non-banking financial services, so even with the additional two variables, substantial differences remain from the FDR index, leading to somewhat different results. These differences do not affect the validity of the methodology – they merely highlight the sensitivity of comparisons among countries to how financial development is conceived of and measured. We also constructed four other indices, measuring openness, technological sophistication, business sophistication and other aspects of institutional environment. Calculations involving these four indices or components of financial development are reported in the Appendix.

Finally, with respect to the data, we focus on 14 economies from the Asia Pacific, or East Asia region, and compare financial development across these economies. They are listed in Table 2, and include developed as well as emerging economies, with seven economies in each of those two broad categories. In fact, the variation in per capita GDP among these countries is substantial, with the richest being 15 times as well-off as the poorest, even at purchasing power parity. The set includes all eight economies that were analyzed in the 'East Asian Miracle' study of the World Bank (1993), as well as all 11 economies considered in Kaur and Singh (2014).

3.2. Methodology

We will denote the value of an indicator n for country i by x_{in}. An indicator here refers to a potential component of a financial development index (FDIndex), and we assume that all indicators have already been converted to a common scale (1–7 in the case of our data). For example, a weighted average of the components will yield an index defined by:

$$\bar{x}_i(w) = \sum_1^N w_n x_{in} \tag{1}$$

where the weights are assumed to sum to one. The left-hand side of this equation therefore measures the level of financial development for country i, based on the index formula chosen.

In this case, the *Level Distance* between country i and country j is simply $\bar{x}_i(w) - \bar{x}_j(w)$. This number may be positive or negative, of course. When considering regional financial integration, we may be interested in how close a single economy in the region is to the other economies in that region, in terms of financial development. Note that we are not measuring integration, but rather financial development as a precursor for integration. With 14 economies in our set of analysis, we would have 13 bilateral Level Distances. It is reasonable to summarize this information with an average over the 13 distance measures. Simply summing the individual distances and averaging will cancel out positives and negatives. In order to avoid this, one can use absolute values or squares, prior to summing up. We choose the latter, giving the general formula as below, with $I = 14$ for the calculations performed here.

$$\overline{LD_i} = \frac{1}{I-1} \sqrt{\sum_{j \neq i} [\bar{x}_i(w) - \bar{x}_j(w)]^2} \tag{2}$$

Hence, economies in the region with higher values of this measure are, on average, further in levels of financial development from their regional counterparts.

In constructing this measure of average Level Distance, differences in patterns are irrelevant, since they disappear into the aggregation. Instead, consider the entire vector of indicators for economy i, before any aggregation. Denote this by $x_i = (x_{i1}, \ldots, x_{iN})$. Differences in these vectors across countries can be thought of as capturing differences in patterns of financial development. Therefore, we define the *Pattern Distance* between two economies by:

$$PD_{ij} = 1 - corr(x_i, x_j) \tag{3}$$

In terms of the concept of distance, a higher correlation denotes a lower pattern distance.[13] Hence, if two economies have a correlation of 1 in their vector measures of financial development, their pattern difference would be the lowest possible. This is incorporated into our formula by subtracting the correlation from 1: the pattern distance measure therefore ranges from 0 to 2. Note that using the correlation coefficient removes the simple mean of the components of the vector. If the level index is constructed with equal weights, the index is the simple average of the components of the vector of financial development measures.

---

[13] Implicitly, this calculation treats all the components of the index as having equal weights. This is not an issue in our calculations, since the index we use weights components equally.

If we average across all such transformed correlations for country i, we obtain the average Pattern Distance for country i. Note that the correlation coefficient does not have the interpretation usually associated with random variables – it is simply a convenient summary measure.[14] For this calculation to make sense, all the components should be on the same scale, which is the case with the GCI data. Also, the calculation here can be contrasted with the correlations which are part of principal components analysis, since those are calculated between vectors of individual components, so that each country's value for that component is an element of the I-vector of country values. Therefore, differences in patterns of financial development, as calculated here are capturing something quite different from anything associated with principal components.

4. Results

We begin by reporting the levels of financial development for the 14 countries in the analysis. The individual country levels are reported in Table 3, for two years (2010 and 2014) and four different specifications of the financial development index. FDIndex8 is a slight modification of the measure of financial market development that is used in the GCI report, with equal weights for all eight components, rather than the two-tier weighting scheme used in that report. FDIndex7 removes Legal Rights of Investors from the index calculation. FDIndex10 adds our measures of business environment and institutional environment to the original eight components, while FDIndex9 adds these two to the seven components, excluding legal rights.[15] All the sub-components or variables included in these two additional components used in FDIndex10 and FDIndex9 are listed in tables in the Appendix. Removing the legal rights component reduces the financial development index levels slightly, on average, but adding the two 'environment' components does not affect the overall levels. The range of variation of the index levels across countries is not much affected by the differences in choice of components, across the four indices.

The relative and absolute levels of financial development in Table 3 are not surprising. Overall values of the index are in a tight range, quite far from the extremes of 1 and 7. There are strong associations between levels of financial development and GDP per capita, although Korea stands out as a considerable exception on the low side, while Malaysia has exceptionally high measures of financial development. Japan also has somewhat of a low score, given its high-income status. We will not go into the contribution of different components of the indices to the variations observed in the levels in Table 3. We mainly want to emphasize that the levels are fairly constant over this short span of time, and especially that they are not much affected by changes in the composition of the index, at least for the four alternatives considered here. However, it is useful to illustrate the patterns of financial development graphically, which we do in Figures 1 and 2, for FDIndex8 for 2014: Figure 1 shows the seven advanced economies of the region in our sample, and Figure 2 shows the other seven.[16] As noted, Korea stands out in the first case, while Malaysia is an outlier in

---

[14] In other words, the components of the vector are not draws from a single distribution, since they are measures of different aspects of financial development.

[15] The legal rights measure is actually included in the institutional environment component, but is only one of several institutional factors in that case.

[16] We are indebted to our discussant, Siu Fung Yiu, for suggesting construction of these graphs.

Table 3. Financial development index levels.

	FDIndex8		FDIndex7		FDIndex10		FDIndex9	
	2010	2014	2010	2014	2010	2014	2010	2014
AUS	5.24	5.18	5.07	4.92	5.27	5.20	5.14	5.00
CHN	4.22	4.26	4.17	4.29	4.17	4.21	4.12	4.23
HKG	5.60	5.77	5.41	5.60	5.56	5.74	5.40	5.60
IDN	4.23	4.44	4.43	4.50	4.14	4.35	4.29	4.39
JPN	4.44	4.86	4.33	4.82	4.53	4.94	4.46	4.91
KHM	3.63	3.63	3.31	3.32	3.54	3.55	3.29	3.30
KOR	3.75	3.65	3.54	3.34	3.90	3.83	3.75	3.61
MYS	5.22	5.48	4.97	5.26	5.09	5.39	4.88	5.21
NZL	4.91	5.53	4.70	5.32	5.05	5.58	4.90	5.42
PHL	3.94	4.33	4.11	4.46	3.82	4.24	3.93	4.33
SGP	5.51	5.67	5.30	5.48	5.55	5.68	5.39	5.54
THA	4.35	4.54	4.49	4.62	4.27	4.43	4.37	4.48
TWN	4.73	4.88	4.92	5.01	4.76	4.91	4.92	5.02
VNM	4.03	3.65	3.77	3.35	3.96	3.63	3.75	3.39

Figure 1. Patterns of financial development, developed economies, 2014.

the second set, although overall the emerging economies seem to show greater variation in their financial development patterns.

We next turn to the measurement of distances between economies of levels and patterns of financial development. Each pair of the 14 economies can be compared in terms of each of these measures, which implies 91 numbers for each measure. We report instead the average for each economy, of 13 pairwise distances with the other economies in the region that are in our set of analysis. Prior to examining these country averages, regional averages are reported in Table 4. For the region as a whole, the first index suggests that distances in financial development levels did not vary too much across countries and years. However, average distances in patterns of financial development, while similar when averaging across the region, showed considerably greater variation across economies for FDIndex7 in 2014 versus 2010, as evidenced in the higher range. Removing the legal rights component from the index had small effects on level distances, but large impacts on pattern distances – the

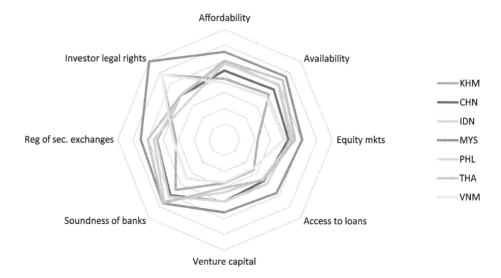

Figure 2. Patterns of financial development, emerging economies, 2014.

Table 4. Regional summary statistics.

	Level distance				Pattern distance			
Year	Average	Range	Min	Max	Average	Range	Min	Max
				FDIndex8				
2010	0.25	0.17	0.18	0.35	0.37	1.35	0.01	1.36
2014	0.29	0.16	0.21	0.37	0.35	1.06	0.00	1.06
				FDIndex7				
2010	0.24	0.20	0.18	0.38	0.09	0.34	0.01	0.35
2014	0.30	0.21	0.22	0.43	0.11	0.63	0.01	0.64
				FDIndex10				
2010	0.26	0.16	0.19	0.35	0.40	1.24	0.02	1.26
2014	0.29	0.17	0.22	0.39	0.39	1.03	0.02	1.05
				FDIndex9				
2010	0.25	0.20	0.18	0.38	0.20	0.73	0.02	0.95
2014	0.29	0.21	0.22	0.43	0.22	0.71	0.02	0.93

Source: The World Economic Forum, Global Competitiveness Index Report, 2015

latter were much lower on average (as a result of higher average correlations), and especially in the lower tail of the regional distribution.[17] Interestingly, adding in the two components measuring business environment and institutional environment had small impacts on pattern distances in the case where the legal rights index was included (FDIndex10), but large impacts when it was excluded (FDIndex9). However, the pattern distances in the case of FDIndex9 are lower than in the case of FDIndex8, implying that the differences in measured patterns of financial development are driven significantly by the single component of legal rights of investors.

Tables 5 through 8 provide economy-level averages for the level and pattern distances, for each of the four financial development indices. The average level distances depend

---

[17] In this context, the observations of the IMF (2015) report are of interest, 'Differences in financial regulation between countries are important determinants of financial integration, as investors may be reluctant to carry out financial transactions with entities in countries whose regulations and institutions are very different from their own.'

Table 5. Level and pattern differences FDIndex8.

Country	Level distance				Pattern distance			
	Average	Range	Min	Max	Average	Range	Min	Max
				Year 2010				
AUS	0.27	1.98	−0.37	1.61	0.24	0.96	0.02	0.98
CHN	0.21	1.98	−1.38	0.59	0.22	0.68	0.08	0.76
HKG	0.35	1.89	0.09	1.98	0.26	1.09	0.04	1.13
IDN	0.20	1.98	−1.38	0.60	0.90	1.18	0.18	1.36
JPN	0.18	1.98	−1.16	0.82	0.23	0.76	0.06	0.82
KHM	0.32	1.85	−1.98	−0.13	0.37	1.31	0.05	1.36
KOR	0.29	1.98	−1.85	0.13	0.26	1.04	0.03	1.07
MYS	0.26	1.98	−0.38	1.59	0.34	1.30	0.03	1.33
NZL	0.21	1.98	−0.69	1.29	0.27	1.04	0.02	1.06
PHL	0.25	1.98	−1.66	0.32	0.42	0.68	0.01	0.69
SGP	0.33	1.98	−0.09	1.89	0.29	1.20	0.03	1.23
THA	0.19	1.98	−1.25	0.72	0.40	0.68	0.01	0.69
TWN	0.19	1.98	−0.87	1.11	0.58	0.81	0.10	0.91
VNM	0.24	1.98	−1.58	0.40	0.33	1.24	0.03	1.27
				Year 2014				
AUS	0.25	2.14	−0.59	1.55	0.23	0.53	0.00	0.53
CHN	0.25	2.14	−1.52	0.62	0.39	0.84	0.07	0.91
HKG	0.37	2.04	0.10	2.14	0.22	0.5	0.01	0.51
IDN	0.22	2.14	−1.34	0.80	0.44	0.95	0.04	0.99
JPN	0.21	2.14	−0.91	1.23	0.22	0.38	0.09	0.47
KHM	0.37	2.12	−2.14	−0.02	0.43	0.89	0.08	0.97
KOR	0.37	2.14	−2.12	0.02	0.33	0.78	0.03	0.81
MYS	0.31	2.14	−0.29	1.85	0.37	0.87	0.03	0.9
NZL	0.32	2.14	−0.24	1.90	0.22	0.51	0.00	0.51
PHL	0.24	2.14	−1.44	0.70	0.48	1.02	0.04	1.06
SGP	0.35	2.14	−0.10	2.04	0.23	0.54	0.02	0.56
THA	0.22	2.14	−1.23	0.91	0.35	0.79	0.04	0.83
TWN	0.22	2.14	−0.89	1.25	0.48	0.90	0.07	0.97
VNM	0.37	2.14	−2.12	0.02	0.49	1.01	0.05	1.06

Source: The World Economic Forum, Global Competitiveness Index Report, 2015

on where the economy is in the ranking of levels, with high and low levels of financial development tending to have higher average distances. However, the average distance also depends on the overall distribution. Thus, in Table 5, Korea has a higher average level distance than Indonesia, even though its level of financial development is higher. This is because Indonesia is part of a cluster of economies in this regional group with relatively low levels of financial development. If we look at average level distances (again using Table 5 to illustrate), Indonesia was similar to several other economies on this measure (China, Japan, New Zealand, Taiwan, and Thailand), but very much an outlier in its pattern distance, which was much greater than any of the other economies in the set. This illustrates a key general point, that economies can be similar in levels of financial development, or in their closeness of levels on average, but quite different in their specific patterns of financial development. This point is explored further later in this section, through an explicit cluster analysis.

The pattern differences in Table 5 are not as large, on the whole, as those measured in Kaur and Singh (2014), using date from the WEF FDR. This reflects the different composition of the indices, based on different data and a somewhat different conceptualization of financial development. Significantly, when only one of the components, the index of

Table 6. Level and Pattern Differences FDIndex7.

Country	Level distance				Pattern distance			
	Average	Range	Min	Max	Average	Range	Min	Max
			Year 2010					
AUS	0.25	2.09	−0.33	1.76	0.08	0.20	0.78	0.98
CHN	0.20	2.09	−1.24	0.85	0.07	0.14	0.83	0.97
HKG	0.32	1.99	0.10	2.09	0.07	0.09	0.89	0.98
IDN	0.18	2.09	−0.98	1.11	0.13	0.30	0.65	0.95
JPN	0.18	2.09	−1.07	1.02	0.08	0.19	0.78	0.97
KHM	0.38	1.86	−2.09	−0.23	0.17	0.26	0.65	0.91
KOR	0.32	2.09	−1.86	0.23	0.08	0.24	0.75	0.99
MYS	0.23	2.09	−0.44	1.65	0.06	0.10	0.89	0.99
NZL	0.19	2.09	−0.70	1.39	0.11	0.27	0.71	0.98
PHL	0.21	2.09	−1.30	0.79	0.06	0.11	0.88	0.99
SGP	0.30	2.09	−0.10	1.99	0.08	0.15	0.82	0.97
THA	0.18	2.09	−0.92	1.17	0.06	0.13	0.86	0.99
TWN	0.22	2.09	−0.48	1.61	0.14	0.24	0.71	0.95
VNM	0.27	2.09	−1.63	0.46	0.09	0.24	0.75	0.99
			Year 2014					
AUS	0.24	2.28	−0.68	1.60	0.07	0.24	0.75	0.99
CHN	0.23	2.28	−1.30	0.97	0.11	0.31	0.66	0.97
HKG	0.36	2.16	0.12	2.28	0.06	0.31	0.68	0.99
IDN	0.22	2.28	−1.10	1.18	0.09	0.22	0.74	0.96
JPN	0.23	2.28	−0.78	1.50	0.08	0.33	0.66	0.99
KHM	0.43	2.26	−2.28	−0.02	0.29	0.53	0.36	0.89
KOR	0.42	2.28	−2.26	0.02	0.09	0.34	0.64	0.98
MYS	0.29	2.28	−0.33	1.94	0.08	0.24	0.74	0.98
NZL	0.30	2.28	−0.28	2.00	0.07	0.27	0.72	0.99
PHL	0.22	2.28	−1.13	1.14	0.06	0.22	0.77	0.99
SGP	0.33	2.28	−0.12	2.16	0.08	0.28	0.70	0.98
THA	0.22	2.28	−0.98	1.29	0.07	0.26	0.73	0.99
TWN	0.25	2.28	−0.59	1.69	0.12	0.44	0.54	0.98
VNM	0.42	2.28	−2.25	0.03	0.25	0.55	0.36	0.91

The World Economic Forum: Global Competitiveness Index
Excludes: Legal Right Index of the 8th Pillar

legal rights of investors, is removed, the pattern distances almost disappear, as can be seen in Table 6. Even when broader measures of institutional environment and business environment are included, to bring the index somewhat closer to that calculated in the FDR, the pattern distances are higher than in the case of the original eight components, although higher than the narrowest index of seven components (Tables 7 and 8). In all of these cases, level distances are relatively insensitive to changes in the index construction, just as was the case for the levels themselves (Table 3), although there are exceptions.

Figures 3 through 10 are useful in visualizing and summarizing the data in the tables. Each figure displays the combinations of level distance and pattern distance for the economies in the regional group. Figures 3 and 4 present the results for FDIndex8, corresponding to the data in Table 1. Clearly, Indonesia is an outlier in 2010, but its pattern distance changes dramatically in 2014. Figure 4, in particular, drives home the point that there is no obvious relationship between distances in levels of financial development and distances in patterns of financial development. Thus, while Vietnam is clearly furthest from other countries in the region on average, in both dimensions, Hong Kong and Singapore, while having the highest levels of financial development, and thus the greatest average

Table 7. Level and pattern differences FDIndex10.

Country	Level distance				Pattern distance			
	Average	Range	Min	Max	Average	Range	Min	Max
AUS	0.28	2.01	−0.29	1.73	0.27	0.95	0.00	0.95
CHN	0.22	2.01	−1.39	0.62	0.26	0.58	0.31	0.89
HKG	0.35	2.01	0.00	2.01	0.29	1.02	−0.07	0.95
IDN	0.22	2.01	−1.42	0.59	0.89	1.03	−0.26	0.77
JPN	0.19	2.01	−1.02	0.99	0.28	0.79	0.11	0.90
KHM	0.34	1.74	−2.01	−0.27	0.39	1.20	−0.26	0.94
KOR	0.26	2.01	−1.66	0.35	0.38	1.08	−0.18	0.90
MYS	0.24	2.01	−0.47	1.55	0.38	1.12	−0.17	0.95
NZL	0.24	2.01	−0.50	1.51	0.34	1.07	−0.12	0.95
PHL	0.28	2.01	−1.74	0.27	0.44	0.63	0.35	0.98
SGP	0.35	2.01	0.00	2.01	0.32	1.14	−0.21	0.93
THA	0.20	2.01	−1.29	0.72	0.42	0.64	0.34	0.98
TWN	0.20	2.01	−0.79	1.22	0.62	0.79	0.04	0.83
VNM	0.25	2.01	−1.60	0.41	0.35	1.14	−0.19	0.95
				Year 2014				
AUS	0.26	2.18	−0.54	1.64	0.26	0.53	0.45	0.98
CHN	0.25	2.18	−1.53	0.65	0.41	0.83	0.10	0.93
HKG	0.37	2.13	0.05	2.18	0.24	0.47	0.50	0.97
IDN	0.23	2.18	−1.38	0.80	0.48	0.93	0.03	0.96
JPN	0.22	2.18	−0.80	1.38	0.28	0.40	0.50	0.90
KHM	0.39	2.11	−2.18	−0.08	0.44	0.90	0.01	0.91
KOR	0.33	2.18	−1.91	0.27	0.47	0.80	0.04	0.84
MYS	0.29	2.18	−0.35	1.83	0.41	0.86	0.05	0.91
NZL	0.33	2.18	−0.16	2.02	0.26	0.53	0.45	0.98
PHL	0.25	2.18	−1.50	0.68	0.49	1.01	−0.05	0.96
SGP	0.35	2.18	−0.05	2.13	0.26	0.57	0.41	0.98
THA	0.22	2.18	−1.31	0.88	0.38	0.78	0.18	0.96
TWN	0.22	2.18	−0.82	1.36	0.52	0.84	0.01	0.85
VNM	0.37	2.18	−2.11	0.08	0.51	0.92	−0.05	0.87

The World Economic Forum: Global Competitiveness Index

distances from the other countries, have low levels of average distance in patterns of financial development. Taiwan and the Philippines, on the other hand, have low average level distances, but high average pattern distances.

Figures 5 and 6 provide the scatter plot for the data from Table 6, where the index of legal rights of investors has been removed from the overall index of financial development. In this case, the pattern distance collapses for most of the countries in the regional set (except for Cambodia and Vietnam). However, without these two outliers, there is again no clear relationship between distance in levels and distance in patterns of financial development. The increase in pattern distance from 2010 to 2014 for Cambodia and Vietnam is noteworthy in the context of increasing financial flows in the region over this time period.

The scatter plots for the data in Tables 7 and 8 are presented in Figures 7 through 10. The results for these measures of financial development, using broader sets of components, are somewhere in between the earlier two cases (Figures 3 and 4 versus Figures 5 and 6), and provide similar visualizations of the central point, that measuring and comparing patterns of financial development provides different information than comparing levels of financial development. Figures 9 and 10, based on FDIndex9, displays increases in pattern distances

Table 8. Level and pattern differences FDIndex9.

Country	Level distance				Pattern distance			
	Average	Range	Min	Max	Average	Range	Min	Max
				Year 2010				
AUS	0.27	2.10	−0.25	1.85	0.16	0.40	0.54	0.94
CHN	0.21	2.10	−1.28	0.82	0.14	0.27	0.69	0.96
HKG	0.32	2.10	0.00	2.10	0.12	0.27	0.69	0.96
IDN	0.19	2.10	−1.11	0.99	0.40	0.58	0.25	0.83
JPN	0.18	2.10	−0.93	1.17	0.18	0.43	0.48	0.91
KHM	0.38	1.64	−2.10	−0.46	0.22	0.37	0.54	0.91
KOR	0.28	2.10	−1.64	0.46	0.30	0.65	0.25	0.90
MYS	0.22	2.10	−0.52	1.59	0.16	0.41	0.56	0.97
NZL	0.22	2.10	−0.49	1.61	0.24	0.59	0.35	0.94
PHL	0.24	2.10	−1.47	0.64	0.17	0.37	0.61	0.98
SGP	0.32	2.10	0.00	2.10	0.18	0.49	0.44	0.93
THA	0.18	2.10	−1.03	1.07	0.14	0.31	0.67	0.98
TWN	0.22	2.10	−0.48	1.62	0.24	0.33	0.54	0.87
VNM	0.27	2.10	−1.64	0.46	0.14	0.19	0.74	0.93
				Year 2014				
AUS	0.24	2.29	−0.60	1.69	0.15	0.25	0.72	0.97
CHN	0.24	2.29	−1.37	0.92	0.22	0.60	0.35	0.95
HKG	0.36	2.23	0.06	2.29	0.12	0.28	0.68	0.96
IDN	0.22	2.29	−1.20	1.09	0.24	0.69	0.27	0.96
JPN	0.23	2.29	−0.69	1.60	0.17	0.35	0.63	0.98
KHM	0.43	2.21	−2.29	−0.08	0.34	0.48	0.34	0.82
KOR	0.36	2.29	−1.99	0.30	0.42	0.52	0.27	0.79
MYS	0.28	2.29	−0.39	1.90	0.22	0.60	0.33	0.93
NZL	0.32	2.29	−0.18	2.11	0.16	0.28	0.70	0.98
PHL	0.23	2.29	−1.27	1.02	0.18	0.58	0.40	0.98
SGP	0.34	2.29	−0.06	2.23	0.15	0.29	0.69	0.98
THA	0.22	2.29	−1.12	1.17	0.17	0.48	0.50	0.98
TWN	0.25	2.29	−0.58	1.71	0.20	0.43	0.51	0.94
VNM	0.41	2.29	−2.21	0.08	0.32	0.56	0.34	0.90

for Korea as well as Cambodia and Vietnam, and a decrease for Indonesia. These heterogeneous movements in patterns of financial development could have implications for further financial integration in the region.

It is also helpful to illustrate the variations in level distance and pattern distance against the actual levels of financial development.[18] Since, as noted earlier, these levels are quite insensitive to the choice of year of components of the index, we only provide scatter plots for the case of eight index components, and the year 2014. Figure 11 shows how average level distances vary with levels for 2014: the pattern mostly reflects the fact that economies with low or high levels of financial development tend to be further away from their regional counterparts on average, as compared to economies with intermediate levels of financial development.

Figure 12 shows how average pattern distances vary with levels, for FDIndex8 in 2014. There is some clustering of average pattern distances for five of the advanced economies in the region, but the other nine economies have higher average pattern distances, and there is no relationship between the pattern distances and the overall levels of financial development for these economies. This reinforces the basic idea that collapsing different

---

[18] We are again indebted to our discussant, Siu Fung Yiu, for suggesting construction of these figures.

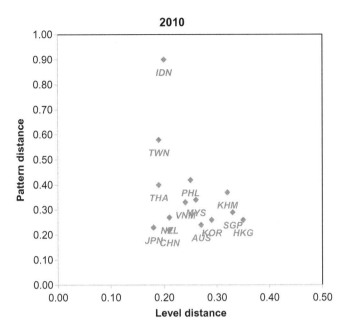

Figure 3. Level and pattern distance, FDIndex8. 2010.

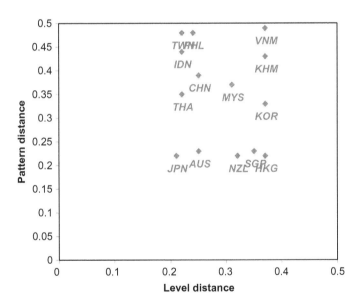

Figure 4. Level and Pattern Distance, FDindex8, 2014.

dimensions of financial development into a single index can hide underlying differences in financial development across economies.

As a final exercise, we conduct a cluster analysis to examine how closeness in levels and patterns of financial development emerges among subgroups of the set of 14 countries.[19]

---

[19] Once more, we are indebted to our discussant, Siu Fung Yiu, for suggesting that we conduct a cluster analysis.

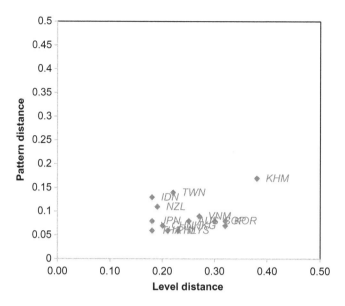

Figure 5. Level and pattern distance, FDIndex7, 2010.

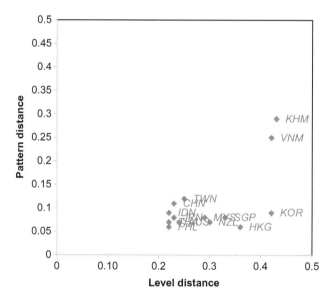

Figure 6. Level and pattern distance, FDIndex7, 2014.

This is particularly pertinent for thinking about financial integration, although the precise implications of closeness in financial development for financial integration depend on the specifics of each: in some cases, specialization in aspects of finance may support integration, whereas, in other dimensions, integration may best occur when financial development is similar across countries.

Our application of clustering analysis uses bilateral differences in levels and patterns of financial development, rather than trade intensity or FDI intensity, which have been used

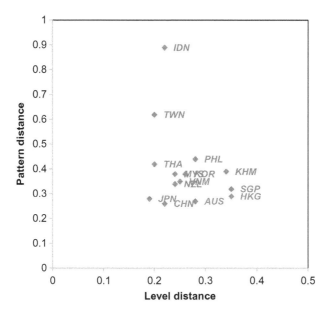

Figure 7. Level and pattern distance, FDIndex10, 2010.

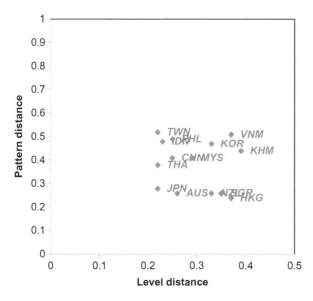

Figure 8. Level and pattern distance, FDIndex10, 2014.

in previous applications.[20] Otherwise, the procedure is the same: at the first step, the two economies that are closest in distance are combined into a cluster, and this cluster is treated as a single observation (with averaged values) for the second step. At the next stage, either another economy is added to this cluster, or a second cluster is formed, and so on. The sequence of steps is shown in Tables 9 and 10, for levels and patterns, respectively.

---

[20] For cluster analysis based on trade intensity, see Huang, Huang and Sun (2006); for analysis based on FDI intensity, see Yang and Huang (2014).

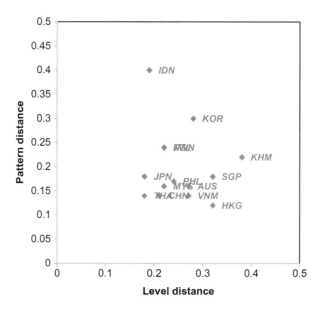

Figure 9. Level and Pattern Distance, FDIndex9, 2010.

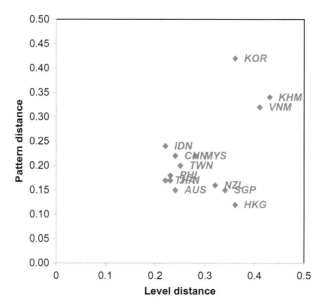

Figure 10. Level and pattern distance, FDIndex9, 2014

The process of creating clusters based on levels of financial development is initially as one would expect, with economies with high, medium and low levels of financial development tending to be assigned to the same clusters (Table 9). The initial exceptions to these clusters lining up with per capita incomes are the outliers, Korea and Malaysia. The initial clusters tend to emerge in the middle and lower end of the distribution of levels of financial development, with the most financially developed economies, Hong Kong and Singapore, being clustered only in the seventh step of the process. At the end, the final two clusters

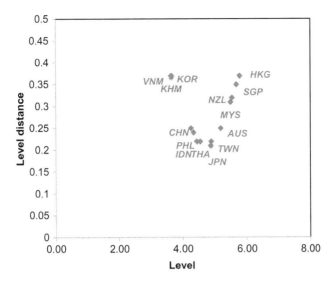

Figure 11. Level distances vs. levels, FDIndex8, 2014.

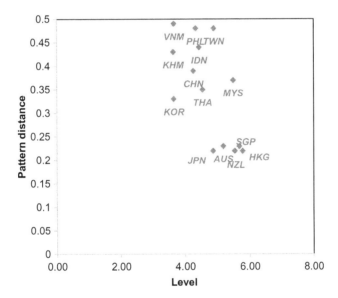

Figure 12. Pattern distances vs. levels, FDIndex8, 2014.

are quite heterogeneous, in per capita incomes as well as levels of financial development. Of course, the entire exercise can be very sensitive to the choice of measure of financial development.[21]

In the case of patterns of financial development (Table 10), the manner in which clustering proceeds is quite different. The first three steps involve a clustering of Australia,

---

[21] For example, we discovered that the clustering was quite sensitive to the way in which the original measure of investor legal rights was converted to the 1–7 scale.

Table 9. Clustering based on Levels of Financial Development.

AUS	AUS	AUS	AUS	AUS	AUS	AUS	AUS	AUS	AUS			
KHM	KHM	KHM										
CHN	CHN	CHN	CHN	CHN	CP	CP	CP	CPITh	CPITh	CPITh		
HKG	HKG	HKG	HKG	HKG	HKG	HKG	HS	HS				
IDN	IDN	IDN	IDN	IDN	IDN	ITh	ITh					
JPN	JPN	JTw	JTw	JTw	JTw	JTw	JTw	JTw	JTw	JTwA	JTwACPITh	JTwACPIThMNHS
KOR	KoV	KoV	KoVKh	KoVKh	KoVKh	KoVKh	KoVKh	KoVKh	KoVKh	KoVKh	KoVKh	KoVKh
MYS	MYS	MYS	MYS	MN	MN	MN	MN	MN	MNHS	MNHS	MNHS	
NZL	NZL	NZL	NZL									
PHL	PHL	PHL	PHL	PHL								
SGP	SGP	SGP	SGP	SGP	SGP	SGP						
TWN	TWN											
THA	THA	THA	THA	THA	THA							
VNM												

Table 10. Clustering based on patterns of financial development.

AUS	AN	ANS	ANSH	ANSH	ANSH	ANSH	ANSH	ANSH	ANSH	ANSHJ	ANSHJKoMV	ANSHJKoMVKh
KHM	KHM	KHM	KHM	KHM	KHM	KHM	KHM	KHM	KHM	KHM	KHM	
CHN	CHN	CHN	CHN	CHN	CHN	CHN	CHN					
HKG	HKG	HKG										
IDN	IDN	IDN	IDN	IP	IP	IPTh	IPTh	IPThC	IPThCTw	IPThCTw	IPThCTw	IPThCTw
JPN	JPN	JPN	JPN	JPN	JPN	JPN	JPN	JPN	JPN			
KOR	KOR	KOR	KOR	KOR	KoM	KoM	KoMV	KoMV	KoMV	KoMV		
MYS	MYS	MYS	MYS	MYS								
NZL												
PHL	PHL	PHL	PHL									
SGP	SGP											
TWN	TWN	TWN	TWN	TWN	TWN	TWN	TWN	TWN				
THA	THA	THA	THA	THA	THA							
VNM	VNM	VNM	VNM	VNM	VNM	VNM						

New Zealand, Singapore and Hong Kong. However, the similarity of patterns of financial development creates clusters that are quite different from those involving similarity of levels, so that Korea and Malaysia are clustered,[22] and Taiwan is added at step nine to a cluster of economies with lower per capita incomes and lower financial development measures. Japan, however, ends up in the higher income cluster, but the final two clusters of economies with similar patterns of financial development are somewhat different than those based on similarities of levels.

5. Conclusion

Even after the global financial crisis, which included financial contagion across national boundaries, there is a continued interest in financial integration, especially in East Asia or the Asia Pacific region. Recent empirical analyses suggest that financial integration within the region has been increasing, but still remains below what might be most beneficial. It is difficult to weigh benefits and risks of financial integration, so assertions of 'too much' or 'too little' financial integration have to be very tentative.

---

[22] Vietnam, which is initially clustered with Korea in the levels analysis, later gets added to this cluster based on patterns. Sahay et al. (2015) also discuss the comparison of South Korea and Vietnam, where both countries have similar private credit but differ strongly along the financial access dimension.

The literature on financial integration does make reference to the need for adequate levels of financial development, especially in the case of financial market regulation, but typically does not go further in empirically associating financial integration and financial development. On the other hand, there is a large literature on financial development and its impacts, especially on economic growth. This literature has tended to measure financial development simply as financial depth, but recently broader-based indices of financial development have begun to be constructed. In some cases, such as Aizenman et al. (2015) and Sahay et al. (2015), there have been attempts to differentiate between different dimensions of financial development, such as quantity versus quality, or depth versus efficiency and access.

In this paper, we have argued that even a sophisticated index is limited because it seeks to reduce the complexities of financial development to a single dimension. As an alternative, we have proposed and constructed a measure of differences in patterns of financial development, and compared measured differences in patterns with differences in levels of financial development. Note that our measure is only operative in capturing the distance between two economies, as opposed to an index (or vector) that measures financial development in a single economy. Measuring differences in patterns of financial development (as opposed to differences in levels) extends the multidimensional approach to characterizing financial development. One could potentially apply a measure of pattern difference to components of financial development that capture quantity versus those that capture quality. This would refine the idea of measuring patterns of financial development, and remains an avenue of future research.

For 14 economies of the Asia Pacific region, we have calculated differences in levels and patterns of financial development for different years and different vectors of components of overall financial development. We also illustrated how groupings of countries can be constructed through cluster analysis, and how the clustering differed when based on patterns versus levels of financial development. We suggest that these kinds of calculations can be a useful preliminary tool for assessing prospects for beneficial financial integration among a given set of economies. In particular, since the components of financial development include various aspects of financial market institutions, as well as regulatory and governance institutions, focusing on patterns and sub-patterns of financial development provides a more systematic way of assessing potential regulatory reform and coordination, and possible regional risk management policies and institutions, both as precursors to, and aspects of, financial integration. Developing these linkages analytically might contribute to regional policy efforts to develop bond markets in various regional member economies (e.g., Lim & Lim, 2012), and to assess the balance between bank and non-bank financing channels, for example.

Acknowledgements

This is a revised version of a paper presented at the Inaugural International Conference on Evolving Finance, Trade and Investment in Asia, held at the Centre on Asia and Globalisation, Lee Kuan Yew School of Public Policy, National University of Singapore, on 16–17 September 2015. We are grateful to conference participants, and particularly to Siu Fung Yiu, our discussant, for extremely valuable comments and suggestions. We are also grateful to the conference co-organizer and special issue editor, Tomoo Kikuchi, for valuable help. All remaining shortcomings are solely our responsibility.

References

Adnan, N. (2011). *Measurement of financial development: A fresh approach*. Eighth International Conference on Islamic Economics and Finance.

Aizenman, J., Chinn, M., & Ito, H. (2013). The 'Impossible Trinity' hypothesis in an era of global imbalances: Measurement and testing. *Review of International Economics*, 21, 447–458.

Aizenman, J., Jinjarak, Y., & Park, D. (2015). Financial development and output growth in developing Asia and Latin America: A comparative sectoral analysis. National Bureau of Economic Research, Working Paper 20917, January.

Aizenman, J., Pinto, B., & Radziwill, A. (2007). Sources for financing domestic capital: Is foreign saving a viable option for developing countries? *Journal of International Money and Finance*, 26, 682–702.

Arcand, J. L., Berkes, E., & Panizza, U. (2015a). Too much finance? *Journal of Economic Growth*, 20, 105–148.

Arcand, J. L., Berkes, E., & Panizza, U. (2015b). Too much finance or statistical illusion: A comment. Working Paper N IHEIDWP12-2015, Graduate Institute of International and Development Studies, International Economics Department, Geneva, Switzerland.

Athukorala, P.-C. (2014). Global production sharing and trade patterns in East Asia. In I. Kaur & N. Singh (Eds.), *Oxford Handbook of the Economics of the Pacific Rim* (pp. 333–361). New York: Oxford University Press.

Bhagwati, J. (1998). The capital myth: the difference between trade in widgets and dollars. *Foreign Affairs*, 77, 7–12.

Borensztein, E., & Loungani, P. (2011). Asian financial integration; Trends and interruptions. International Monetary Fund IMF Working Papers 11/4.

Cline, W. R. (2015). Too much finance, or statistical illusion? Peterson Institute for International Economics Policy Briefs PB15-9.

Cooper, R. N. (1999). Should capital controls be banished? *Brookings Papers on Economic Activity*, 1, 89–141.

Demetriades, P., & Law, S. H. (2006). Finance, institutions and economic development. *International Journal of Finance & Economics*, 11, 245–260.

Eichengreen, B. (2003). What to do with the Chiang Mai Initiative., *Asian Economic Papers*, 2(1), 1–49.

Feldstein, M., & Horioka, C. (1980). Domestic saving and international capital flows. *The Economic Journal*, 90, 314–329.

Financial Services Institute of Australasia (2015). *Financial Integration in the Asia-Pacific: Fact and Fiction*. FINSIA: Sydney, Australia.

Fung, L. K.-p., Tam, C.-s., & Yu, I,-w. (2008). Assessing the integration of Asia's equity and bond markets. In BIS Papers, No 42, *Regional Financial Integration in Asia: Present and Future. Proceedings of the First Workshop of the Asian Research Network for Financial Markets and Institutions*, pp. 1–37.

García-Herrero, A., Yang, D.-y., & Wooldridge, P. (2008). Why is there so little regional financial integration in Asia? *Press & Communications* CH 4002 Basel, Switzerland, 38.

Ghosh, A., Goretti, M., Joshi, B., Ramakrishnan, U., Thomas, A., & Zalduendo, J. (2008). Capital inflows and balance of payments pressures – tailoring policy responses in emerging market economies. *IMF Policy Discussion Paper*, PDP/08/2.

Henry, P. B. (2007). Capital account liberalization: Theory, evidence, and speculation. *Journal of Economic Literature*, 45, 887–935.

Herwartz, H., & Walle, Y. M. (2014). Determinants of the link between financial and economic development: Evidence from a functional coefficient model. *Economic Modelling*, 37, 417–427.

Hoxha, I., Kalemli-Ozcan, S., & Vollrath, D. (2009). How big are the gains from international financial integration? National Bureau of Economic Research Working Paper 14636.

Hoxha, I., Kalemli-Ozcan, S., & Vollrath, D. (2013). How big are the gains from international financial integration? *Journal of Development Economics*, 103, 90–98.

Huang, D.-S., Huang, Y.-Y., & Sun, Y.-C. (2006). Production specialization and trade blocks, *Journal of Economic Integration, 21*, 474–495.

IMF (2015). *Regional Economic Outlook: Asia and Pacific – Stabilizing and Outperforming Other Regions*. World Economic and financial Surveys, April.

Kaur, I. (2014). Are the geese still flying? Catch-up industrialization in a changing international economic environment. In I. Kaur & N. Singh (Eds.), *Oxford Handbook of the Economics of the Pacific Rim* (pp. 395–414). New York: Oxford University Press.

Kaur, I., & Singh, N. (2014). Financial integration and financial development in East Asia. *Millennial Asia, 5*(1), 1–22.

Kose, M. A., Prasad, E. S., & Terrones, M. E. (2009). Does openness to international financial flows raise productivity growth? *Journal of International Money and Finance, 28*, 554–580.

Law, S. H., & Singh, N. (2014). Does too much finance harm economic growth? *Journal of Banking & Finance, 41*, 36–44.

Law, S. H., Azman-Saini, W. N. W., and Ibrahim, M. H. (2013). Institutional quality thresholds and the finance Growth nexus. *Journal of Banking & Finance, 37*, 5373–5381.

Lee, H.-H., Park, D., & Yi, I. (2013). Impact of the global financial crisis on the degree of financial Integration among East Asian Countries. *Global Economic Review, 42*, 425–459.

Lim, M.-H., & Lim, J. (2012). Asian initiatives at monetary and financial integration: A critical review. Background Paper No. 4, UNCTAD Program on the Rise of the South and New Paths of Development in the 21st Century, March.

Obstfeld, M. (2009). International finance and growth in developing countries: What have we learned? *IMF Staff Papers, 56*(1), 63–111.

Ostry, J. D., Ghosh, A. R., Chamon, M., & Qureshi, M. S. (2012). Tools for managing financial-stability risks from capital inflows. *Journal of International Economics, 88*, 407–421.

Ostry, J. D., Ghosh, A. R., Habermeier, K. F., Laeven, L., Chamon, M., Qureshi, M. S., & Kokenyne, A. (2011). Managing capital inflows: What tools to use? International Monetary Fund IMF Staff Discussion Notes 11/06.

Park, C. Y., & Lee, J.-W. (2011). Financial integration in emerging Asia: Challenges and prospects. ADB Working Paper Series on Regional Economic Integration, No. 79, http://hdl.handle.net/11540/2031.

Pongsaparn, R., & Unteroberdoerster, O. (2011). Financial integration and rebalancing in Asia. International Monetary Fund, IMF Working Papers 11/243.

Rajan, R. G., & Zingales, L. (2003). The great reversals: The politics of financial development in the twentieth century. *Journal of Financial Economics, 69*(1), 5–50.

Rey, H. (2013). Dilemma not trilemma: The global cycle and monetary policy independence. *Proceedings – Economic Policy Symposium – Jackson Hole*.

Rodrik, D. (1998). Who needs capital-account convertibility? In *Should the IMF Pursue Capital-Account Convertibility*. Essays in International Finance, 207, Princeton University.

Saci, K., Holden, K. (2008). Evidence on growth and financial development using principal components. *Applied Financial Economics, 18*, 1549–1560.

Sahay, R., Cihak, M., N'Diaye, P., Barajas, A., Pena, D. A., Bi, R., Gao, Y., Kyobe, A., Nguyen, L., Saborowski, C., Svirydzenka, K., & Yousefi, R. (2015). Rethinking financial deepening: Stability and growth in emerging markets. International Monetary Fund IMF Staff Discussion Notes 15/8.

Schularick, M., & Taylor, A. M. (2012). Credit booms gone bust: Monetary policy, leverage cycles, and financial crises, 1870-2008. *American Economic Review, 102*, 1029–1061.

Stiglitz, J. E. (2003). *Globalization and its Discontents*. New York: Norton.

World Bank (2013). Global Financial Development Report 2013: Rethinking the Role of the State in Finance. Washington, DC: World Bank.

World Bank (2014). Global Financial Development Report 2014: Financial Inclusion. Washington, DC: World Bank.

Yang, T.-H., & Huang, D.-S. (2014). Multinational enterprises, foreign direct investment, and the East Asian economic integration. In I. Kaur & N. Singh (Eds.), *Oxford Handbook of the Economics of the Pacific Rim* (pp. 415–440). New York: Oxford University Press.

Appendices

Table A1. Institutional environment.

Efficacy of corporate boards
Reliance on professional management
Willingness to delegate authority
Strength of auditing and reporting standards
Ethical behavior of firms
Protection of minority shareholders' interests
Burden of government regulation
Regulation of securities exchanges
Property rights
Intellectual property protection
Diversion of public funds
Public trust in politicians
Legal rights index
Judicial independence
Irregular payments and bribes

Table A2. Business environment.

Quality of management schools
Quality of math and science education
Extent of staff training
Availability of research and training services
Secondary education enrollment, gross %
Tertiary education enrollment, gross %
Quality of the education system
Quality of overall infrastructure
Quality of electricity supply
Individuals using Internet, %
Fixed broadband Internet subscriptions/100 pop.
Fixed telephone lines/100 pop.
Mobile telephone subscriptions/100 pop.
No. procedures to start a business
No. days to start a business

Table A3. Additional components and variables.

Business sophistication
Local supplier quantity
Local supplier quality
State of cluster development
Nature of competitive advantage
Value chain breadth
Control of international distribution
Production process sophistication Extent of marketing
Technology sophistication
Int'l Internet bandwidth, kb/s per user
Mobile broadband subscriptions/100 pop.
Openness
Prevalence of trade barriers
Trade tariffs, % duty
Prevalence of foreign ownership
Business impact of rules on FDI
Burden of customs procedures Imports as a percentage of GDP
Institutional environment2
Favoritism in decisions of government officials
Wastefulness of government spending
Efficiency of legal framework in settling disputes
Efficiency of legal framework in challenging regs
Transparency of government policymaking
Effect of taxation on incentives to invest
Total tax rate, % profits

Table A4. Level and pattern differences FDIndex14.

Country	Level distance				Pattern distance			
	Average	Range	Min	Max	Average	Range	Min	Max
				Year 2010				
AUS	0.24	1.93	−0.42	1.51	0.28	0.73	0.20	0.93
CHN	0.20	1.93	−1.35	0.58	0.25	0.44	0.42	0.86
HKG	0.33	1.93	−0.04	1.89	0.30	0.86	0.07	0.93
IDN	0.21	1.93	−1.39	0.54	0.72	0.91	−0.10	0.81
JPN	0.18	1.93	−0.91	1.01	0.33	0.52	0.38	0.90
KHM	0.32	1.74	−1.93	−0.18	0.40	1.01	−0.10	0.91
KOR	0.23	1.93	−1.52	0.41	0.36	0.75	0.15	0.90
MYS	0.21	1.93	−0.59	1.34	0.35	0.83	0.09	0.92
NZL	0.22	1.93	−0.54	1.39	0.35	0.91	0.02	0.93
PHL	0.27	1.93	−1.74	0.18	0.39	0.58	0.40	0.98
SGP	0.34	1.89	0.04	1.93	0.33	0.99	−0.06	0.93
THA	0.19	1.93	−1.29	0.64	0.38	0.59	0.39	0.98
TWN	0.19	1.93	−0.76	1.16	0.53	0.72	0.14	0.86
VNM	0.24	1.93	−1.57	0.36	0.32	0.89	0.04	0.93
				Year 2014				
AUS	0.22	2.06	−0.63	1.43	0.26	0.41	0.55	0.96
CHN	0.23	2.06	−1.46	0.60	0.40	0.77	0.14	0.91
HKG	0.35	2.03	0.03	2.06	0.26	0.38	0.57	0.95
IDN	0.22	2.06	−1.35	0.71	0.41	0.81	0.13	0.94
JPN	0.22	2.06	−0.68	1.38	0.35	0.37	0.40	0.77
KHM	0.36	2.01	−2.06	−0.05	0.47	0.71	0.10	0.81
KOR	0.27	2.06	−1.69	0.37	0.52	0.62	0.12	0.74
MYS	0.26	2.06	−0.42	1.64	0.36	0.48	0.35	0.83
NZL	0.29	2.06	−0.27	1.79	0.30	0.43	0.52	0.95
PHL	0.24	2.06	−1.48	0.58	0.44	0.89	0.07	0.96
SGP	0.34	2.06	−0.03	2.03	0.29	0.51	0.45	0.96
THA	0.21	2.06	−1.30	0.76	0.36	0.69	0.27	0.96
TWN	0.20	2.06	−0.81	1.25	0.45	0.78	0.10	0.88
VNM	0.35	2.06	−2.01	0.05	0.49	0.74	0.07	0.81

The World Economic Forum: Global Competitiveness Index
Includes: All Eight Sub-Index of the 8th Pillar, Includes: Six Additional Index

Table A5. Level and pattern differences FDIndex13.

Country	Level distance				Pattern distance			
	Average	Range	Min	Max	Average	Range	Min	Max
				Year 2010				
AUS	0.23	1.98	−0.41	1.58	0.20	0.26	0.65	0.91
CHN	0.19	1.98	−1.27	0.71	0.17	0.22	0.70	0.92
HKG	0.31	1.98	−0.04	1.94	0.17	0.26	0.66	0.92
IDN	0.18	1.98	−1.17	0.81	0.34	0.49	0.40	0.89
JPN	0.17	1.98	−0.85	1.14	0.26	0.29	0.61	0.90
KHM	0.34	1.60	−1.98	−0.39	0.28	0.38	0.49	0.87
KOR	0.23	1.98	−1.50	0.49	0.30	0.42	0.48	0.90
MYS	0.19	1.98	−0.63	1.35	0.18	0.35	0.60	0.95
NZL	0.20	1.98	−0.54	1.45	0.28	0.52	0.40	0.92
PHL	0.24	1.98	−1.56	0.43	0.17	0.32	0.66	0.98
SGP	0.32	1.94	0.04	1.98	0.22	0.46	0.46	0.92
THA	0.18	1.98	−1.11	0.87	0.16	0.31	0.67	0.98
TWN	0.20	1.98	−0.54	1.44	0.23	0.29	0.57	0.86
VNM	0.25	1.98	−1.60	0.39	0.16	0.16	0.75	0.91
				Year 2014				
AUS	0.21	2.12	−0.68	1.45	0.21	0.33	0.61	0.94
CHN	0.22	2.12	−1.34	0.79	0.29	0.73	0.20	0.93
HKG	0.34	2.10	0.03	2.12	0.20	0.41	0.51	0.92
IDN	0.21	2.12	−1.22	0.90	0.28	0.72	0.23	0.95
JPN	0.22	2.12	−0.59	1.53	0.28	0.38	0.47	0.85
KHM	0.38	2.07	−2.12	−0.06	0.46	0.33	0.39	0.72
KOR	0.29	2.12	−1.72	0.40	0.55	0.61	0.14	0.75
MYS	0.25	2.12	−0.45	1.67	0.31	0.79	0.14	0.93
NZL	0.28	2.12	−0.29	1.84	0.26	0.53	0.41	0.94
PHL	0.22	2.12	−1.31	0.81	0.21	0.63	0.34	0.97
SGP	0.33	2.12	−0.03	2.10	0.24	0.41	0.53	0.94
THA	0.20	2.12	−1.17	0.95	0.21	0.53	0.44	0.97
TWN	0.22	2.12	−0.64	1.48	0.22	0.44	0.45	0.89
VNM	0.37	2.12	−2.07	0.06	0.39	0.42	0.40	0.82

The World Economic Forum: Global Competitiveness Index
Excludes: Legal Right Index of the 8th Pillar, Includes: Six Additional Index

Regional Financial Integration in East Asia against the Backdrop of Recent European Experiences

Ulrich Volz

SOAS, University of London, UK; German Development Institute

ABSTRACT
This article discusses recent trends in regional financial integration in East Asia and the current efforts of the Association of Southeast Asian Nations (ASEAN) member countries to foster regional financial integration against the backdrop of three decades of experience with financial integration in Europe. It reviews the two major crisis episodes of the recent European financial history to illustrate the risks associated with comprehensive capital account liberalisation and financial integration without commensurate supervisory structures. The article highlights the importance of targeted macroprudential policies and the development of an adequate region-wide regulatory and supervisory framework to reduce the risks associated with regional – and hence international – financial integration.

1. Introduction

Cross-border bank lending has increased substantially in the Asia-Pacific region since the Global Financial Crisis of 2007–2009 (Remolona & Shim, 2015). The region has also seen an increase in intra-regional portfolio investments. The growing importance of intra-regional cross-border lending and investment is a break from the past in which (long-term) financial investments primarily went to the US and Europe, only to be partly channelled back to the East Asian region in the form of short-term lending and investment. This round-tripping of capital and the reliance on financial intermediation in the financial centres of the West has for long increased the vulnerability to the developing and emerging economies of East Asia. It has also held back the development of banking and capital markets in the East Asian region and perpetuated the dependency on the US dollar as the dominant trade and investment currency for the region and indeed the world economy.

A lesser reliance on Western financial markets should, in principle, be welcomed not only in East Asia. Deeper and more robust and stable financial systems in the East Asian region that are less exposed to shocks emanating in the US or Europe will also increase the resilience of the global financial system. A further development of deep and liquid local currency sovereign and corporate bond markets that provide means for much needed long-term investment in infrastructure and elsewhere can provide an important bedrock for sustainable development of the region. Likewise, the development of a solid region-wide banking system that offers important services in transaction banking, especially in trade finance, and in wholesale banking, especially in infrastructure finance, can contribute to sustainable regional economic development.

Yet regional financial integration also carries risks. Liberalising the capital account is a risky affair in general and, unlike in trade where rules of origin allow for discrimination, in finance it is difficult if not impossible to distinguish between 'regional' and 'global' capital flows. In East Asia, the Asian Financial Crisis of 1997–1998 has illustrated both the risks of badly managed capital account liberalisation and the risk of contagion of financial crisis along regional lines (Glick & Rose, 1999). Recent European experiences with financial integration and crises underscore these risks. Against the background of current efforts to boost regional financial integration among the ten member countries of the Association of Southeast Asian Nations (ASEAN), this article reviews two crisis episodes of recent European financial history to illustrate the risks associated with comprehensive capital account liberalisation and efforts to promote regional financial integration across the European Union. Although there are substantial differences between the two regions, the European experiences suggest that ASEAN countries need to be very cautious in implementing their ambitious financial integration agenda. The article highlights the importance of targeted macroprudential policies and the development of an adequate region-wide regulatory and supervisory framework to minimise risks associated with regional financial integration.

The next section re-examines the policy efforts to reduce barriers to financial integration in Europe since the late 1970s and discusses the roles that financial integration has played in the crisis of the European Monetary System (EMS) in 1992 and in the euro crisis since 2010, respectively. Section 3 will subsequently consider recent trends in regional financial integration in East Asia and policy efforts to promote further regional financial integration among ASEAN and the associated risks. Section 4 concludes.

2. Experiences with Financial Integration in Europe

2.1. *Financial Integration and Liberalisation of Cross-border Flows in Europe*

European countries gradually dismantled restrictions to cross-border financial flows from the second half of the 1970s onwards. Fostering financial market integration was commonly seen as way of supporting further trade integration. Liberalising barriers to capital flows and integrating regional financial markets was expected to improve the allocation of capital and unleash the growth potential of the member states. European financial integration was in principal fostered through market deregulation, especially an abolition of capital account restrictions, and an agreement on common legislative standards. The European Community's *First* and *Second Banking Directives* were the centrepieces for the harmonisation of regulation and financial integration. The *First Banking Directive on the Co-ordination of Laws, Regulations and Administrative Provisions Relating to the Taking Up and Pursuit of Credit Institutions* was adopted in 1977. It was the first step towards the harmonisation of banking regulation across (then Western) Europe. It applied the principle of non-discrimination against businesses from other member states to the banking sector. The *First Banking Directive* also established the principle of home country control,

Table 1. Liberalisation of banking activities in EU member states

	Lifting of capital controls	Interest rate deregulation	First Banking Directive	Second Banking Directive
Belgium	1991	1990	1993	1994
Denmark	1982	1988	1980	1991
France	1990	1990	1980	1992
Germany	1967	1981	1978	1992
Greece	1994	1993	1981	1992
Ireland	1985	1993	1989	1992
Italy	1983	1990	1985	1992
Luxembourg	1990	1990	1981	1993
Netherlands	1980	1981	1978	1992
Portugal	1992	1992	1992	1992
Spain	1992	1992	1987	1994
UK	1979	1979	1979	1993

Source: Buch and Heinrich (2003).

which maintains that responsibility for the supervision of a bank rests with the supervisory authority of the home country of the parent institution.

The *Second Banking Directive* of 1989 established a 'single passport' for banks, granting permission to any bank licensed in a member state to operate freely across the European Economic Area.[1] Banks continued to be supervised by their home country regulator. The *Second Banking Directive* also required member states to harmonise capital adequacy standards. It did not envisage a role for a region-wide regulatory authority. The *Second Banking Directive* was fully implemented by the beginning of 1993.

The early 1990s also saw the complete elimination of capital controls across the European Community. The liberalisation of capital flows was necessary as the *Single European Act* of 1986 required all member countries to remove all legal barriers to an internal market, including barriers to competition and factor mobility in financial services.[2] In 1988, the European Council adopted a *Capital Liberalisation Directive* requiring member countries to remove of all remaining exchange controls by mid-1990, with longer transition periods granted for Greece, Ireland, Portugal and Spain. Since 1993, the freedom of capital movements has the same status as the other internal market freedoms. Since 1 January 1994 all restrictions on capital movements and payments between EU member states have been prohibited, as well as restrictions between EU member states and third countries.

As can be seen in Table 1 and Figure 1, besides Germany and the UK, which abolished all capital controls in 1967 and 1979, respectively, all other Western European countries maintained a substantial degree of capital controls throughout most of the 1980s. Several countries, including Belgium (1991), France (1990), Greece (1994), Luxembourg (1990), Portugal (1992) and Spain (1992), maintained capital controls until the early 1990s.

The *Financial Services Action Plan* (FSAP) was adopted in May 1999 and included numerous initiatives to ensure the full integration of EU banking and capital markets by 2005. The FSAP had three strategic objectives: (i) establishing a single EU market in wholesale financial services; (ii) making retail markets open and secure; and (iii) development of state-of-the-art prudential rules and supervision. Implementation of the FSAP started in 2001.

---

[1] The European Economic Area consists of the member countries of the European Union (previously European Community) as well as Iceland, Liechtenstein and Norway.

[2] On capital market liberalisation see, for instance, NIESR (1997).

The various legislative regulatory harmonisation policies in financial services contributed notably to the deepening of European financial markets and banking integration (Kalemli-Ozcan, Papaioannou, & Peydró, 2010). As shown by Kalemli-Ozcan et al. (2010, p. 77), 'cross-border banking activities increased significantly among European countries that quickly adopted the financial services Directives of the FSAP'.

A further boost to financial integration came from monetary unification. The alleged disappearance of currency risk (which was rediscovered in 2010) for cross-border lending

Figure 1. Capital account openness in European countries, 1970–2013.
Source: Compiled with the KAOPEN dataset from Chinn and Ito (2006).
Note: A higher value of the Chinn-Ito Index indicates a more open capital account. A value of −2.5 indicates a completely closed capital account, while a value of 2.5 indicates a completely liberalised capital account.

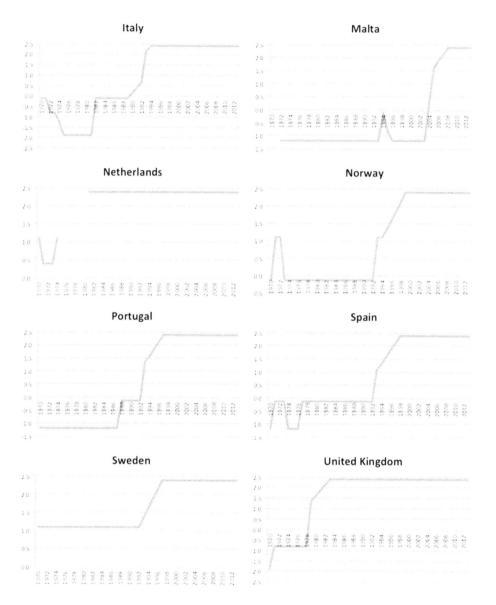

Figure 1. Continued.

and investment within the European Economic and Monetary Union (EMU) had a 'catalytic effect' and led to 'a continuing process of integration in European financial markets' (ECB, 2012, p. 108). By some estimates, cross-border bilateral bank holdings and transactions rose by about 40% among euro member countries in the decade after the launch of the euro (Kalemli-Ozcan et al., 2010).

2.2. Two European Crises Related to Liberalised Capital Flows

Since the liberalisation of capital account restrictions, Europe has experienced two major financial crises on a region-wide scale: the EMS crisis in 1992–1993 and the euro crisis that has rattled Europe since 2010. Both crises were related to liberalised capital flows in different ways.

2.2.1. The ESM crisis: currency speculation in the face of liberalised cross-border capital flows

The EMS crisis was a crisis that resulted from speculative attacks on the fixed but adjustable exchange rate pegs that were part of the European Exchange Rate Mechanism (ERM).[3] The ERM was the centrepiece of the EMS, which was established in 1979 as a European 'mini-Bretton Woods system' (Cooper, 1999, p. 100). Like the Bretton Woods system in the 1950s and 1960s at the global level, the EMS provided the exchange rate stability that enabled a deepening of trade and investment ties across Western Europe in the 1980s. Throughout the existence of the EMS, exchange rate realignments – which were explicitly envisaged as part of the system – were necessary to cope with macroeconomic imbalances which at times created devaluation pressure on EMS member countries with current account deficits. None of these realignments, however, were the cause of greater concern or trigger of further financial instability.

This was different when macroeconomic imbalances arose across the EMS countries in the course of Germany's economic post-reunification boom in 1991–1992. Germany's Bundesbank, the *de facto* lead central bank in the EMS (Reade & Volz, 2011), raised interest rates in the face of inflationary pressures in Germany at a time when other EMS countries were in a recession. This coincided with a negative referendum in Denmark on membership in the EMU in June 1992, causing concern that the entire monetary union project may never be realised. Given that membership in the EMS was a precondition for membership in the EMU, speculators thought it less likely that countries would accept high central bank interest rates to stay within the system at a time when unemployment was already high. The imbalances led to massive speculative attacks on several EMS currencies, including the British pound and the Italian lira, both of which were ultimately forced to exit the ERM.

While speculative attacks on fixed exchange rate systems were nothing new at the time (be it in Europe or elsewhere), the EMS crisis was of a new quality as the crisis was not primarily due to fundamental macroeconomic imbalances but rather a concerted, self-fulfilling speculative attack (which subsequently led to the development of so-called second generation models of currency crises).[4] Indeed, the EMS crisis can be described as the first of a new kind of crisis that would later strike in numerous emerging market economies, including Thailand, Malaysia, Indonesia and Korea in 1997–1998.

The major reason why the EMS crisis had this new quality is straightforward: there were no limits to currency transactions. As Wyplosz (2004, p. 262) puts it:

> In the 10 years between its creation in 1979 and 1990, when capital accounts were freed, there were 12 realignments, most of them involving several currencies. With few exceptions, these realignments came in the wake of speculative attacks, yet the system survived. The first attack that occurred after capital liberalization was lethal.

The EMS crisis demonstrated forcefully what the string of emerging market crises confirmed in the 1990s: maintaining a fixed exchange rate regime akin to the EMS

---

[3] See, for instance, Buiter, Corsetti, and Pesenti (1998), Eichengreen and Wyplosz (1993) and Volz (2006).
[4] The first second generation crisis model was developed by Obstfeld (1996).

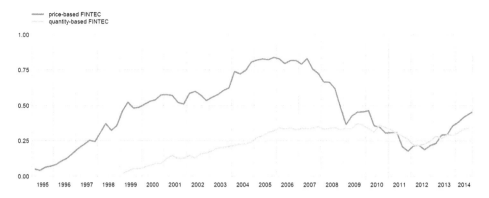

Figure 2. Price-based and quantity-based financial integration composites (FINTECs).
Source: ECB, Financial Integration in Europe, April 2015
Notes: The price-based FINTEC aggregates ten indicators covering the period from the first quarter of 1995 to the fourth quarter of 2014, and the quantity-based FINTEC aggregates five indicators available from the first quarter of 1999 to the third quarter of 2014. The FINTEC is bounded between zero (full fragmentation) and one (full integration). Increases in the FINTEC signal higher financial integration.

becomes almost impossible in the face of a completely liberalised capital account (Volz, 2006).

Given that the level of financial integration in Europe was still relatively low at the time of the EMS crisis, financial system instabilities were largely contained to the national level. This was very different when the euro crisis broke out in 2010.

2.2.2. The Euro crisis: a capital flow bonanza ending in tears

As mentioned above, the introduction of the euro gave a further boost to regional financial integration. Indeed, as described by the ECB (2012, p. 108, cf. Figure 2) the creation of the EMU led to 'a surge in intra-euro area crossborder investment'. Importantly, by joining the euro, member countries with previously weaker currencies experienced a significant drop in nominal and real interest rates, converging to the much lower interest rate level Germany had enjoyed for a long time (cf. Figure 3). The booms in the periphery countries sparked by the drop in real interest rates gave rise to a European capital flow bonanza. Low interest rates and inflowing capital fuelled unsustainable developments in periphery countries, including excessive credit dynamics and real estate bubbles in Ireland and Spain and excessive fiscal spending in Greece. Moreover, while Germany (which in the first part of the 2000 s was commonly referred to as the 'sick man of Europe') experienced a period of slow economic growth and low wages grow, the peripheral boom economies saw compensation grow much faster than productivity (Figure 4).[5] The consequence were real exchange rate appreciations and growing current account deficits in the later crisis countries and real exchange rate depreciation and growing current account surpluses in Germany (Figure 5). The role of capital flows is described by the ECB (2012, p. 10) as follows:

> Increased public and current account deficits were fuelled by freely flowing capital within the Single Market. The strong cross-border capital flows into the non-tradable sector (and into

---

[5] The slow growth in Germany was partly related to entering the euro at an overvalued exchange rate.

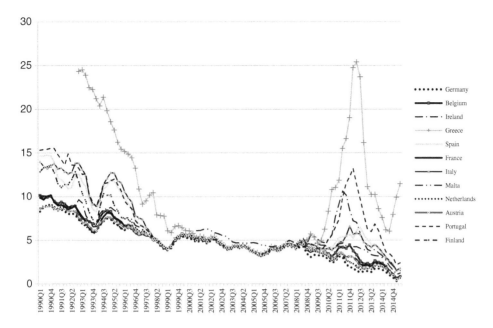

Figure 3. Ten-year government bond yields (% p.a.), 1990:Q1 – 2015:Q2.
Source: Compiled with data from Eurostat.

government debt and interbank markets) financed demand rather than supply and imports rather than exports, leading to imbalances that turned out to be unsustainable. As current account deficits widened, countries became increasingly dependent on capital inflows, and a sudden stop of capital inflows could cause financial disruption and severely impact growth. Indeed, when the crisis hit, private capital flows to the euro vulnerable countries reversed and financing constraints became apparent. In some vulnerable countries, private capital flows were largely replaced with ECB and official financing.

The macroeconomic imbalances that built up in the first decade of the euro's existence provided the ground for the euro crisis. Even though the ECB (2015, p. 27) still maintains that '[u]nder full financial integration, banking markets would efficiently allocate resources to the most productive investment opportunities across the euro area, without frictions in the flow of funds across borders' it is quite clear with hindsight that the allocation of capital was not very efficient in the run-up to the crisis. In many ways the economic crises in Greece, Ireland, Italy, Spain and Portugal resembled the many emerging market crises in which capital flow bonanzas ended with a 'sudden stop' (Calvo, 1998) and a reversal of capital flows (Reinhart & Reinhart, 2009). The capital flow bonanzas in the euro area's periphery countries were made possible because of unrestricted capital flows and tightly integrated banking and capital markets.

The crisis was compounded by severe sovereign-bank interdependences where a worsening of the sovereign's credit position would put the domestic banking system under pressure as the latter has been heavily exposed to the sovereign's debt - which was and still is treated as zero-risk assets by European financial regulators and the Eurosystem. At the same time, the weakening banking sectors would increase the risk that the government would have to bail out the domestic banking system, in turn worsening the credit standing of the sovereign.

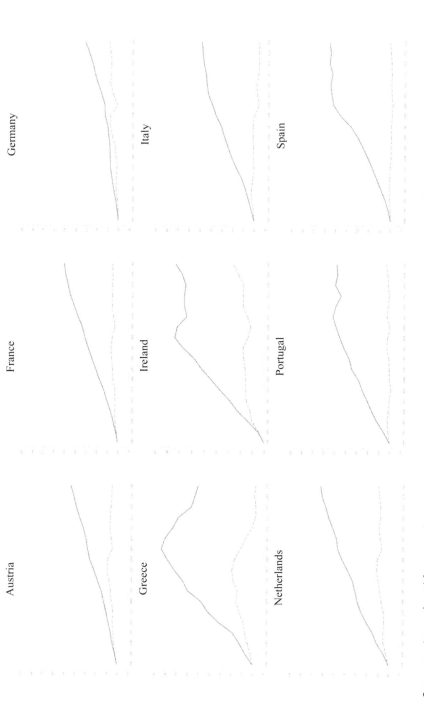

Figure 4. Compensation and total factor productivity developments (dotted line) in selected euro area countries (1998 = 100), 1998–2015.
Source: Compiled with data from the European Commission's Annual Macro-economic Database.

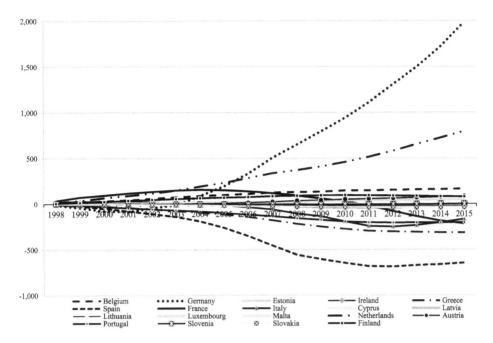

Figure 5. Cumulated current account balance of Eurozone countries (in billion €), 1998–2015.
Source: Compiled with data from the European Commission's Annual Macro-economic Database.

The crisis was also worsened by the fact that the financial systems of the Eurozone had become increasingly intertwined and complex. Notwithstanding far-reaching regional financial integration, regulation – albeit harmonised – was still the domain of national regulatory and supervisory authorities that failed to cooperate among each other. As acknowledged by the European Commission (2009), '[n]ationally based supervisory models have lagged behind the integrated and interconnected reality of today's European financial markets, in which many financial firms operate across borders. The crisis exposed serious failings in the cooperation, coordination, consistency and trust between national supervisors.'

The crisis demonstrated forcefully that it is not sustainable to foster financial integration but leave regulation and supervision entirely in the hands of national authorities. Schoenmaker and Oosterloo (2008) have referred to this as the 'financial trilemma', a situation where it is impossible to achieve at the same time financial stability, financial integration and maintain national financial policies.

But regulatory failure not only occurred due to a lack of regulation on the regional level. There was also a failure of national and European financial and monetary authorities to look beyond microprudential risk. As can be seen in Table 2, the various regulatory measures that are today commonly referred to as macroprudential regulation (including loan-to-value ratios, debt-to-income ratios, limits on foreign currency loans, reserve requirement ratios) were hardly used in Europe. Irish financial authorities made no attempts to restrain the country's developing asset and property bubbles. Spanish authorities, which also saw the growth of a large property bubble financed by the domestic banking system in the years prior to the crisis, did actually employ loan-to-value ratios but not other loan-terms-based instruments that can be used to contain property lending, such

Table 2. Macroprudential index for European economies

	2000	2001	2002	2003	2004	2005	2006	2007	2008	2009	2010	2011	2012	2013	CB
Austria	0	0	0	0	0	0	0	0	0	0	1	2	2	2	0
Belgium	2	2	2	2	2	2	2	2	2	2	2	2	2	2	0.5
Estonia	0	0	0	0	0	0	0	0	0	0	0	0	0	0	–
Finland	0	0	0	0	0	0	0	0	0	0	0	0	0	1	0
France	2	2	2	2	2	2	2	2	2	2	2	3	3	3	0
Germany	0	0	0	0	0	0	0	0	0	0	2	2	2	2	0.5
Iceland	1	2	2	2	2	2	2	2	2	2	2	2	2	2	0
Ireland	0	0	0	0	0	0	0	0	0	0	0	0	0	0	–
Italy	2	2	2	2	2	2	2	2	2	2	2	2	2	2	1
Latvia	0	0	0	0	0	0	0	1	1	1	1	2	2	2	0
Lithuania	0	0	0	0	0	0	0	0	0	0	0	2	2	2	1
Malta	0	0	0	0	0	0	0	0	0	0	0	0	0	0	–
Netherlands	0	0	0	0	0	0	0	0	0	0	0	0	1	3	0
Poland	1	1	1	1	1	1	1	1	1	1	2	2	2	2	0
Portugal	0	0	0	0	0	0	0	0	0	1	1	1	2	2	0.5
Slovakia	1	1	1	1	1	1	1	1	1	1	1	2	2	2	0
Slovenia	0	0	0	0	0	0	0	0	0	0	0	0	0	0	–
Spain	3	3	3	3	3	3	3	3	3	3	3	3	3	3	0.3
Sweden	0	0	0	0	0	0	0	0	0	0	0	1	1	1	0
United Kingdom	0	0	0	0	0	0	0	0	0	0	0	0	0	0	–

Source: Compiled with dataset from Cerutti, Claessens, and Laeven (In press).
Note: The macroprudential index ranges from 0 to 12. The higher the index, the more of the following macroprudential tools are employed: Loan-to-Value Ratio Caps, Debt-to-Income Ratio, Time-Varying/Dynamic Loan-Loss Provisioning, General Countercyclical Capital Buffer/Requirement, Leverage Ratio, Capital Surcharges on Systemically Important Financial Institutions, Limits on Interbank Exposures, Concentration Limits, Limits on Foreign Currency Loans, FX and/or Countercyclical Reserve Requirements, Limits on Domestic Currency Loans, Levy/Tax on Financial Institutions. CB stands for fraction of macroprudential instruments that are controlled by the central bank as of 2013 and ranges from 0 to 1.

as loan-to-income ratios, debt-to-income or debt-service-to-income ratios. Also, Spanish authorities did not use capital-based instruments that take into account sectoral and cyclical conditions. In both countries, the burst of property bubbles proved extremely costly – not only for the domestic banks that had financed the property investment but also for the governments that found themselves in a position where they had to bail out the banks, ultimately leaving the bill with the taxpayer.

3. Regional Financial Integration in East Asia – Benefits and Dangers

3.1. Recent Trends in Regional Financial Integration in East Asia

Since the Global Financial Crisis, the East Asian region has seen a trend towards greater regional financial integration (Remolona & Shim, 2015).[6] While European banks, which had been very active in dollar lending in the years prior to the crisis, have considerably cut down their exposure to the region since the outbreak of the crisis, this gap has been filled by banks from within the region. As a consequence, 'the bulk of the intermediation is now conducted within the region' (Remolona & Shim, 2015, p. 119).[7]

Moreover, there has also been a growing importance of intra-regional portfolio investment. The assets invested in the East Asian region as a share of total international investments have increased substantially in the region's two leading financial centres (Singapore

---

[6] For a recent survey of financial integration in Asia see Genberg (in press).
[7] See also Avdjiev, McCauley, and Shin (2015).

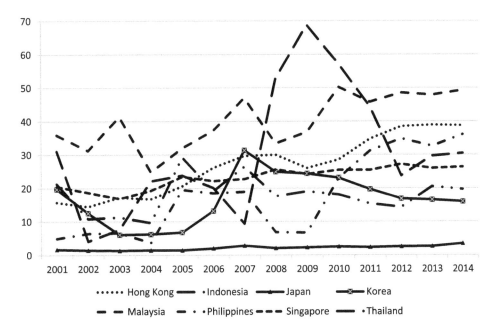

Figure 6. Assets invested in the East Asian region as share of total international asset investments (in percent).
Source: Compiled with data from the IMF's Coordinated Portfolio Investment Survey (CPIS).
Note: Data are for investment in ASEAN, China, Japan, Korea, Hong Kong, Macao and Taiwan. *Data for investment in Japan is missing for Singapore.

and Hong Kong) since the early 2000 s (Figure 6). Singapore has developed into an important hub for wealth management for regional investors as well as for intermediating flows from outside the region. While a large share – 32.3% in 2014 – of Hong Kong's total international portfolio investment is directed towards China, it is more modest in the case of Singapore (8.6% in 2014).

The intra-regional portfolio investments of Malaysia and the Philippines have also increased substantially. While Thailand has seen a recent decline in the share of intra-regional investment, this is due to a significant drop of portfolio investment in Korea (from US$15.1 trillion in 2009 to US$2.0 trillion in 2014). Leaving out data for Korea, the share of Thai intra-regional portfolio investments has increased since the Global Financial Crisis. In Korea, the share of intra-regional investments has decreased since 2007 due to a decline of investment in China, which has only recently stabilised again.

Despite the recent trends towards greater regional financial integration, the current level of regional financial integration is still low. This is in part related to the fact that many East Asian economies still maintain relatively tight capital controls (Figure 7), but also to the fact that regional capital markets remain rather shallow, with the exception of the major regional financial centres. As mentioned earlier, the historic reliance on financial intermediation in the financial centres of the West hampered the development of capital markets in the East Asian region. This essentially led to a vicious circle of financial underdevelopment and reliance on extra-regional investment and financial intermediation. But it seems that this vicious circle has been broken.

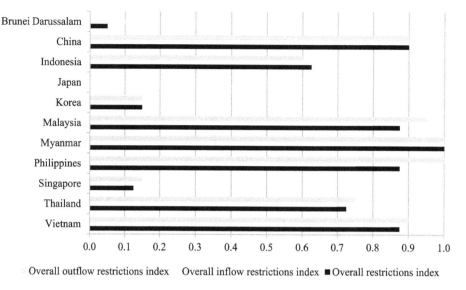

Figure 7. Capital inflow and outflow restrictions of East Asian countries in 2013.
Source: Compiled with dataset from Fernandez, Klein, Rebucci, Schindler, and Uribe (2015).
Note: A higher value indicates more restrictions. A value of 0 indicates a completely liberalised capital account.

The vulnerabilities of emerging East Asian economies that stemmed from an excessive reliance on financial intermediation in the US and Europe and the associated round-tripping of capital (as well as the dangers of premature capital account liberalisation) were painfully illustrated by the Asian Financial Crisis. In the wake of the crisis, East Asian countries put in concerted efforts to develop local currency bond markets, which have expanded rapidly since the late 1990s.[8] The crisis also led to efforts at strengthening the regional financial architecture through initiatives such as the Chiang Mai Initiative, which was established by the ASEAN Plus Three Finance Ministers Meeting in 2000. The Global – or North-Atlantic – Financial Crisis gave further impetus for developing local and regional markets and reducing dependency on Anglo-Saxon financial markets. It also led to the conviction, especially in China, that the region needed to reduce its dependency on the US dollar.

The general view is that deeper regional financial integration will lessen East Asian economies' reliance on global financial markets for funding and the resulting vulnerabilities to global shocks (e.g. Park & Shin, 2015). Moreover, developing deep and liquid local currency sovereign and corporate bond markets can facilitate much needed long-term investment in infrastructure and other areas needed for sustainable development in the region. Likewise, the development of a solid region-wide banking system that offers important services such as trade and infrastructure finance can contribute to sustainable economic development.

---

[8] Initiatives to foster bond market development include the ASEAN+3 Asian Bond Market Initiative and the Asian Bond Fund initiatives of the Executives' Meeting of East Asia Pacific Central Banks (EMEAP). See Park (in press).

3.2. ASEAN Financial Integration

As recently noted by the *Financial Times*, financial integration of ASEAN countries is still 'embryonic' (Kynge, 2015). To change this, the ten ASEAN member countries have adopted an ambitious agenda of regional financial integration. Plans to foster regional financial integration date back to the late 1990 s. In 1997, the ASEAN heads of state and government proclaimed the *ASEAN Vision 2020* with the goal of building 'a stable, prosperous and highly competitive ASEAN Economic Region in which there is a free flow of goods, services and investments, *a freer flow of capital*, equitable economic development and reduced poverty and socio-economic disparities' (ASEAN, 1997, emphasis added). The *ASEAN Vision 2020* included plans to 'promote financial sector liberalisation and closer cooperation in money and capital market, tax, insurance and customs matters as well as closer consultations in macroeconomic and financial policies' (ASEAN, 1997). In 2003, the ASEAN finance ministers adopted a *Roadmap for Monetary and Financial Integration of ASEAN*, with concrete measures, timelines and indicators for promoting capital market development, the liberalisation of financial services and capital accounts, and for currency cooperation (ASEAN, 2016). Various working committees have since been set up to flesh out the details of ASEAN's developing financial integration framework. In 2007, the heads of state and government approved the *ASEAN Economic Community (AEC) Blueprint* for establishing the AEC by 2015. The *AEC Blueprint* comprises comprehensive provisions regarding financial services sector liberalisation among member states and various measures for advancing capital market development and integration.[9] In 2011, the ASEAN central bank governors agreed on the *ASEAN Financial Integration Framework* (AFIF), which was also endorsed by the ASEAN finance ministers. With the AFIF, the ASEAN members aim for 'a semi-integrated financial region by 2020' (ASEAN, 2015a, p. 1). AFIF calls for 'remov[ing] restrictions to the intra-ASEAN provision of financial services by ASEAN financial institutions; build[ing] capacity and infrastructure to develop and integrate the ASEAN capital markets; liberalis[ing] the flow of capital across the ASEAN region; harmonis[ing] payments and settlements systems; [and] strengthen[ing] capacity building, regional financing arrangements, and regional surveillance' (Menon, 2015, pp. 2–3). Figure 8 provides an overview of the different elements of ASEAN financial integration, comprising the *ASEAN Banking Integration Framework* (ABIF), the *ASEAN Insurance Integration Framework*, and various initiatives to foster the integration of capital markets.[10]

While the AEC was formally established at the end of 2015, many of the aims set out in the *AEC Blueprint* remain unaccomplished.[11] In November 2015, the *ASEAN Economic Community Blueprint 2025* (ASEAN, 2015c) was published, setting out the agenda for fostering financial integration, financial inclusion and financial stability (Box 1). While pushing for further liberalisation of financial services and capital account restrictions, the *AEC Blueprint 2025* adopts a rather cautious tone, emphasising that countries should '[a]llow adequate safeguards measures against potential macroeconomic instability and

---

[9] For a discussion of these provisions, see Volz (2013b).

[10] These include, among others, the ASEAN Trading Link, which electronically connects exchanges in Malaysia, Singapore and Thailand; the ASEAN Disclosure Standards (which have been signed up to by Malaysia, Thailand and Singapore) to facilitate multi-jurisdictional offering of equity and debt; the ASEAN Corporate Governance Scorecard aiming to raise corporate governance standards and practices; and the ASEAN Bond Market Development Scorecard, which monitors the development of bond markets, cf. ASEAN (2015a).

[11] ASEAN (2015a) provides an overview of the 'achievements' of ASEAN financial integration. See also Menon (2015).

ASEAN Framework Agreement on Services (AFAS)		
Banking	**Insurance**	**Capital markets**
ASEAN Banking Integration Framework	ASEAN Insurance Integration Framework	ASEAN Trading Link
		ASEAN Disclosure Standards
		ASEAN Corporate Governance Scorecard
		Bond market development
Payment and settlement systems		
Capital account liberalisation		
Capacity building		

Figure 8. ASEAN financial integration.
Source: Adapted from ASEAN (2015a, p. 2).

systemic risks that may arise from the liberalisation process, including the right to adopt the necessary measures to ensure macroeconomic and financial stability' (ASEAN, 2015c, §18.1.b).[12] Given the European experiences discussed above, this caution is warranted.

However, the risks of badly managed capital account liberalisation cannot be overemphasised. Especially for economies with very shallow financial systems, the risks associated with large-scale capital inflows are immense. Against this backdrop, the view expressed in a recent study published jointly by the Asian Development Bank (ADB) and the ASEAN Secretariat that '[f]ull and complete capital account and financial services liberalization is ultimately key to the success of the AEC' (ADB and ASEAN, 2013, p. 27) is questionable. Although the same study concedes that 'a gradual and judicious approach is the only pragmatic and feasible option at the present', it advises that 'this must be considered as a step toward the eventual elimination of all restrictions on crossborder capital flows and financial services' (ADB and ASEAN, 2013, p. 27).[13] Aiming for a complete 'elimination of all restrictions on crossborder capital flows and financial services' for developing and emerging economies may be a recipe for financial crisis.

An important issue that needs to be addressed by policymakers is whether ASEAN countries will be willing to create an ASEAN-wide regulatory structure that matches the comprehensive plans for regional financial integration. The *AEC Blueprint 2025* calls for '[i]ntensify[ing] the existing process of macroeconomic and financial surveillance through identifying financial system risks and vulnerabilities, and intensifying exchange of key macroeconomic information among monetary and fiscal authorities' (§17.iii.a). It also demands ASEAN member countries to '[f]urther enhance cross-border cooperative arrangements in relation to the implementation of the ABIF' (§17.iii.b) and to '[m]ake prudential regulations more cohesive [in order to achieve] greater consistency with international best practices and regulatory standards' (§17.iii.c). The question needs to be asked whether this will suffice to ensure financial stability, given the degree of integration that is to be achieved.

---

[12] This provision is also included in the original *AEC Blueprint*.
[13] The study, which was launched on the sidelines of the Ninth ASEAN Central Bank Governors meeting in Brunei in April 2013, was endorsed by the ASEAN Central Bank Governors (2013) 'as an important reference for ASEAN to further guide its financial integration process.'

Box 1. AEC Blueprint 2025 provisions on financial integration, financial inclusion and financial stability

16. Ensuring that the financial sector is inclusive and stable remains a key goal of regional economic integration. The financial sector integration vision for 2025 encompasses three strategic objectives, namely financial integration, financial inclusion, and financial stability, and three crosscutting areas (Capital Account Liberalisation, Payment and Settlement Systems, and Capacity Building).

17. Strategic measures include the following:
i. Strengthen financial integration to facilitate intra-ASEAN trade and investment by increasing the role of ASEAN indigenous banks, having more integrated insurance markets, and having more connected capital markets. These will be supported by robust financial market infrastructure that is safe, cost-efficient, and more connected. Financial liberalisation will be undertaken with greater regulatory cohesiveness to keep requirements for regulatory compliance to a minimum to reduce costs, while remaining prudent.
   The key measures are as follows:

(a) Further commit to liberalise financial services sector through the ATISA [ASEAN Trade in Services Agreement], which will serve as a platform to link financial markets within the region and with Dialogue Partners;
(b) Provide greater market access and operational flexibility for Qualified ASEAN Banks (QABs) through the ASEAN Banking Integration Framework (ABIF), based on each country's readiness and on a reciprocal basis, thereby reducing gaps in market access and operational flexibility across ASEAN;
(c) Promote deeper penetration in insurance markets through the ASEAN Insurance Integration Framework (AIIF), with greater risk diversification, deeper under-writing capacity, improved and strengthened insurance sector supervision and regulatory frameworks;
(d) Further deepen and interlink capital markets by progressing towards more con-nectivity in clearing settlement and custody linkages to facilitate investment in the region, and allow investors and issuers to tap cross-border ASEAN capital markets efficiently, in line with the objective of ASEAN Capital Market Infrastructure (ACMI) Blueprint. This will ensure that the benefits of such connectivity are shared by all ASEAN Member States; and
(e) Promote the development of sovereign bond markets as well as corporate issuances that will diversify risks from the banking system and provide savers with greater opportunities to invest.

ii. Promote financial inclusion to deliver financial products and services to a wider community that is under-served, including MSMEs [micro, small and medium enterprises]. This would also include initiatives to address the uneven digital gap in the region and reflect changes in the demographic structure, as some countries become aging societies. Key measures are as follows:

(a) Enhance the financing ecosystem in the region to benefit MSMEs, including through cross-collaboration among various working groups in ASEAN. Initiatives to be explored may include the establishment of credit bureaus to facilitate the MSMEs in establishing credit standing to improve access to financing, credit guarantee institutions to provide credit enhancement to MSMEs that do not have collateral, other appropriate facilities or mechanisms that will provide financial access for MSMEs, as well as debt resolution agencies to assist distressed but viable MSMEs;

(b) Expand the scope of financial access and literacy, as well as intermediary and distribution facilities, such as digital payment services to promote cost-reducing technologies and the development of financial services for smaller firms and lower income groups. Enhance discussion channels in ASEAN to develop best practices and exchange information as well as strengthen cooperation;

(c) Intensify the implementation of financial education programmes and consumer protection mechanisms to bolster financial management capacity and encourage take up of financial services. These include raising awareness of personal safeguard measures against deceptive practices as well as enhancing technical countermeasures against threats of digital fraud; and

(d) Promote the expansion of distribution channels which improve access to and reduce cost of financial services, including mobile technology and microinsurance.

iii. Ensure financial stability through the continuous strengthening of regional infrastructure, particularly in times of regional stress. Key measures are as follows:

(a) Intensify the existing process of macroeconomic and financial surveillance through identifying financial system risks and vulnerabilities, and intensifying exchange of key macroeconomic information among monetary and fiscal authorities. Discussions may complement ongoing efforts by the Financial Stability Board (FSB) at the global level;

(b) Further enhance cross-border cooperative arrangements in relation to the implementation of the ABIF with the emergence of regionally active banks during both crisis and in the normal course of business. In the near term, existing regional and bilateral cooperation platforms for macro-surveillance and supervision will continue to perform an integral role. Furthermore, closer dialogues between authorities may be achieved through regional supervisory colleges; and

(c) Make prudential regulations more cohesive, aimed at achieving greater consistency with international best practices and regulatory standards.

18. The measures under the three key cross-cutting areas are as follows:
    i. Enhance capital account liberalisation to encourage greater flows of capital among ASEAN Member States to facilitate cross-border investment and lending in the region, following these guiding principles:

(a) Ensure an orderly capital account liberalisation, consistent with ASEAN Member States' national agenda and the readiness of their economies;

(b) Allow adequate safeguards measures against potential macroeconomic instability and systemic risks that may arise from the liberalisation process, including the right to adopt the necessary measures to ensure macroeconomic and financial stability; and

(c) Ensure the benefits of liberalisation are shared by all ASEAN Member States. ASEAN will continue to monitor the progress of capital account liberalisation among ASEAN Member States by utilising the ASEAN Capital Account Liberalisation Heatmap and Individual Milestones Blueprint.

ii. Payment and Settlement Systems will be further enhanced in several areas such as promoting standardisation and developing settlement infrastructure for cross-border trade, remittance, retail payment systems and capital markets. This will provide an enabling environment to promote regional linkages and payment systems that are safe, efficient and competitive. This will also require a certain level of harmonisation of standards and market practices based on international best practices (such as ISO 20022) to foster stability and efficiency within as well as outside the region.

iii. Capacity Building will help to narrow the financial development gap in the region. This can be achieved through the conduct of learning programmes and exchanges of knowledge and experiences, and best practices in areas relevant to financial integration and development, such as financial regulation and supervision, financial inclusion, and payment and settlement systems.

Source: ASEAN (2015c).

The ABIF is a case in point. Once fully implemented, the ABIF will give so-called Qualified ASEAN Banks (QABs) greater market access in other ASEAN countries.[14] The AIIB will be therefore somewhat comparable to the single passport for banks in Europe, which has granted permission to any bank licensed in a member state to operate freely across the European Economic Area since the early 1990 s. As discussed, it has become evident in Europe that regional banking integration, which relied solely on supervision by home country regulators has failed, even though regulation was harmonised. For the time being, ASEAN countries will rely on 'existing regional and bilateral cooperation platforms for macro-surveillance and supervision' while aiming to develop 'closer dialogues between authorities [. . .] through regional supervisory colleges' (§17.iii.b). Such supervisory colleges may be sufficient as long as QAB status will be extended only to a few banks, or QABs will be active in only few ASEAN countries. But once ABIF is fully implemented region-wide, regulatory harmonisation and regional supervisory colleges will not suffice to ensure regional financial stability. The European experience suggests that from a certain level of regional financial integration a region-wide regulator is needed. Given this would involve a transfer of sovereignty to the regional level – which ASEAN countries have shown no inclination for whatsoever – this may be politically impossible to achieve. For the time being the level of ASEAN financial integration is still at a fairly low level, but complexity has been

---

[14] The ABIF was endorsed by the ASEAN Central Bank Governors in December 2014. For the moment, QAB status will be granted through reciprocal bilateral agreements between two ASEAN central banks. These agreements will specify details of home-host regulatory and supervisory cooperation to ensure effective surveillance and supervision of QABs. Banks that have achieved QAB status will be allowed to operate in both countries involved (not in the entire ASEAN area) and will be granted the same operational flexibilities of domestic banks in the respective host country.

Table 3. Macroprudential index for East Asian economies

	2000	2001	2002	2003	2004	2005	2006	2007	2008	2009	2010	2011	2012	2013	CB
Brunei	0	0	0	0	0	1	1	1	1	1	1	1	3	3	1
Cambodia	2	2	2	2	2	2	2	2	2	2	2	2	2	2	1
China	1	1	1	2	4	4	4	4	5	5	5	7	7	8	0.3
Hong Kong	3	3	3	3	3	3	3	3	3	3	3	3	3	3	1
Indonesia	0	0	0	0	0	1	1	1	1	1	1	1	2	2	0.5
Japan	1	1	1	1	1	1	1	1	1	1	1	1	1	1	0
Lao PDR	2	2	2	2	2	2	2	2	2	2	2	2	2	2	1
Malaysia	2	2	2	2	2	2	2	2	2	2	2	2	2	2	1
Philippines	1	1	2	2	2	2	2	2	2	2	2	2	2	2	0.5
Singapore	1	1	2	2	2	2	2	2	2	2	2	2	2	5	0.8
South Korea	0	0	1	1	1	2	2	3	3	3	3	4	4	4	0.5
Thailand	0	0	0	1	1	1	1	1	1	1	1	1	2	2	1
Timor-Leste	1	1	1	1	1	1	1	1	1	1	1	1	1	1	1

Source: Compiled with dataset from Cerutti et al. (In press).

Note: The macroprudential index ranges from 0 to 12. The higher the index, the more of the following macroprudential tools are employed: Loan-to-Value Ratio Caps, Debt-to-Income Ratio, Time-Varying/Dynamic Loan-Loss Provisioning, General Countercyclical Capital Buffer/Requirement, Leverage Ratio, Capital Surcharges on Systemically Important Financial Institutions, Limits on Interbank Exposures, Concentration Limits, Limits on Foreign Currency Loans, FX and/or Countercyclical Reserve Requirements, Limits on Domestic Currency Loans, Levy/Tax on Financial Institutions. CB stands for fraction of macroprudential instruments that are controlled by the central bank as of 2013 and ranges from 0 to 1.

rising already. Efforts to enhance the capacity and resources of the ASEAN Integration Monitoring Office to develop surveillance reports, monitoring tools and capacity building programmes (ASEAN, 2015b) are hence appropriate. Moving forward, a more complex and integrated ASEAN banking system would make regional banking supervision obligatory.

To be able to cope with greater cross-border capital flows, the *AEC Blueprint 2025* rightly calls for making prudential regulations more cohesive across ASEAN. At the moment, the use of macroprudential measures varies substantially across ASEAN (Table 3).[15] While risks arising from credit booms and capital inflow volatility can be mitigated by adequate macroprudential measures (Bruno, Shim, & Shin, 2015), regional coordination is important to reduce the risk of cross-border distortions and spillovers arising from unilateral action by member countries. The same holds for capital flow measures; empirical evidence shows that capital flows can be diverted to other economies when one economy imposes capital flow controls (Forbes, Fratzscher, Kostka, & Straub, 2012; Lambert, Ramos-Tallada, & Rebillard, 2011).

However, it is not only important to have the 'right' frameworks and policies for maintaining financial and macroeconomic stability. Saiki, Chantapacdepong, and Volz (2016) highlight the importance of institutional capacities and good governance for effectively dealing with capital inflow surges. This remains a big challenge especially in the CLMV countries (Cambodia, Laos, Myanmar, Vietnam). In these countries, efforts should be focused on developing human capacity, institutions and infrastructure in the financial system. Peer-to-peer learning among ASEAN countries and technical assistance from central banks of advanced ASEAN countries can play important roles in capacity building. The ASEAN finance ministers' agreement to continuously strengthen and intensify capacity building efforts (ASEAN, 2015b) should be thus made a priority.

---

[15] For an overview of macroprudential regulation and capital flow management measures in Asia see Chantapacdepong (in press).

4. Conclusions

The literature on (regional) financial integration has long highlighted the potential benefits of integration. Meanwhile, recent crisis experiences in Europe and elsewhere have
demonstrated the risks to financial and macroeconomic stability arising from regional and
international financial integration. Although there are substantial differences between the
EU and ASEAN, the European experiences suggest that ASEAN member countries need
to be very cautious in implementing their ambitious financial integration agenda. Based on
a brief review of two European crisis episodes related to regional financial integration, this
article has discussed the risk arising from badly managed integration. The lesser developed
ASEAN countries need to be cautious with gradual capital account liberalisation and work
on strengthening domestic financial systems and capacities for financial governance. The
European experiences clearly show the importance of targeted macroprudential policies
in the absence of capital controls. They also underpin the importance of developing an
adequate region-wide regulatory and supervisory framework to minimise risks associated
with regional financial integration.

Acknowledgements

This article is a revised and updated version of a paper prepared for the conference on 'Evolving Trade and Investment in Asia' at the Lee Kuan Yew School of Public Policy in Singapore,
16–17 September 2015. This article builds on the author's earlier work in this area (Volz, 2013a,
2013b). Helpful comments by conference participants and especially my discussant Siu Fung Yiu are
gratefully acknowledged.

References

ADB and ASEAN (2013). *The road to ASEAN financial integration: A combined study on assessing the
financial landscape and formulating milestones for monetary and financial integration in ASEAN.*
Manila: Asian Development Bank.

ASEAN (1997). ASEAN vision 2020. Kuala Lumpur, 15 December. Retrieved from http://www.asean.
org/news/item/asean-vision-2020

ASEAN (2015a). Summary of achievements of ASEAN financial integration. Document prepared
by the ASEAN Senior Level Committee for the First ASEAN Finance Ministers' and Central Bank Governors' Meeting. Retrieved from http://www.kemenkeu.go.id/sites/default/files/SP_
2732015.pdf

ASEAN (2015b). Joint statement of the First ASEAN Finance Ministers' and Central Bank Governors' Meeting. Kuala Lumpur, 21 March. Retrieved from http://www.kemenkeu.go.id/sites/
default/files/SP_2732015.pdf

ASEAN (2015c). *ASEAN Economic Community Blueprint 2025.* Jakarta: ASEAN Secretariat.

ASEAN (2016). ASEAN Finance Ministers Meeting (AFMM). Regional cooperation in finance.
Retrieved from http://www.asean.org/asean-economic-community/asean-finance-ministers-
meeting-afmm/overview/

Avdjiev, S., McCauley, R. N., & Shin, H. S. (2015). *Breaking free of the triple coincidence in
international finance (BIS Working Paper No. 524).* Basel: Bank for International Settlements.

Bruno, V., Shim, I., & Shin, H. S. (2015). Effectiveness of macroprudential and capital flow measures
in Asia and the Pacific. *BIS Papers, 82,* 185–192.

Buch, C. M., & Heinrich, R. P. (2003). Financial integration in Europe and banking sector performance. In P. Cecchini, F. Heinemann, & M. Jopp (Eds.), *The incomplete European market for
financial services* (pp. 31–64). Heidelberg: Physica Verlag.

Buiter, W. H., Corsetti, G., & Pesenti, P. A. (1998). *Financial markets and European monetary cooperation. The lessons of the 1992-93 Exchange Rate Mechanism crisis.* Cambridge: Cambridge University Press.

Calvo, G. A. (1998). Capital flows and capital-market crises: The simple economics of sudden stops. *Journal of Applied Economics, 1,* 35–54.

Cerutti, E., Claessens, S., & Laeven, L. (In press). The use and effectiveness of macroprudential policies: New evidence. *Journal of Financial Stability.*

Chantapacdepong, P. (In press). Macroprudential regulation and capital flow management measures in Asia. In U. Volz & N. Yoshino (Eds.), *Routledge handbook of banking and finance in Asia.* London: Routledge.

Chinn, M. D., & Ito, H. (2006). What matters for financial development? Capital controls, institutions, and interactions. *Journal of Development Economics, 81,* 163–192.

Cooper, R. N. (1999). Exchange rate choices. In J. Sneddon Little & G. P. Olivei (Eds.), *Rethinking the international monetary system* (pp. 99–123). Boston, MA: Federal Reserve Bank of Boston.

ECB (2012). *Financial integration in Europe.* Frankfurt am Main: European Central Bank.

ECB (2015). *Financial integration in Europe.* Frankfurt am Main: European Central Bank.

Eichengreen, B. J., & Wyplosz, C. (1993). The unstable EMS. *Brookings Papers on Economic Activity, 1,* 51–143.

European Commission (2009). European financial supervision. Communication from the Commission COM 2009 252 final, Brussels, May 27.

Fernandez, A., Klein, M., Rebucci, A., Schindler, M., & Uribe, M. (2015). *Capital control measures: A new dataset (NBER Working Paper No. 20970).* Cambridge, MA: National Bureau of Economic Research.

Forbes, K. J., Fratzscher, M., Kostka, T., & Straub, R. (2012). *Bubble thy neighbor: Portfolio effects and externalities from capital controls (NBER Working Paper 18052).* Cambridge, MA: National Bureau of Economic Research.

Genberg, H. (In press). *Financial integration in Asia.* In U. Volz & N. Yoshino (Eds.), *Routledge handbook of banking and finance in Asia.* London: Routledge.

Glick, R., & Rose, A. K. (1999). Contagion and trade: Why are currency crises regional? *Journal of International Money and Finance, 18,* 603–617.

Kalemli-Ozcan, S., Papaioannou, E., & Peydró, J.-L. (2010). What lies beneath the euro's effect on financial integration? *Currency risk, legal harmonization, or trade? Journal of International Economics, 81,* 75–88.

Kynge, J. (2015). Creation of economic community forges new Asean era. *Financial Times,* 10 December. Retrieved from http://www.ft.com/intl/cms/s/3/cc929732-9dc5-11e5-b45d-4812f209 f861.html#axzz3wxfIkx6C

Lambert, F., Ramos-Tallada, J., & Rebillard, C. (2011). *Capital controls and spillover effects: Evidence from Latin-American countries (Working Paper No. 357).* Paris: Banque de France.

Menon, R. (2015). ASEAN financial integration – Where are we, where next? Keynote address by Mr Ravi Menon, Managing Director of the Monetary Authority of Singapore, at the ASEAN Banking Council Meeting, Singapore, 12 June. Retrieved from http://www.bis.org/review/r150707c.htm

National Institute of Economic & Social Research (NIESR) (1997). *Capital market liberalization.* Prepared for the European Commission's 1996 Single Market Review Series, Subseries III: Dismantling of Barriers, Vol. 5. London: Kogan Page/Earthscan.

Obstfeld, M. (1996). Models of currency crises with self-fulfilling features. *European Economic Review, 40,* 1037–1047.

Park, C.-Y. (In press). Developing Asian bond markets. In U. Volz & N. Yoshino (Eds.), *Routledge handbook of banking and finance in Asia.* London: Routledge.

Park, D., & Shin, K. (2015). *Financial integration in asset and liability holdings in East Asia (ADB Economics Working Paper No. 444).* Manila: Asian Development Bank.

Reade, J. J., & Volz, U. (2011). Leader of the pack? German monetary dominance in Europe prior to EMU. *Economic Modelling, 28,* 239–250.

Reinhart, C. M., & Reinhart, V. R. (2009). Capital flow bonanzas: An encompassing view of the past and present. In: *NBER International Seminar on Macroeconomics 2008* (pp. 9–62). Cambridge, MA: National Bureau of Economic Research.

Remolona, E., & Shim, I. (2015). The rise of regional banking in Asia and the Pacific. *BIS Quarterly Review*, September, 119–135.

Saiki, A., Chantapacdepong, P., & Volz, U. (2016). *Dealing with QE spillovers in East Asia: The role of institutions and macroprudential policies (ADBI Working Paper)*. Tokyo: Asian Development Bank Institute.

Schoenmaker, D., & Oosterloo, S. (2008). Financial supervision in Europe: A proposal for a new architecture. In L. Jonung, C. Walkner, & M. Watson (Eds.), *Building the financial foundations of the Euro. Experiences and challenges* (pp. 337–354). London: Routledge.

Volz, U. (2006). On the feasibility of a regional exchange rate system for East Asia: Lessons of the 1992/1993 EMS crisis. *Journal of Asian Economics*, *17*, 1107–1127.

Volz, U. (2013a). Lessons of the European crisis for regional monetary and financial integration in East Asia. *Asia Europe Journal*, *11*, 355–376.

Volz, U. (2013b). ASEAN financial integration in the light of recent European experiences. *Journal of Southeast Asian Economies*, *30*, 124–141.

Wyplosz, C. (2004). Regional exchange rate arrangements: Lessons from Europe for East Asia. In Asian Development Bank (Ed.), *Monetary and financial integration in East Asia. The way ahead* (Vol. 2, pp. 241–284). Houndmills: Palgrave Macmillan.

Does Inflation Targeting in Asia Reduce Exchange Rate Volatility?

Alice Y. Ouyang[a] & Ramkishen S. Rajan[b]

[a]Chinese Academy of Public Finance and Public Policy, Central University of Finance and Economics, Beijing, China; [b]Lee Kuan Yew School of Public Policy, National University of Singapore and School of Policy, Government and International Affairs, George Mason University, USA

ABSTRACT
Inflation targeting has become a popular option among many developing economies, including those in Asia. Despite a gradual move towards inflation targeting, many Asian economies remain concerned about exchange rate variability. Motivated by this, this paper is interested in the impact of inflation targeting on real exchange rate volatility in the Asian economies. In particular, using a panel of developing countries that includes many from Asia for the period 2007–2012, the paper explores the impact of inflation targeting on real exchange rate volatility as well as in terms of its two component parts, i.e. relative tradable prices across countries (external prices) and the sectoral prices of tradables and non-tradables within countries (internal prices). The paper also compares the inflation and growth effects of inflation targeting regimes with non-inflation targeters.

1. Introduction

Since the Asian Financial Crisis (AFC) in 1997–1998, many Asian economies have forsaken their soft-pegged regimes and have moved towards adopting more flexible exchange rate frameworks (Gerlach & Tillmann, 2011), see Table 1. Along with de-pegged exchange rate regimes, monetary policy anchored around inflation targeting has become increasingly popular worldwide and viewed as 'state of the art monetary policy' (Blanchard, 2011, p. 6). As Posen (2008) indicated, the main reason for the worldwide interest in inflation targeting is the lack of a nominal anchor for inflation expectations in most countries that have moved to a more flexible regime. The first actual inflation targeter was the Reserve Bank of New Zealand in 1989, followed by the Bank of Canada in 1991 and then the Bank of England in 1992 (Posen, 2008). According to Hammond (2012), 27 countries had adopted inflation targeting regimes as of 2009. This number climbed to 34 by 2014.[1] Since then, there have been a few more notable entrants to this 'club', including India in March 2015.

---

[1] Sourced from the IMF's *Annual Report on Exchange Arrangements and Exchange Restriction*. See IMF (2014, p. 14).

Table 1. De facto classification of Asian and pacific exchange rate arrangements, 30 April 2014.

Exchange rate arrangement (number of countries)	Monetary Policy Framework						
	Exchange rate anchor				Monetary aggregate target	Inflation targeting framework	Other
	US dollar	Euro	Composite	Other			
No separate legal tender	Timor-Leste; Marshall Islands; Micronesia; Palau			Kiribati; Tuvalu			
Currency board	Hong Kong SAR			Brunei Darussalam			
Conventional peg	Bahrain; Jordan; Oman; Qatar; Saudi Arabia; Turkmenistan; United Arab Emirates		Fiji; Kuwait; Samoa	Bhutan; Nepal			Solomon Islands
Stabilized arrangement	Iraq; Kazakhstan (02/14); Lebanon; Maldives		Singapore; Vietnam		Bangladesh (02/13); Sri Lanka (10/13); Tajikistan; Yemen		
Crawl-like arrangement					China; Uzbekistan;		Lao P.D.R.
Pegged exchange rate within horizontal bands			Tonga				
Other managed arrangement	Cambodia			Iran; Syria	Myanmar		Vanuatu; Kyrgyz Rep; Malaysia; Pakistan (12/13)
Floating					Afghanistan; Papua New Guinea	Indonesia (08/13); Korea; Philippines; Thailand; Mongolia; New Zealand	India
Free floating						Australia; Japan	

Source: IMF AREAER 2014, Table 2.

The initial adoption of an inflation targeting arrangement in Asian economies was partly driven by recommendations from the International Monetary Fund (IMF) (especially for those under IMF rescue packages). For instance, Indonesia, Korea, Thailand as well as the Philippines in Asia adopted inflation targeting regimes in the late 1990s.[2] However, the experiences of many developed countries that seemed to have had significant success – in

---

[2] For discussions of the performance of inflation targeting regimes in these economies, see Inoue, Toyoshima, and Hamori (2012).

terms of macroeconomic outcomes – following the adoption of such regimes, have also been a driving factor (Portugal, 2007; Roger, 2010).

Many emerging and developing economies have become enthusiastic about inflation targeting regimes as they move towards greater exchange rate flexibility. As stated by Filardo and Genberg (2009, p. 251) '[c]entral banks in Asia and the Pacific have over-whelmingly chosen inflation as the principal objective of monetary policy. Some central banks have declared themselves to be inflation targeters, while others pursue their objective without referring to this particular label.' As summarized in Table 2, New Zealand and Australia adopted inflation targeting in 1989 and 1993 respectively, followed by Indonesia (1999), Thailand (2000), Philippines (2001) and more recently by Japan (2013).

As Table 2 notes, the broad characteristics of inflation targeters in Asia are as follows. First, most Asian inflation targeters de-pegged and transitioned to an inflation targeting regime after the Asian financial crisis. Second, headline consumer price index (CPI) has been more commonly adopted in these countries than core CPI. Third, most countries announced precise inflation targets with a time frame that is usually set by a monetary policy committee, reflecting the commitment of the central banks to implement an inflation targeting regime. Fourth, it appears that only the Philippines and Korea explicitly announced their escape clauses for inflation targeting regime. Furthermore, in terms of policy accountability and transparency, more than half of the listed countries release quarterly monetary policy, suggesting that monetary policy becomes more transparent under inflation targeting regimes. Table 3 lists the monetary policy framework of some of the non-inflation targeting regimes in the Asian region.

Despite this move towards inflation targeting regimes, many Asian economies remain concerned about exchange rate variability given its potential negative impact of trade and investment.[3,4] Motivated by this, our paper is specifically interested in assessing the impact of inflation targeting on real exchange rate (RER) volatility in Asian economies, also in terms of its two component parts, i.e. relative tradable prices across countries as well as sectoral prices of tradables and non-tradables within countries. The paper is also related to two other strands of literature, namely the impact of fixed versus flexible regimes on RER volatility, including the so-called 'Mussa puzzle' (Mussa, 1986; Stockman, 1983) as well as the literature on RER decomposition into its two sub-components – external prices (deviation from purchasing power parity (PPP)) and internal prices (relative price of tradables and non-tradables) à la Engle (1999). The paper also compares the impact of inflation targeting regimes on inflation and output.

The remainder of the paper is organized as follows. Section 2 presents a brief literature review. Section 3 discusses the relevant definitions and hypotheses about the impact of inflation targeting on RER volatility. Section 4 outlines the methodology and data sources. Section 5 presents the empirical results. In addition to examining the impact of inflation targeting on RER volatility, we also examine its impact on inflation and growth. Section 6 concludes the paper.

---

[3] While the general literature on the impact of exchange rate volatility on growth has found rather small negative effects, there is more recent evidence that suggests that the negative impacts are of particular concern at low levels of financial development (Nicolas & Héricourt, 2010).

[4] In response to the concerns about allowing benign neglect of the exchange rate, there has been a literature on how exchange rates might be incorporated explicitly in an inflation targeting framework. This is referred to as the 'flexible inflation targeting', which most economies in Asia seem to favour. See Cavoli and Rajan (2006, 2007); Nordstrom et al. (2009); Ostry, Ghosh, and Chamon (2012); and Volz (2015).

Table 2. Highlights of inflation targeting arrangements in selected Asian and Pacific economies as of September 2015.

Country	Date of initiation of inflation targeting arrangement	Target price index	Target rate	Target horizon	Escape clauses	Accountability	Target set by	Publication and accountability
Indonesia	May 1999	Headline CPI	4.5% with ±1% deviation (2012–2014) 4% with ±1% deviation (2015)	3 years	None	None, but parliament can request reports at any time	Government in consultation Central Bank	Quarterly Monetary Policy Report and Annual report to public
Philippines	Dec 2001	Headline CPI. Also monitors Core CPI (excluding agricultural products and petroleum products)	4% with ±1% deviation (2012–2014) 3% with ±1% deviation (2015–2018)	2 years	Yes, in the event of oil price shocks, food supply shocks and significant government policies	Public explanation of the nature of the breach and steps to address it	Government in consultation Central Bank	Quarterly inflation report, publication of monetary policy meetings
Thailand	Apr 2000	Core CPI (quarterly average, excluding fresh food and energy) (2010–2014) Headline CPI (annual average) (2015)	0.5–3% (2010–2014) 2.5% with ±1.5% deviation (2015)	1 year	None	Public explanation of breach and steps taken to address it	Central Bank in consultation with Government	Monetary Policy Report, inflation forecasts and publication of models used
Korea	Jan 1998	Headline CPI	2.5–3.5% (2013–2015)	3 years	Changes caused by major force	None	Central Bank in consultation with Government	Monetary Policy report and submission to parliament, publication of monetary policy meetings
Australia	Jun 1993	Headline CPI over medium Term	2–3%	No time frame	——	Report twice a year to the House of Parliamentary committees	Central Bank	Quarterly Statement on Monetary Policy and Bulletin

New Zealand	Dec 1989	Headline CPI over medium Term	1-3%	Not explicit	—	Review of monetary policy statement by a Select Parliamentary committee	Target set by agreement between government and central bank	Quarterly monetary policy statement
Japan	Jan 2013	The year-over-year rate of change in the consumer price index	2%	Not explicit	—	Release MPMs minutes; submits the Semiannual Report on Currency and Monetary Control to the Diet; the House of Diet/Representatives/Councillors can request clarification	Central Bank	Quarterly Outlook for Economic Activity and Prices
Mongolia	2014–2015	CPI	5-7%	2014-2015	—	Press Conference; Report to the Parliament	Central Bank and the government	Annual Monetary Policy Guidelines

Source: Filardo and Genberg (2010, p. 5, Table 2) and updated by the authors from central bank websites.

Table 3. Institutional frameworks for monetary policy for selected non-inflation targeting Asian central banks.

	Targeting arrangement
China	The objective of the monetary policy is to maintain the stability of the value of the currency and thereby promote economic growth. Reference to money growth targets.
Hong Kong	Currency board: target range centred on HKD 7.8 = USD 1. The Currency Board system requires the Monetary Base to be fully backed by foreign reserves.
India	Multiple objectives of monetary policy: maintaining price stability, ensuring adequate flow of credit to sustain the growth momentum, and securing financial stability. The RBI has agreed on a monetary policy framework that will make managing inflation the main basis of monetary policy decisions.
Malaysia	Monetary policy aims to maintain price stability while remaining supportive of growth through managing interest rate, quarterly policy announcement, foreign exchange rate market intervention, etc.
Singapore	The Singapore dollar is managed against a basket of currencies of major trading partners; the primary objective of Singapore's exchange rate-based monetary policy is to promote medium term price stability as a sound basis for sustainable economic growth.

Source: Filardo and Genberg (2010, p. 5, Table 2) and updated by the authors from central bank websites.

2. Literature Review

There has been considerable academic interest exploring the macroeconomic impacts of inflation targeting. A large body of empirical literature has claimed to find that, compared with other monetary policy frameworks, inflation targeting regimes tend to enhance macroeconomic performance by way of controlling inflation and inflationary expectations as well as managing long-term interest rates, hence contributing to higher GDP growth and reduced volatility (Barnebeck, Malchow-Møller, & Nordvig, 2014; Bernanke, Laubach, Mishkin, & Posen, 1999; Roger, 2010). In addition, Debelle, Masson, and Savastano (1998) have opined that inflation targeting compels central banks to look ahead and make policy decisions before situations (inflationary pressures) get out of hand.

Nevertheless, a well-cited paper by Ball and Sheridan (2003) measured the effects of inflation targeting on the macroeconomic performance of 20 Organization for Economic Cooperation and Development (OECD) countries, seven of which adopted inflation targeting before 1999.[5] The authors concluded that there was no evidence that inflation targeting improved the macroeconomic performance (inflation, output and interest rates). Their results suggested that the larger decrease of inflation rates for targeters compared with non-targeters was probably due to their high initial inflation rates and the phenomenon of regression to the mean. Furthermore, as the authors noted, one possible reason for the seeming success of inflation targeting countries is that targeters and non-targeters pursued similar interest rate policies.

Focusing specifically on inflation targeting in Asia,[6] especially for the period of 1996–2005, Filardo and Genberg (2009, 2010) also observed that it was difficult to document significant differences in inflation performance between explicit inflation targeters and non-inflation targeters, with inflation having come down generally in the region (from 5.8% in 1990–1997 to 3.0% in 1999–2008). The authors offered two explanations for this pattern. One view claims that 'inflation dynamics in the region have been dominated by common nominal shocks' (Filardo & Genberg, 2009, p. 262). Another view emphasizes

---

[5] The seven countries are Australia, Canada, Finland, Spain, Sweden, the UK and New Zealand.

[6] Countries are Australia, New Zealand, Korea, Indonesia, Thailand, Philippines, Singapore, China, India, Malaysia, Hong Kong, Japan,

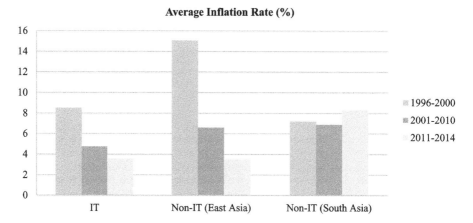

Figure 1. The inflation record for developing Asia countries.
Note: IT countries include South Korea, Indonesia, Philippines and Thailand. Non-IT countries include Brunei, Cambodia, China, Laos, Myanmar, Singapore (East Asia); Bangladesh, Bhutan, India, Nepal, Pakistan, Sri Lanka (South Asia).

the role of central bank mindsets, i.e. there has been a definite 'social consensus about importance of inflation control' and general improvement in overall governance (Filardo & Genberg 2009, p. 262) in the region regardless of whether one is an inflation targeter or not. As the authors note:

> the results confirm that greater emphasis on targeting inflation – though not explicit inflation targeting – has been important in the Asia-Pacific region. Central bank inflation fighting credibility appears to have generally risen, reflecting the intellectual, social and economic consensus that central banks control the inflation destiny of a country and that low, stable inflation promotes sustainable growth. But the initial motivation for this study remains an open empirical question: what is the marginal contribution of explicit versus implicit inflation targeting? The panel evidence in this section suggests that the contributions are not so obvious but subtle differences might be linked to the particular features of explicit inflation targeting regimes.(p. 261)

Consistent with the above findings, Figure 1 highlights that the inflation record in East Asia is in some ways more impressive in the case of non-inflation targeters than countries that have conducted monetary policy using the inflation targeting framework.[7]

While average inflation rates may not differ significantly between Asian inflation targeting and non-inflation targeting, Gerlach and Tillmann (2011) found differences in the extent of inflation persistence between inflation targeting and non-inflation targeting countries (they use a moving 40-quarter window). They found that for the period 1985 to 2010,[8] inflation persistence fell in the Asian inflation targeting group as a whole but remained roughly unchanged in the Asian non-inflation targeting group. Moreover, the rolling window evidence showed there was significant heterogeneity in the behaviour of inflation persistence across inflation targeting regimes. Inflation persistence in Korea and

---

[7] In Figure 1, inflation targeting countries include Korea, Indonesia, Philippines and Thailand. Non-inflation targeting countries include Brunei, Cambodia, China, Laos, Myanmar, Singapore (East Asia); Bangladesh, Bhutan, India, Nepal, Pakistan, Sri Lanka (South Asia).

[8] The authors studied 19 countries in total: six Asian inflation targeting countries, seven non-Asian inflation targeting countries, six Asian non-inflation targeting countries.

Thailand fell immediately after the new monetary regime became effective but much later for the Philippines and especially Indonesia. They hypothesize that this could have been something to do with managing exchange rates, with exchange rate volatility remaining a persistent concern in emerging Asian economies.

Using a panel of more than 170 small economies, Rose (2014) noted that during and post the global financial crisis (GFC) period (2007–2012) there was little difference in the macroeconomic performance of countries with inflation targeting regimes and hard fixers when measured in terms of inflation or growth rates. Gagnon (2013) countered that the foregoing findings might be biased towards hard fixers. Specifically, Rose's (2014) analysis had not included those countries that were originally hard fixers in 2006 but ceased to be so for at least one year thereafter due to their inability to maintain a hard fix during the GFC period.[9] After accounting for this, Gagnon (2013) found that countries with inflation targeting regimes have performed better in terms of durability (in the sense that almost no country has forsaken the regime under duress),[10] inflation, unemployment rate, and the changes of these variables.

Overall, there has been a great deal of focus on the impact of inflation targeting regimes on various indicators of macroeconomic performance.[11] However, the literature on the effect of inflation regimes on real exchange rate (RER) volatility has been rather sparse. There have only been a handful of papers to date on this specific issue. Using a sample of seven countries over the period 1985–2005, Edwards (2006) examined whether exchange rate volatility differed in inflation targeting regimes compared with countries not operating such regimes. He concluded that volatility rises with inflation targeting as a result of flexible exchange rate regimes, but after controlling for exchange rate variability per se, the result is overturned. In other words, the adoption of inflation targeting regimes per se did not increase the extent of exchange rate volatility.

Rose (2007) explored this issue (among others) using monthly data between 1990 and 2005 for 42 countries and found that inflation targeting leads to lower real effective exchange rate (REER) volatility than in alternative regimes. Berganza and Broto (2012) examined the effects of inflation targeting adoption and foreign exchange intervention (proxied imperfectly by actual foreign exchange movements) on RER volatility. They estimated a panel data model for 37 inflation targeting and non-inflation targeting emerging economies. While they found that exchange rates were more volatile under inflation targeting than under other regimes in their sample, foreign exchange interventions in inflation targeting countries seemed more effective in containing exchange rate volatility than in non-inflation targeting countries. This suggests that exchange rate volatility under inflation targeting countries with 'managed' regimes tends to be lower than those with flexible regimes.[12]

---

[9] There are other slight differences in the dataset. For instance, Gagnon treats the smaller euro area countries as a separate group (six countries).

[10] See Rose (2007) and Gagnon (2013). Durability in turn has positive effects on the macro-economy, especially inflation (Mihov & Rose, 2007).

[11] Other studies have suggested that, other things being equal, inflation targeting regimes foster greater fiscal discipline (Minea & Tapsoba, 2014) and reduce risk premia (Fouejieu & Roger, 2013).

[12] Two related works are worth noting. Gonçalves and Carvalho (2009) consider the reverse causality and find that the volatility of the RER is not a statistically significant determinant of the probability of inflation targeting adoption. Using a quarterly panel of 16 emerging economies for the period 1989–2004, Aizenman, Hutchison, and Noy (2010) find that countries with inflation targeting regimes tend to respond less strongly to RER changes, unless they are exporters of basic commodities.

Building on this literature, this paper revisits the comparison of the effects of inflation targeters versus hard peggers and intermediate exchange rate regimes. In particular, this paper is interested in exploring the impact of inflation targeting on RER volatility in Asian countries as well as in terms of its two component parts, i.e. relative tradable prices across countries (external prices) and sectoral prices of tradables and non-tradables within countries (internal prices). To do so, the paper uses a panel data of 34 developing economies over the period 2007–2012.

3. Definition and Hypotheses[13]

3.1. Understanding the Real Exchange Rate (RER)

The RER is a measure of internal and external price competitiveness. The former refers to the relative price of tradables to non-tradables within the country and the latter refers to the relative price of tradables across countries (see Ouyang & Rajan, 2013 and references cited within).

In particular, the (log) aggregate price index can be expressed as a weighted-average of the price of tradables (T) and non-tradables (N):

$$p_t = (1 - \alpha)p_t^T + \alpha p_t^N, \text{ for the domestic country} \tag{1}$$

and,

$$p_t^* = (1 - \beta)p_t^{T*} + \beta p_t^{N*}, \text{ for the foreign country} \tag{2}$$

As often noted, the RER can be written as the sum of the relative price of traded goods between economies (a) and the relative price of non-traded to traded goods within each economy (b).

$$
\begin{aligned}
rer_t &= e_t + p_t - p_t^* \\
&= (e_t + p_t^T - p_t^{T*}) + \alpha(p_t^N - p_t^T) - \beta(p_t^{N*} - p_t^{T*}) \\
&= \underbrace{e_t + p_t^T - p_t^{T*}}_{(a)} + \underbrace{(p_t - p_t^T) - (p_t^* - p_t^T)}_{(b)} \\
&= rer_t^T + rer_t^N \tag{3}
\end{aligned}
$$

where p_t^* denotes the prices in foreign country, p_t refers to domestic prices and e_t denotes the nominal exchange rate of the foreign currency to the domestic currency. Denoting α (β for foreign) as the share of non-tradables in the determination of the aggregate price level, we decompose the RER into two sets of prices: rer_t^T, or external prices, and rer_t^N, or internal prices. All the exchange rates and prices are in logarithmic form.

3.2. Nexus between RER volatility and inflation targeting regimes

What is the impact of inflation targeting regimes on RER volatility? There are three related hypotheses that we explore (Ouyang & Rajan, 2015).

---

[13] This section draws on Ouyang and Rajan (2015).

Hypothesis 1a:

Inflation targeting regimes may lead to greater RER volatility as more flexible regimes are prone to 'excessive variability,' which in turn should be driven largely by the relative price of tradables.

Hypothesis 1b:

To the extent that inflation targeting regimes and concomitant flexible exchange rate regimes allow countries to use monetary policy tools to manage the economy more effectively it might lead to lower RER volatility, largely due to relative stability in internal prices.

Hypothesis 1c:

To the extent that developing countries often undertake necessary preconditions (Portugal, 2007) prior to implementing inflation targeting regimes or implementing inflation targeting regimes post-structural reforms, inflation targeting regimes should be associated with more stable RER, largely due to relative stability in internal prices.

4. Data Sources and Methodology

4.1. Methodology

To test the foregoing hypotheses we focus on the impacts of regime choices on the volatility of real effective exchange rate (REER) and its two components, i.e. relative tradable prices across countries (external prices) and relative prices of tradables and non-tradables within countries (internal prices).

Following Rose (2007) we outline the broad empirical model to be estimated below:

$$
y_{i,t} = \beta_0 + \beta_1 IT_{i,t} + \beta_2 IT_{i,t}^{Asia} + \beta_3 \left(\frac{CA}{GDP} \right)_{i,2006} + \beta_4 \ln \left(\frac{Trade}{GDP} \right)_{i,2006}
$$

$$
+ \beta_5 \ln(Pop)_{i,2006} + \beta_6 \ln(RGDPPC)_{i,2006} + \beta_7 \left(\frac{Budget}{GDP} \right)_{i,2006}
$$

$$
+ \sum_t \gamma_t T_t + v_i + \varepsilon_{i,t} \tag{4}
$$

where: $y_{i,t}$ is the volatility of REER (in logarithms) in aggregate as well as the volatility of external prices (REERT) and internal prices (REERN). $IT_{i,t}$ is an inflation targeting dummy that takes the value 1 if the country i is an inflation targeter over period t and 0 otherwise. $IT_{i,t}^{Asia}$ is the interactive term of IT dummy and Asia dummy, so it takes the value 1 if the country i is an Asian inflation targeter over period t and 0 otherwise. The control variables include current account over GDP, fiscal balance over GDP, logarithm of trade balance over GDP, total population and real GDP per capita. To limit endogeneity concerns, all the control variables are dated as of 2006. T_t controls for time effect while v_i is country specific random effects.

4.2. Data Sources

Our database consists of 34 developing countries in total over the period 2007–2012, nine of which are Asian (Table 4).[14] Among these, 13 economies are classified as inflation

---

[14] Three high income Asian countries are also included, i.e. Hong Kong, South Korea and Singapore.

Table 4. Sample countries: 34 developing countries.

Asian Inflation Targeting Countries between 2006-2012 (4)	**Indonesia**, **South Korea**, **Philippines**, **Thailand**,
Other Inflation Targeting Countries between 2006-2012 (9)	Armenia, Brazil, Chile, Colombia, Mexico, Peru, Romania, South Africa, Turkey
Non-IT Countries (21)	Argentina, Belarus, Bulgaria, **China,** Costa Rica, Egypt, El Salvador, **Hong Kong**, Jordan, Kazakhstan, Lithuania, **Malaysia,** Morocco, Paraguay, Panama, Russian Federation, **Singapore**, **Sri Lanka**, Tunisia, Uruguay, Venezuela

Note: To ensure that the IT-group and non-IT group are comparable, we restrict non-IT countries with (a) the average real GDP per capita between 2007 to 2012 at least as high as those of the poorest IT countries (i.e. the Philippines), and (b) average population between 2007–2012 at least as big as those of the smallest IT country (i.e. Armenia). Based on these restrictions, India and Pakistan are dropped because they fail the first criteria, while Cyprus, Estonia, Latvia, Macedonia, Slovenia, and Trinidad and Tobago are dropped because they fail the second criteria. The countries in bold are Asian countries.

targeters, of which four are Asian (Indonesia, Korea, Malaysia and Thailand). All the country classifications are listed in Table 4. To ensure that the inflation-targeting group and non-inflation-targeting group are comparable, we restrict non-inflation-targeting countries to those for who (a) the average real GDP per capita between 2007 to 2012 is at least as high as those of the poorest inflation targeting countries (i.e. the Philippines), and (b) average population between 2007–2012 is at least as big as those of the smallest inflation targeting country (i.e. Armenia).[15]

All the data are taken from *World Development Indicator Database (WDI)* except REER, which we compute based on the bilateral RERs among a set of 70 economies, geometrically-weighted by their bilateral trade. The data on bilateral trade are taken from the IMF's *Direction of Trade Statistics (DOTs)* database. To track the dynamic movement of the trade weights over time we use the shares of exports and imports in the total trade under consideration each year to calculate the effective exchange rate. The formula for calculating the trade weights is as follows:

$$w_{i,j,t} = \left[\frac{Export_{i,j,t} + Import_{i,j,t}}{\sum_{j=1}^{70}(Export_{i,j,t} + Import_{i,j,t})} \right] \tag{5}$$

where $w_{i,j,t}$ is the trade weight between domestic economy i and country j in year t; $Export_{i,j,t}$ is the free on board (f.o.b.) merchandise exports from domestic economy i to country j in year t; $Import_{i,j,t}$ is the cost insurance and freight (c.i.f.) imports from country j to domestic economy i in year t. We attribute equal weights to both exports and imports.[16] The REER (in logarithms) for country i is calculated as follows:

$$reer_{i,t} = \sum_{j=1,j\neq i}^{70} (rer_{i,j,t} \times w_{i,j,t}) \tag{6}$$

Following the same logic applied to equation (6) we calculate the REER (in logarithms) for external ($reert_{i,t}$) and internal prices ($reern_{i,t}$) as well. The CPI is generally used to compute the RER, while producer price index (PPI) is used to proxy the prices for tradable

---

[15] Based on these restrictions, India and Pakistan are dropped because they fail the first criteria, while Cyprus, Estonia, Latvia, Macedonia, Slovenia, and Trinidad and Tobago are dropped because they fail the second criteria.

[16] Since we only have annual data for exports and imports we apply the same trade weights for the 12 months within a year.

goods. Data on monthly bilateral exchange rates, consumer price index (CPI) and PPI are used to calculate the REER. We rescaled all the price indices to the base year of the first month of 2010. We further decompose the REER into two sets of relative prices as outlined in Section 2. We then use the standard deviation of monthly REERs within a year to proxy the annual volatility of REERs.

Table 5. The effects of inflation targeting on volatility of real exchange rates (2007–2012).

Random effect model with robust errors	Vol(reer)	Vol(reert)	Vol(reern)	Vol(reer)	Vol(reert)	Vol(reern)
Constant	0.0629	0.00835	**0.0910***	0.0714	0.0101	**0.0941***
	(0.0485)	(0.0371)	(0.0483)	(0.0507)	(0.0372)	(0.0519)
IT	0.00287	**−0.00863***	**−0.00847****	0.00568	−0.00807	**−0.00745***
	(0.00479)	(0.00503)	(0.00423)	(0.00650)	(0.00607)	(0.00440)
IT^{Asia}	–	–	–	−0.00955	−0.00193	−0.00347
				(0.00869)	(0.00825)	(0.00633)
$(CA/GDP)_{2006}$	0.0223	−0.0174	−0.0284	0.0237	−0.0172	−0.0279
	(0.0218)	(0.0385)	(0.0285)	(0.0224)	(0.0382)	(0.0287)
$\ln(Trade/GDP)_{2006}$	**−0.0171*****	**−0.0104***	−0.00577	**−0.0145*****	−0.00986	−0.00483
	(0.00444)	(0.00548)	(0.00421)	(0.00498)	(0.00694)	(0.00435)
$\ln(Pop)_{2006}$	−0.00242	0.000259	−0.000904	−0.00189	0.000366	−0.000712
	(0.00160)	(0.00150)	(0.00165)	(0.00143)	(0.00174)	(0.00168)
$\ln(RGDPPC)_{2006}$	−0.000459	0.00111	**−0.00711****	−0.00255	0.000693	**−0.00787***
	(0.00339)	(0.00275)	(0.00315)	(0.00461)	(0.00355)	(0.00420)
$(Budget/GDP)_{2006}$	0.0114	0.124	**0.180***	0.0214	0.126	**0.183***
	(0.0576)	(0.0807)	(0.0962)	(0.0635)	(0.0858)	(0.0985)
$H_0: IT + IT^{Asia} = 0$	–	–	–	−0.0039	−0.0100	**−0.0109***
				[0.53]#	[2.15]	[2.80]
Observations	186	184	184	186	184	184
Number of Countries	31	31	31	31	31	31
R-squared	0.274	0.258	0.292	0.281	0.259	0.293

Notes: (1) Time effects are considered in the model but not reported.
(2) #: The value in brackets is the χ^2 value in Wald test.
(3) Values in bold refer to statistically significant variables; *, **, *** represent significance at 10, 5, and 1 percent, respectively.

Table 6. The effects of inflation targeting on volatility of real exchange rates non-Asia developing countries (2007-2012)

Random effect model with robust errors	Vol(reer)	Vol(reert)	Vol(reern)
Constant	0.0539	−0.0154	0.0786
	(0.0658)	(0.0497)	(0.0565)
IT	0.00654	−0.00833	**−0.00890***
	(0.00658)	(0.00658)	(0.00475)
$(CA/GDP)_{2006}$	0.0328	−0.0117	−0.0399
	(0.0284)	(0.0459)	(0.0330)
$\ln(Trade/GDP)_{2006}$	−0.00985	−0.00383	−0.00594
	(0.00881)	(0.0109)	(0.00582)
$\ln(Pop)_{2006}$	−0.000989	0.00282	0.000573
	(0.00264)	(0.00293)	(0.00228)
$\ln(RGDPPC)_{2006}$	−0.00209	−0.000841	**−0.00872***
	(0.00555)	(0.00464)	(0.00472)
$(Budget/GDP)_{2006}$	−0.00471	0.105	**0.226****
	(0.0778)	(0.103)	(0.107)
Observations	150	149	149
Number of Countries	25	25	25
R-squared	0.253	0.245	0.314

Notes: (1) Time effects are considered in the model but not reported.
(2) Values in bold refer to statistically significant variables; *, **, *** represent significance at 10, 5, and 1 percent, respectively.

5. Empirical Results

We use a random effect panel regression with time fixed effect and robust error correction model to estimate the effects of inflation targeting on the REER volatility and its components. We start with all developing economies including Asia (Table 5) and then split the subsamples into non-Asia (Table 6) and Asia (Table 7).

Table 7. The effects of inflation targeting on volatility of real exchange rates – Asia developing countries (2007–2012).

Random effect model with robust errors	Vol(reer)	Vol(reert)	Vol(reern)
Constant	0.0251*	0.0440***	0.322***
	(0.0139)	(0.00958)	(0.0304)
IT	−0.00386***	−0.00579***	−0.0222***
	(0.00149)	(0.000733)	(0.00183)
$(CA/GDP)_{2006}$	−0.0106	0.00618**	0.0217*
	(0.00779)	(0.00306)	(0.0129)
$\ln(Trade/GDP)_{2006}$	−0.0228***	−0.0202***	−0.0257***
	(0.00265)	(0.00119)	(0.00427)
$\ln(Pop)_{2006}$	−0.00251***	−0.00272***	−0.0109***
	(0.000622)	(0.000300)	(0.00107)
$\ln(RGDPPC)_{2006}$	0.00526***	0.00293***	−0.0117***
	(0.000543)	(0.000267)	(0.00130)
$(Budget/GDP)_{2006}$	0.0880***	0.187***	0.436***
	(0.0243)	(0.0100)	(0.0459)
Observations	54	53	53
Number of Countries	9	9	9
R-squared	0.493	0.601	0.539

Notes: (1) Time effects are considered in the model but not reported.
(2) Values in bold refer to statistically significant variables; *, **, *** represent significance at 10, 5, and 1 percent, respectively.

Table 8. The effects of inflation targeting on inflation and real GDP per capita growth (2007–2012).

Random effect model with robust errors	Inflation	Real GDP per capita Growth
Constant	0.0918	11.30
	(0.123)	(9.664)
IT	−0.0470**	−0.419
	(0.0206)	(0.913)
IT^{Asia}	0.0240	−1.344
	(0.0337)	(1.828)
$(CA/GDP)_{2006}$	0.0554	3.129
	(0.0983)	(3.487)
$\ln(Trade/GDP)_{2006}$	−0.0336	0.583
	(0.0270)	(1.236)
$\ln(Pop)_{2006}$	−0.00517	0.245
	(0.00597)	(0.519)
$\ln(RGDPPC)_{2006}$	0.00875	−1.428*
	(0.0169)	(0.851)
$(Budget/GDP)_{2006}$	−0.0502	7.818
	(0.294)	(8.933)
$H_0: IT + IT^{Asia} = 0$	−0.0231	−1.7626
	[0.83]#	[1.33]
Observations	186	180
Number of Countries	31	30
R-squared	0.147	0.427

Notes: (1) Time effects are considered in the model but not reported.
(2) #: The value in brackets is the χ^2 value in Wald test.
(3) Values in bold refer to statistically significant variables; *, **, *** represent significance at 10, 5, and 1 percent, respectively.

Results in Table 5 suggest that inflation targeting regimes do not appear to be associated with any greater REER volatility compared with other regimes. However, there is evidence that the volatility of both external and internal prices decline, with the latter being slightly more statistically significant than the former. Within the same sample, after separating the Asian inflation targeters from the other inflation targeters, we see that the only robust result is that both the Asian and non-Asian inflation targeters appear to experience somewhat lower internal price variability than all others. This is consistent with Hypothesis 1c.

Table 6 re-estimates the regression but excludes all Asian economies. We see that the basic results do not change, namely that non-Asia inflation targeters appear to experience

Table 9. The effects of inflation targeting on inflation and real GDP per capita growth – non-Asia developing countries (2007–2012).

Random effect model with robust errors	Inflation	Real GDP per capita growth
Constant	−0.148	**15.78****
	(0.208)	(7.283)
IT	**−0.0391****	0.331
	(0.0181)	(0.782)
$(CA/GDP)_{2006}$	0.154	5.710
	(0.126)	(4.031)
$\ln(Trade/GDP)_{2006}$	0.0208	0.197
	(0.0356)	(1.491)
$\ln(Pop)_{2006}$	0.00777	**−0.581***
	(0.00935)	(0.310)
$\ln(RGDPPC)_{2006}$	0.0142	−0.414
	(0.0216)	(0.703)
$(Budget/GDP)_{2006}$	−0.295	2.519
	(0.340)	(7.669)
Observations	150	144
Number of Countries	25	24
R-squared	0.161	0.476

Notes: (1) Time effects are considered in the model but not reported.
(2) Values in bold refer to statistically significant variables; *, **, *** represent significance at 10, 5, and 1 percent, respectively.

Table 10. The effects of inflation targeting on inflation and real GDP per capita growth – Asia developing countries (2007–2012).

Random effect model with robust errors	Inflation	Real GDP per capita growth
Constant	**0.615*****	0.451
	(0.0237)	(3.733)
IT	**−0.0452*****	**−4.557*****
	(0.00200)	(0.443)
$(CA/GDP)_{2006}$	**−0.0425*****	**−5.860*****
	(0.0119)	(2.101)
$\ln(Trade/GDP)_{2006}$	**−0.0599*****	**−2.272*****
	(0.00412)	(0.744)
$\ln(Pop)_{2006}$	**−0.0219*****	**0.584*****
	(0.000972)	(0.170)
$\ln(RGDPPC)_{2006}$	**−0.0184*****	**−0.415*****
	(0.00126)	(0.145)
$(Budget/GDP)_{2006}$	**0.616*****	**36.29*****
	(0.0419)	(6.418)
Observations	54	54
Number of countries	9	9
R-squared	0.698	0.699

Notes: (1) Time effects are considered in the model but not reported.
(2) Values in bold refer to statistically significant variables; *, **, *** represent significance at 10, 5, and 1 percent, respectively.

somewhat lower internal price variability than other non-Asian economies, with this result being statistically significant at the 10% level.

Table 7 undertakes the same regression for the Asian economies in our sample. We now see that the inflation targeting regimes do in fact appear to experience lower REER volatility than other Asian economies in our sample, and interestingly they experience lower REER volatility in both external and internal prices, with the latter being especially economically significant (both are statistically significant at the 1% level).

Beyond REER volatility, it would be of interest to examine the relative performance of inflation targeting regimes in terms of inflation and growth. As shown in Table 8, what stands out is that inflation targeting regimes seem to experience lower inflation rates than other types of regimes, but there is no evidence that Asian inflation targeters experience any differences in inflation or growth rates compared with other countries in the sample. This result regarding non-Asian inflation targeting regimes experiencing lower inflation rates than other countries is also apparent from Table 9 which separates out the Asian economies from the non-Asian ones. Table 10 reveals that, within the Asian sub-sample, inflation targeting regimes seem to experience lower inflation but have also faced lower real GDP per capita growth rates.

6. Conclusion

Even though inflation targeting regimes have been lauded as being highly successful on a number of counts (Walsh, 2009), the Global Financial Crisis has led to some reconsideration about it. For example, Posen (2008, p. 17) has noted '[o]ne concern is that if you set the target inflation rate too low or enforce it too strictly, you could end up with scenarios where you are tightening monetary policy more aggressively and more often than necessary.' Moreover, concerns have also been expressed that traditional inflation targeting as a monetary policy framework may be too narrow; should central banks be concerned about the monetary policy effects of financial stability, for instance?[17]

Despite these concerns in the developed world, many economies in Asia and elsewhere have continued to embrace an inflation targeting regime. India is the most recent entrant to the inflation targeting club in the region, having adopted the recommendations of the Urjit Patel Committee Report in January 2014. This committee proposed that India move to a flexible inflation-targeting regime with CPI of 4% (with a ±2% band) for the financial year 2016–2017.[18] Apart from India, 'the National Bank and the Government of the Republic of Kazakhstan made the decision to start implementing a new monetary policy based on the inflation targeting regime, to abandon the foreign exchange band and to move to the free-floating exchange rate, effective August 20, 2015.'[19] In similar vein, the Deputy Central

---

[17] For instance, Vredin (2015) and Woodford (2012). Also see Filardo and Genberg (2009) and Volz (2015).

[18] See 'India Adopts Flexible Inflation Targeting' http://www.business-standard.com/article/economy-policy/india-adopts-flexible-inflation-targeting-115030201251_1.html. Also see the goals of monetary policy from the Reserve Bank of India https://www.rbi.org.in/scripts/FS_Overview.aspx?fn = 2752. For early discussion of the possibility of India adopting an inflation targeting framework, see Cavoli and Rajan (2007, 2008).

[19] National Bank of Kazakhstan, 'Joint Statement of the Government of the Republic of Kazakhstan and the National Bank of the Republic of Kazakhstan on transition to a new economic policy: to reforms in the real economy and new monetary policy regime', 26 August 2015. http://www.nationalbank.kz/?docid = 949&switch = english

Bank Governor Nandalal Weerasinghe of Sri Lanka also expressed interest in the country adopting 'flexible inflation targeting.'[20]

This paper examined the impact of inflation targeting on RER volatility in developing countries as well as in terms of its two component parts, namely relative tradable prices across countries as well as sectoral prices of tradables and non-tradables within countries. The paper set out a series of hypotheses regarding the expected impact of an inflation targeting regime on RER volatility. Based on a panel of 34 developing countries over the period 2007–2012, we find that while there is no evidence that inflation targeting regimes have faced greater REER volatility than other regimes. Both Asian and non-Asian inflation targeting regimes seem to experience lower variability in internal prices than other countries. Among all developing countries in our sample, inflation targeters tend to have lower inflation compared with other regimes. Compared with other Asian economies, Asian inflation targeters experience lower inflation rate, although this seems to be at the expense of lower growth rates as well.

A weakness with most prevailing studies – including the current one – on exchange rate impacts is that they do not fully account for the self-selection concerns of policy adoption (Lin, 2010), i.e. do countries with more or less volatile exchange rates choose to adopt a certain type of exchange rate regime? Given the heterogeneity of exchange rate regimes in Asia, this would be an important area for future research.

Acknowledgment

Financial support from the Program for Innovation Research in the Central University of Finance and Economics and comments by participants at the Centre on Asia and Globalisation (CAG) at the Lee Kuan Yew School of Public Policy, National University of Singapore are greatly acknowledged. The usual disclaimer applies.

References

Anand, R., Ding, D., & Peiris, S. J. (2011). *Toward Inflation Targeting in Sri Lanka*. Working Paper WP/11/81, Asia and Pacific Department, International Monetary Fund.

Aizenman, J., Hutchison, M., & Noy, I. (2010). Inflation targeting and real exchange rates in emerging markets. *World Development*, 39, 712–724.

Ball, L. & Sheridan, N. (2003). Does inflation targeting matter? In B. Bernanke, & M. Woodford (Eds.), *The Inflation Targeting Debate* (pp. 249–276). Chicago: The University of Chicago Press.

Barnebeck, T., Malchow-Møller, N., & Nordvig, J. (2014). *Inflation-targeting, Flexible Exchange Rates and Macroeconomic Performance since the Great Recession*. Discussion Papers No. 394, University of Southern Denmark.

Berganza, J. C., & Broto, C. (2012). Flexible inflation targets, Forex interventions and exchange rate volatility in emerging markets. *Journal of International Money and Finance*, 31, 428–444.

Bernanke, B., Laubach, T., Mishkin, F., & Posen, A. (1999). *Inflation Targeting: Lessons from the International Experience*. Princeton: Princeton University Press.

Blanchard, O. (2011). Monetary policy in the wake of the crisis. Paper presented at the IMF Macro Conference, 7–8 May. Washington, DC: International Monetary Fund.

Cavoli, T., & Rajan, R. S. (2006). Monetary policy rules for small and open developing economies: A counterfactual policy analysis. *Journal of Economic Development*, 31(1), 89–111.

---

[20] Information is derived from 'Sri Lanka for Flexible Inflation Targeting', Economynext, 27 July 2015. http://www.economynext.com/Sri_Lanka_for_flexible_inflation_targeting-3-2472.html. For an earlier examination of the impact and implication of Sri Lanka moving to an inflation targeting-based framework, see Anand, Ding, and Peiris (2011).

Cavoli, T., & Rajan, R. S. (2007). Inflation targeting arrangements in Asia and elsewhere: Exploring the role of the exchange rate. *Briefing Notes in Economics* No. 74.

Cavoli, T., & Rajan, R. S. (2008). Open economy inflation targeting arrangements and monetary policy rules: Application to India. *India Growth and Development Review*, 1, 237–251.

Debelle, G., Masson, P., & Savastano, M. (1998). Inflation targeting as a framework for monetary policy. *Economic Issues No 15*, International Monetary Fund.

Edwards, S. (2006). The relationship between exchange rates and inflation targeting revisited. In F. Mishkin, & K. Schmidt-Hebbel (Eds.), *Monetary Policy under Inflation Targeting* (pp. 373–413). Santiago: Banco Central de Chile.

Filardo, A., & Genberg, H. (2009). *Targeting Inflation in Asia and the Pacific: Lessons from the Recent Past*. BIS Working Paper Series No 52, Bank for International Settlements.

Filardo, A., & Genberg, H. (2010). *Monetary Policy Strategies in the Asia and Pacific Region: What Way Forward?* Working Paper Series No 195, Tokyo: Asian Development Bank Institute: ADBI.

Fouejieu, A. A., & Roger, S. (2013). *Inflation Targeting and Country Risk: An Empirical Investigation*. Working Paper WP/13/21, International Monetary Fund.

Gagnon, J. (2013). *Stabilizing Properties of Flexible Exchange Rates: Evidence from the Global Financial*. No. PB 13-28, Washington, DC: Peterson Institute.

Gerlach, S., & Tillmann, P. (2011). *Inflation Targeting and Inflation Persistence in Asia-Pacific*. HKIMR Working Paper No. 25/2011, Hong Kong Institute for Monetary Research.

Gonçalves, E. C., & Carvalho, A. (2009). Inflation targeting matters: Evidence from OECD economies' sacrifice ratios. *Journal of Money, Credit and Banking*, 41, 233–243.

Hammond, G. (2012). *State of the Art of Inflation Targeting*. CCBS Handbook No. 29, Bank of England.

International Monetary Fund (2014). *Annual Report on Exchange Arrangements and Exchange Restrictions*. Washington, DC: International Monetary Fund.

Inoue, T., Toyoshima, Y., & Hamori, S. (2012). *Inflation Targeting in Korea, Indonesia, Thailand, and the Philippines: The Impact on Business Cycle Synchronization between Each Country and the World*. IDE Discussion Paper No.328, Japan: Institute of Developing Economies.

Lin, S. (2010). On the international effects of inflation targeting. *Review of Economics and Statistics*, 92, 195–199.

Mihov, I., & Rose, A. K. (2007). *Is Old Money Better than New? Duration and Monetary Regimes*. Discussion Papers No.6529, CEPR.

Minea, A., & Tapsoba, R. (2014). Does inflation targeting improve fiscal discipline? *Journal of International Money and Finance*, 40, 185–203.

Mussa, M. (1986). Nominal exchange rate regimes and the behavior of real exchange rates: evidence and implications. *Carnegie-Rochester Conference Series on Public Policy*, 25, 117–214.

Nicolas, B., & Héricourt, J. (2010). Financial factors and the margins of trade: Evidence from cross-country firm-level data. *Journal of Development Economics*, 93, 206–217.

Nordstrom, A., Roger, S., Stone, M. R., Shimizu, S., Kisinbay, T., & Restrepo, J. (2009). *The Role of the Exchange Rate in Inflation-Targeting Emerging Economies*. IMF Occasional Paper No. 267, International Monetary Fund.

Ostry, J. D., Ghosh, A. R., & Chamon, M. (2012). *Two Targets, Two Instruments: Monetary and Exchange Rate Policies in Emerging Market Economies*. IMF Staff Discussion Note, Research Department, International Monetary Fund.

Ouyang, A. Y., & Rajan, R. S. (2013). Real exchange rate fluctuations and the relative importance of nontradables. *Journal of International Money and Finance*, 32, 844–855.

Ouyang, A. Y., & Rajan, R. S. (2015). Exchange rate regimes and real exchange rate volatility: Does inflation targeting help or hurt? Mimeo.

Portugal, M. (2007). Perspectives and lessons from country experiences with inflation targeting. Remarks at a panel on inflation targeting, 17 May. Washington, DC: International Monetary Fund.

Posen, A. (2008). The future of inflation targeting. *Challenge*, 51, 5–22.

Roger, S. (2010). Inflation targeting turns 20. *Finance and Development*, 12(March), 46–49.

Rose, A. K. (2007). A stable international monetary system emerges: Inflation targeting is Bretton Woods, reversed. *Journal of International Money and Finance, 26*, 663–681.

Rose, A. K. (2014). Surprising similarities: Recent monetary regimes of small economies. *Journal of International Money and Finance, 49*, 5–27.

Stockman, A. (1983). Real exchange rates under alternative nominal exchange-rate systems. *Journal of International Money and Finance, 2*, 147–166.

Volz, U. (2015). On the future of inflation targeting in East Asia, *Review of Development Economics, 19*, 638–652.

Vredin, A. (2015). *Inflation Targeting and Financial Stability: Providing Policymakers with Relevant Information.* BIS Working Papers No.503, Bank for International Settlements.

Walsh, C. (2009). Inflation targeting: What have we learned? *International Finance, 12*, 195–233.

Woodford, M. (2012). *Inflation Targeting and Financial Stability.* NBER Working Paper Series 17967, April, National Bureau of Economic Research, Inc.

Index

Note: Page numbers in *italic* refer to figures
    Page numbers in **bold** refer to tables

ABIF *(ASEAN Banking Integration Framework)* 121, 122, 125, 125n14
ACMI (ASEAN Capital Market Infrastructure) Blueprint 123
ADB (Asian Development Bank) 122
AEC (ASEAN Economic Community), the 1, 4, 121
AFIF *(ASEAN Financial Integration Framework)* 121
AFTA (ASEAN Free Trade Area) 73
aggregation bias in empirical studies 42, 42n3
AIIB (Asian Infrastructure Investment Bank), the 1
Apple 28 *see also* iPhone, the
ASEAN 73, 109, 121–5, **123–5**
ASEAN+6 FTA **19**, 25 *see also* RCEP (Regional Comprehensive Economic Partnership)
ASEAN Economic Community Blueprint 2025 121, 122, **123,** 126
ASEAN Insurance Integration Framework 121, **123**
ASEAN Vision 2020 121
Asian financial crisis, the 79, 109, 113, 120, 130
Australia 73, 85, 99, 132, **133**; and export trade **55,** 56, **56,** 57

Bali Package, the 70
banking regulation harmonisation in the European Community 109–12, **110**
banking stability and regional development 108–9
Bank of England 130
brands and consumer choice 30
Brunei 7, **126,** *136*
Bundesbank, the 113
buyer-driven chains and GVCs 29, 30

capacity building 125, 126
capital account liberalisation 3–4, 81–2, *111–12,* 114, 121, **124–5**; and risks involved 109, 120, 122 *see also* capital flows
capital allocation and resource efficiencies in the Euro area 115

capital controls 81–2; and financial integration 119, *120,* 127
capital flows 65, 80, 81, 109, 114–15, *120,* 122, **124,** 126; liberalisation of 110
Capital Liberalisation Directive, the 110
central banks and inflation 136
Centre on Asia and Globalisation conferences 1
China 30–1; and export growth 1, 2, 3, 27–8, *34*; and hi-tech exports and GVCs 28, 31, 32–5, *33*; and trade surpluses through ordinary exports 57–8, *58,* 65 *see* processing exports in Chinese bilateral trade
China and machine production networks 1, 5–6, 13, 15, 24–5; and exports to Japan and Korea 18–22, **19,** *21–2*; and percentage of machinery components in total manufactured exports 8, *9*; and world machinery exports 10, **10**
CLMV countries 126
CMI (Chiang Mai Initiative), the 82, 120
comparative advantages in labor-intensive products 28, 30, 32–3, 38
compensation and total factor productivity developments in the Euro area *116*
competitiveness across GVCs 43, 50–1
competitiveness and currency appreciation 65
consumer protection and financial education 124
consumers of developed countries 30
CPI (consumer price index) 132
cross-border bank lending 108, 111–12, 124
cumulated current account balance of Eurozone countries *117*
currency appreciation 3, 32, 37, 42, 61, 65
currency risk in cross-border lending 111–12

data construction and machinery production networks 6–7
devaluation and exchange rate realignments 113
dispute settlement mechanism in the WTO 71, 77
distance measurement between economies of financial development patterns 89–93, **91, 92, 93,** 101

diversification of export destination trends 11–13, *12*

Doha Round (DDA - Doha Development Agenda), the 67, **69,** 69–70, 72, 75, 77; and the Environmental Goods Agreement 70, 76

DOLS estimates of Chinese exports 60–1, **63**

DOTs (Direction of Trade Statistics) database 140

DVA (Domestic Value Added) 2, *33,* 34, 40, 42–3, 44, 45, *45,* **47,** 47–8, 49, *49,* 51

effective protection concept, the 42n2

electrical machinery trade between China, Japan and Korea 20–2, **21**

EMS (European Monetary System), the 109, 113

EMS crisis (1992–93), the 112–13

EMU (European Monetary Union) 113, 114

Enabling Clause of RTAs, the 71

Environmental Goods Agreement of the Doha Round 70, 76

EPR (effective protection rate), the 42n2

EU, the 74, 76

Euro crisis, the 114–17, *115, 116*; and macroprudential regulation 117–18, **118**

exchange-rate adjusted prices in GVCs 2, 50–1

exchange rate classifications **131**

exchange rate elasticities of imports and exports 2, 42, 42n3, *48*; and REER elasticities 46, 47, 48–50, *49*

exchange rate realignments and devaluation 113

exchange rate variability 4, 40–1; and Chinese processed exports 53–4; importance for value-added in processed exports 57, 59–66, **62–3**; trade and real exchange rate variables in imports and exports 43–5, *44,* 50

export flows and product-destination pairs 11–13, *12, 17,* 18

extensive margins in export growth 15, 16, *16*

extensive margins in trade growth **23,** 23–4

FDIndex (Financial Development Index) 85, 88, **89,** 90, **106–7**

FDRs (Financial Development Reports) 83–4, 91

financial integration and financial development 82–4, 119, 120–7, *122,* **123–5, 126**; and capital controls 119, *120,* 127; and distance measurement 89–93, **91, 92, 93,** 101; measurement of 84–5, 86–9, **89, 90,** *90,* 98–101, **100**; and openness 79–82, 83; sub-components and variables **104–5**; and the WEF Global Competitiveness Index 85–6, **86**

financial integration in Europe 109–12, **110,** *111–12,* 114, 117, 125, 127 *see also* Euro crisis, the

financial intermediation 84, 120

FINTECs (financial integration composites) *114*

First Banking Directive, the 109–10

fixed exchange rates and the EMS 113–14

flexible de-pegged exchange rate regimes 130–1, **131**

Foxcon 28

FTAs (free trade agreements) 71–3

FVA (Foreign Value Added) **47,** 47–9, *49,* 59; in a country's exports 2, 40; and export elasticities 49, 49n11; in GVC exports 41, 42, 44, *44,* 44n6, 46

GATT (General Agreement on Tariffs and Trade) 67, 68, 77; and the Uruguay Round 68, **69,** 70

GCI (Global Competitiveness Index) of the WEF Global Competitiveness Report 85–6, **86**

GDP and share of GVC exports 41

GDP per capita growth and inflation targeting **142, 143,** 144

Germany 27, 35; and currency crises 113, 114; and EU capital controls 110, **110**; and machinery exports 10, **10,** 11, 13, 15, 16, *17*; and processing exports from China 35, *35,* 54, **55–6,** 57

global brands and China 30–1

global distribution networks 31–2

global financial crisis, the 5, 79–80, 108, 137

GVCs (Global Value Chains) 28–30, 31, 32–4, 40–1, 42; and exchange-rate adjusted prices 2, 50–1; exports and REER elasticities **47,** *48, 49,* 49–50; and trade and real exchange variables 43–9, *44,* 44n6, *45,* **47,** *48, 49*

harmonisation of standards 125

Hong Kong 36–7, 55, 57, 59, 119, *119*; and financial development **92,** 92–4, **93,** 98; and monetary policy **131, 135**

HS (Harmonized System) product classification 6–7, 11, 26

Huawei 30

ICT (information and communication technology) markets 31

IMF (International Monetary Fund), the 1, 37, 81, 131, 140

index of financial development 84

India 25, 35, 69, 130; and monetary policy 130, **131, 135,** *136,* 144

Indonesia 6n2, 91, 92, 94, 113, **126**; and inflation targeting 131, **131,** 132, **133,** *136,* 136n7, **140**

inflation targeting 4, 130–7, **133–4, 135,** *136,* **143**; impact on RER volatility 138–45, **140, 141, 142**

infrastructural investment 120, 121

institutional quality measures and the finance-growth nexus 83

intensive and margins of trade growth **23,** 23–4

intensive margins in export growth 16

international trade and comparative advantage 30

intra-East Asian machinery exports between China, Japan and Korea 18–24, **19, 21–2, 23**

intra-regional portfolio investment in East Asia 118–19, *119*

iPhone, the 29, 31, 32

Ireland and the Euro crisis 117–18

ITA (Information Technology Agreement) of the Doha Round 70, 76

Japan 1, 13, 16, 73, **126**; and exchange rates 59, 64, *64,* 65, **131**; and exports to China and Korea 18–22, **19**, **21–2**, 24–5, **56**, 57; financial integration and financial development 80, 85, **86**, 88, 91, 100; and inflation targeting 132, **134**; and machinery production 8, **10**, 10–11, *12,* 13, 15, *17*; and processing exports from China 35, *35,* 38, 54, **55**
Johansen MLE estimates for Chinese exports 60, 61, **62**

Kazakhstan 144
Kennedy Round on non-tariff measures 68, **69**
Kimura, Fukunari 1–2
knowledge diffusion and GVCs 31
Korea 3, 64, 65, 91, 119; and exports to China and Japan 18–22, **19**, **21–2**, 24–5; and machinery production networks 1, 5, 8, 11, *17,* 18; and processing exports from China 54, **55–6**

labor-intensive products and comparative advantage 28, 30
Laos 7
least-traded goods 16
'least-traded goods' concept 6
level and pattern distances between economies of financial development **91–4**, 91–7, *95–9,* 101, **106–7**

machinery production networks 1, 5–8, 15–16, 24–5; export flows and product-destination pairs 11–13, *12*; and export growth margins 15–18, *17*; intensive and extensive margins in trade growth 22–4, **23**; intra-East Asian trade between China, Japan and Korea 18–24, **19**, **21–2**, **23**; and product-destination pairs 13–15, *14*; and shares in exports and imports 8, **9**; and trade growth margins 22–4, **23**; and world exports 8, **10**, 10–11
macroeconomic performance and inflation targeting 135, 137
macroprudential index for East Asian economies 126, **126**
macroprudential regulation and the Euro crisis 117–18, **118**
Malaysia 8, 59, 64, 113, 119, **126**; and ASEAN 4 54, **55**, **56**, 121n10; and financial development **86**, 88–9, 98, 100; and machinery exports **10**, *12,* 13, 15; and monetary policy **131**, **135**, **140**
margins of machine export growth 15–16
Marshall-Lerner condition, the 43, 50
mega-FTAs (Free Trade Agreements) 3, 25, 67, 73–7
MNEs (multinational enterprises) 28, 30, 31
monetary policy and inflation targeting **131**, 132, **135**, 144

most-favored nation principle, the 71
MSMEs (micro, small and medium enterprises) 123, 124
multilateral trade liberalization under the GATT and WTO 68–72, **69**, 77–8
Myanmar 7

NAFTA (North American Free trade Agreement) 73
non-zero product-destination pairs 6, 11, *12,* 13, 15

Obashi, Ayako 1–2
OECD (Organisation for Economic Co-operation and Development), the 2, 135
OECD-WTO TiVA database, the 43–4, 44n6
openness and financial integration 79–82, 83
outline of the book 2–4

PAA (processing and assembly) exports 59, 61
payment and settlement systems 125
peripheral EU countries and the Euro crisis 114–15
plurilateral agreements 3, 70, 76–7, 78
processing exports in Chinese bilateral trade 29, 33–5, *34, 35*; and correlation with income of trading partners 35–8, *36,* **37**, 59; and dependence on the exchange rate for value added 53–6, **55–6**, 59–63, **62–3**; and trade surpluses 57, *58*
producer-driven chains and GVCs 29
product-destination pairs in exports 13–15, *14,* 18
production networks and trade 79
property bubbles and the Euro crisis 117–18
PWIM (processing with imported materials) exports 59, 61–3, **62–3**

QABs (Qualified Asian Banks) 125

RCEP (Regional Comprehensive Economic Partnership) 3, 25, 67, 73, 74
real trade balance and REER 50, *50*
REER (real effective exchange rate) weights 42, 43, 45, **62–3**, *64,* 137; and elasticities 48–50, *49*; and exchange rate data 46–9, **47**, 59–60
RER (real exchange rate) volatility 132, 137, 138–41, **140**, 144; and inflation targeting 138–45, **140**, **141**, **142**
Reserve Bank of New Zealand 130
resource allocation efficiencies through international trade specialization 30, 81
risk diversification 123
Roadmap for Monetary and Financial Integration of ASEAN 121
Rodrik, Dani 81–2
RTAs (regional trade agreements) 71, *72*

Second Banking Directive, the 110
Singapore 59, *64,* 79, 92, 98, 118–19; and FDIndex 85, **86**

SITC (Standard International Trade Classification) 7
South Korea *see* Korea
sovereign debt and domestic banking systems 115
Spain and the Euro crisis 117–18
Special Drawing Rights basket 1
specialization and comparative advantage 30
speculative attacks on the ERM (European Exchange Rate Mechanism) 113–14
spillover effects 43, 51; of lead firms' technology innovations 30, 31–2, 33–4
Sri Lanka 145

Taiwan 64, **86,** 91, 93, 100; and trade with China 54, **55,** 56, **56,** 57, 59
tariff rate reductions under FTAs 68–9, 75, 77
ten-year government bond yields *115*
TFA (trade Facilitation Agreement), the 70
Thailand 8, *86,* 91, 113, 119, **126**; and monetary policy **131,** 132, **133,** *136,* 136–7, 140; and trade with China 54, **55, 56**
TiSA (Trade in Service Agreement) of the Doha Round 70, 76
Tokyo Round on trade rules under the GATT 68, **69**
TPP (Trans-Pacific Partnership) 1, 3, 25, 67, 73–4, 75–6
trade and real exchange rate variables in import and export trade 43–9, *44,* 44n6, *45,* **47,** *48, 49*
TTIP (Transatlantic Trade and Investment Partnership), the 3, 67, 73, 74, 75–6

Urjit Patel Committee Report, the 144
Uruguay Round of the GATT/WTO 68, **69,** 70
US, the 74–5, 76; and machine exports 10, **10,** 13, 16, *17*; and processing exports from China 35, *35,* 54, 55, **55–6**
US dollar dependency 120
US-Israel FTA, the 72–3

value added in trade 2

Wal-Mart 32
WDI (World Development Indicator Database) 140
Weerasinghe, Nandalal 145
WEF (World Economic Forum), the 83, 85
weighted exchange rates *64 see also* REER (real effective exchange rate) weights
workers and high productive sectors 78
World Bank, the 37, 83–4
world machinery exports 8, **10** *see also* China and machine production netwworks; machinery production networks
world trade expansion under the GATT 68
WTO (World Trade Organisation), the 3, 67, 69–71, 72, 74; and the entry of China 36, 57; and mega-FTAs 75, 76–7

Xing, Yuqing 2

Yuan appreciation 3, 32, 37

zero export flows 11